THE NECROMANCERS
Dr. Dee and Kelley raising the dead

[Frontispiece

A POPULAR HISTORY OF
WITCHCRAFT

MONTAGUE SUMMERS

Illustrated

DOVER PUBLICATIONS, INC.
Mineola, New York

This offence of Sorcery is so great and comprehensive that it includes in itself almost every other crime.

Paul Laymann, Processus Juridicus contra
Sagas et Veneficos.

Bibliographical Note

This Dover edition, first published in 2006, is an unabridged republication of the work originally published in 1937 by E. P. Dutton & Company, New York.

International Standard Book Number: 0-486-44391-4

Manufactured in the United States of America
Dover Publications, Inc., 31 East 2nd Street, Mineola, N.Y. 11501

CONTENTS

ILLUSTRATIONS

vii

INTRODUCTION

During the eleven years which have passed since I published my *History of Witchcraft and Demonology* a second edition has repeatedly been asked for, and—wisely or no—I have as often delayed this and deferred. The fact is that throughout this time owing to my further researches into an immense subject—as old as the world and as wide as the world—and perhaps more especially owing to the interest and kindness of correspondents from every continent I found that I had accumulated so vast a quantity of new material that in order to include a tithe, and yet keep my work within a reasonable compass, there would have to be frequent excisions from the original pages together with a certain amount of compression. At first I began upon these lines, but I soon recognized that again and again I was at a loss how to abbreviate without in some way impairing the structure and sequence of the chapters, and thus it was a matter of no little difficulty to avail myself to any extent of many recent and extraordinarily interesting narratives and investigations whilst not essentially altering and even recasting the whole.

A considerable amount of time also was taken up in closely examining and discussing cases and incidents which were brought under my notice. Not a few persons were, quite naturally, at first reluctant to give details. The majority shrank from furnishing their names, dates, and the exact localities, such precise information as might bring them into a notice they were far from desiring or indeed would for a moment allow. This, an entirely reasonable and prudent point of view, must often hinder and obstruct the student of these dark and riddling mysteries. Yet he has no right whatsoever to complain or show himself embarrassed by the discretion of a reticence which is perfectly justifiable and fair. It was necessary to poise delicate questions and to probe with great tact in order to obtain knowledge together with the confirmation of knowledge which not unseldom was only supplied on condition that it was not publicly utilized, or, if so employed, disguised in such a way that the informant could not be identified. Persons who have been brought in contact with, and it may be who have hardly escaped from the clutches of, the Satanists are loath that their experiences, however valuable to others, should be published. They are afraid too of the vengeance and pursuit of the witches. This is quite understandable, nor are they to be blamed who lack courage to expose and confront those infernal gangs whose weapons are poisons, black magic, and evil spells.

As time went on and I was even more frequently being requested to issue a second edition of my book it became increasingly difficult satisfactorily to myself to find a happy issue from the impasse. In the view of so much that was new and vitally important I did not wish to send it from the press without certain added matter. I was, too, perpetually being urged by those whose opinion carries no little weight that I would bring the subject right up to the very day of writing, that I would emphasize the oneness of witchcraft throughout the world, the unchangeableness of the church of Satan throughout the centuries, and thus expose the horrid activities and propaganda of the society of devil-worshippers in our midst.

Such arguments were scarcely to be resisted, and I decided that in order to accomplish what was required more efficiently it would be better, rather than to attempt any modification of my first work, to write a new study ; and this I have called *A Popular History of Witchcraft*.

My aim throughout my new work has been to show how the profession and practice of witchcraft are the same always and in all places, be it in some remote English village, in a quiet cathedral city, in the sweltering hinterland of Jamaica, or in savage Africa. In the course of the present study I have concentrated upon England and English witchcraft, although I have freely cited parallel circumstances as revealed in foreign trials.

Since *A Popular History of Witchcraft* is designed for the general reader rather than for the specialist I have been advised not to burden the text with a multiplicity of notes. A reader, unless it be the scholar at his desk, pen in hand, is harassed by, or else ignores, a parade of commentary, the details of which he has no intention, even if he had the opportunity, of verifying by making reference to the original source. In quotations, for the same reason, I have given the newer forms of words rather than strictly adhering to the old spelling, which so many find cumbersome and a nuisance, although I have been scrupulously careful neither to alter nor modify. My citations of texts are from the Authorized Version of the Bible, but these have been checked in each instance by the Douai.

The last chapter, English witchcraft, is necessarily in the nature of a survey, designed to show the continuity of the thing rather than to enter into details of cases, many of which, however important, I have been obliged to pass without mention. For these particulars I must refer the reader to my *Geography of Witchcraft*.

The present work is designed to awaken the general reader to a sense of the dangers with which he is encompassed and beset. Although *A Popular History of Witchcraft* is entirely new I have not hesitated to make use of apposite passages from my previously published works, and even to incorporate one or two sentences, the gist of which I felt I was not able better or more forcibly to express.

Since I published *The History of Witchcraft and Demonology* there has been little or nothing, I believe, which covers the same ground. Professor Lynn Thorndike's work, for example, encyclopædic in extent, was scarcely designed to touch upon the field I review. The *Short Title-Catalogue* of my friend Mr. Harry Price will, of course, be in the hands of, and constantly referred to by, every student of occultism, for whom the *Proceedings* of the National Laboratory of Psychical Research must be an ever ready guide-book, his veritable Baedeker.

During the past decade in various journals and magazines there have been published one or two articles of great value. Such are Lieut.-Colonel Spain's " The Witches of Riding Mill, 1673 ", which appeared in *The Cornhill Magazine*, March, 1929, and Mr. S. Everard's " Oliver Cromwell and Black Magic ", *Occult Review*, April, 1936. Mr. W. Branch Johnson has written a good book in *The Age of Arsenic*, 1931. Two studies by the Rev. Joseph J. Williams, S.J., *Voodoos and Obeahs* and *Psychic Phenomena of Jamaica* are of the first importance, whilst W. B. Seabrook's *The Magic Island* (1929) is very illuminating in reference to Voodoo in Haiti.

With reference to witches in England there have (so far as I am aware) only been three books worthy of note published during the last ten years : Mr. George Lyman Kittredge's *Witchcraft in Old and New England* (1928), Mr. C. L'Estrange Ewen's *Witch Hunting and Witch Trials* (1929), and *Witchcraft and Demonianism* (1933). If I may venture a criticism Mr. Kittredge's book, exhaustive in references and annotation, suffers from presenting a series of unconnected essays, unconnected that is save in so far as they one and all relate to various phases of the same subject. Thus some of the chapters were, I am given to understand, originally published in the *Proceedings of the American Antiquarian Society*, 1907, the *American Historical Review*, 1917, and in other ephemerides. Mr. L'Estrange's works, of the most painstaking scholarship, are indispensable to any student of witchcraft, to whom they supply the amplest and most essential material.

There have been translations of the *Malleus Maleficarum*, of Boguet, Remy, Guazzo, Taillepied, and others. Again, such a reprint as *The Trial of the Lancaster Witches, 1612*, with an introduction by Dr. G. B. Harrison (1929), is a notable piece of no slight value.

I am grateful to many friends and correspondents for their warmly appreciative letters and so widespread an interest that is taken in my work. Since she is no longer with us it will not (I am sure) be invidious to particularize Mrs. Violet Tweedale, whose psychic gifts were so truly remarkable, and whose writings on the occult are so justly admired.

I have to thank Messrs. Maggs for their generous courtesy in granting me permission to quote from their Catalogue of Books on Medicine, Alchemy, Astrology, etc. (No. 520 ; 1929), details concerning the interesting and important MS. Book of Black Magic and Conjurations therein described. I am further indebted to their kindness for the reproduction thence of the drawing of the Demon King Maymon.

In conclusion I would say that the present study aims at presenting a clear view of the Practice and Profession of Witchcraft, as it was carried on in former centuries and now prevails amongst us. I am convinced that it is most necessary to realize that this is no mere historical question, but a definite factor in politics of to-day, as well as in social life and the progress of humanity.

The Black International of Satan—that is the canker which is corrupting and destroying the world.

IN FESTO TRANS. ALMÆ DOMUS LAURETANÆ.
1936.

CHAPTER I

OF THE PROFESSION OF WITCHCRAFT; OF THE CONTRACT, AND OF THE FAMILIAR

In order to the proof that there have been, and are, unlawful
Confederacies *with evil Spirits, by vertue of which the* hellish accomplices *perform things above their natural powers : I must premise that
this being* matter *of* fact, *is onely capable of the evidence of* authority
and sense ; *and by both these the being of* Witches *and* diabolical
Contracts *is most abundantly confirm'd.*
JOSEPH GLANVIL, *Saducismus Triumphatus.*

" A sorcerer is one who by commerce with the Devil
has a full intention of attaining his own ends, and I
give this definition because not only is it necessary for
the full understanding of my book, but also because it
explains and supplies the reason for the divers laws
which in all Christian countries have been directed
against sorcerers, and furthermore because no concise
definition has hitherto been supplied by the many
authorities who have written upon witchcraft, whilst
at the same time it is essential that we should be quite
clear and exact in regard to the use of our terms."
With this sentence the erudite lawyer and politician,
Jean Bodin, one of the most acute and liberal minds
of his age, opens his famous treatise *Demonomania, A
Scourge for Wizards and Witches,* which was first published
at Paris in 1580, and in the opinion of not a few scholars
is still distinguished as being the most copious and
most closely-argued manual of its kind.

It would be, I imagine, hardly possible to discover
a more explicit, precise, comprehensive, and intelligent

I

definition of a Witch. Bodin was thinking only of
European witchcraft, but actually his words carry a
complete and universal connotation, and we find, for
example, that Father Joseph J. Williams, S.J., who is
Professor of Cultural Anthropology at Boston College
Graduate School, in his *Psychic Phenomena of Jamaica*,
writes : " Certainly we have this definition [of Bodin's]
fully verified in the case of the Jamaica obeah-man as
the direct descendant in theory and practice from the
Ashanti *obayifo*," a term which Captain R. Sutherland
Rattray in his *Ashanti Proverbs* (Oxford, 1916), explains
as follows : " Obayifo, deriv. bayi, sorcery (Synonymous term ayen), a wizard, or more generally a witch.
A kind of human vampire, whose chief delight is to
suck the blood of children whereby the latter pine and
die.   Men and women possessed of this black magic
are credited with volitant powers, being able to quit
their bodies and travel great distances in the night.
Besides sucking the blood of victims, they are supposed
to be able to extract the sap and juice of crops. (Cases
of coco blight are ascribed to the work of the obayifo.)
These witches are supposed to be very common, and a
man never knows but that his friend or even his wife
may be one."

Such characteristics can be closely paralleled in the
history of European Witchcraft,   Some are frequent,
others are more rarely met, but all occur, and this in
itself goes far to show how in spite of external differences
and even climatic and regional variations, the horrid
cult is essentially one and the same the wide world
over, the witch near home or in the remotest and most
savage quarters of the globe serves only one master, is
the bondslave of one only lord, the fallen angel who

is the Prince of Darkness, " that old serpent, which is the Devil, and Satan."

It must be borne in mind that the word " witch ", although in recent usage almost invariably applied to a woman, may with perfect correctness be employed of a man, and it seems a pity that the meaning should be narrowed and curtailed. The great *Oxford English Dictionary* defines " witch " (a word of Anglo-Saxon derivation) as " A man who practises witchcraft or magic, a magician, sorcerer, wizard ". Also, and to-day more generally, " A female magician, sorceress ; in later use a woman supposed to have dealings with the devil or evil spirits and to be able by their co-operation to perform supernatural acts." The word " sorcerer " is from the Old French, and is derived from a popular Latin term signifying a caster of lots, a diviner, a charmer.

" The father of the English law," Sir Edward Coke (commonly called Lord Coke), defines a witch as " a person that hath conference with the Devil to take counsel or do some act ".

Whilst he was Bishop of Luçon, and before he had received the red hat, Cardinal Richelieu, in 1618, with considerable pains and application, composed for his diocese a catechism which became famous under the name *A Wholesome Instruction in the Christian Faith*. The Cardinal thus distinguishes between Magic and Sorcery. " Magic is the art of producing extraordinary and supernatural effects by the power of the devil : Sorcery or Witchcraft is the art of injuring men in their persons or their possessions by the power of the devil. The difference between Magic and Sorcery strictly lies in this, that the former has for its chief aim and end the design to excite wonder and vain esteem ; whilst the latter in its malevolence seeks to injure and harm."

Magic, says Swedenborg, is an abuse of the correspondences of the natural world with the spiritual.

Black magic, which is magic proper, produces effects which are beyond the reach of any forces of nature, and which could not be contrived by any skill of legerdemain. These effects, moreover, are produced by the power of the demon, with whom the witch has commerce and has entered into a contract.

In order clearly to understand and fully to realize the shuddering horror and heart-sick dismay any sort of communion between human beings and evil spirits, which is the very core and kernel of Witchcraft, excited throughout the whole of Christendom, to appreciate why tome after tome was written upon the subject by the most learned pens of Europe, why holiest pontiffs and wisest judges, grave philosopher and discreet scholar, king and peasant, careless noble and earnest divine, all alike were of one mind in the prosecution of sorcery ; why in Catholic Spain and in Puritan Scotland, in cold Geneva and at genial Rome, unhesitatingly and perseveringly man sought to stamp out the plague with the most terrible of all penalties, the cautery of fire ; in order that by the misreading of history we should not superficially and foolishly think monk and magistrate, layman and lawyer were mere tigers, mad fanatics—for as such have they, too, often been presented and traduced,—it will be not wholly impertinent briefly to recapitulate the orthodox doctrine of the Powers of Darkness, facts nowadays too often forgotten or ignored, but which to the acute

mediæval mind were ever fearfully and prominently
in view.

And here, as in so many other beliefs, we shall find
a little dogma ; certain things that can hardly be
denied without the note of temerity ; and much concerning which nothing definite can be known, upon
which assuredly no pronouncement will be made.

In the first place, the name Devil is commonly given
to the fallen angels, who are also called Demons. The
precise technical distinction between the two terms
may be seen in the phrase used in a decree of the Fourth
Lateran Council, which was convened under Pope
Innocent III in 1215. The assembled Fathers spoke of
" The Devil and other demons ", i.e. all are demons,
and the chief of the demons is called the Devil.

As Cotton Mather explains in his *The Devil Discovered* : " It is not *One Devil* alone, that has Cunning
or Power enough to apply the Multitudes of *Tempta-
tions*, whereby Mankind is daily diverted from the
Service of God ; No, the *High Places* of Our Air, are
Swarming full of those *Wicked Spirits*, whose Tempta-
tions trouble us. . . . But because those Apostate
Angels, are all *United*, under one Infernal Monarch,
in the Designs of Mischief, 'tis in the Singular Number,
that they are spoken of."

Mention is made of the Devil in many passages both
of the Old and New Testaments. Thus, as he is multi-
fold in evil, so is he known under a variety of names.
Beelzebub is prince of the devils (St. Matthew, xii, 24) ;
he is Satan (St. Luke, x, 18) ; he is Belial (2 Corinthians,
vi, 15) ; he is the angel of the bottomless pit, " whose
name in the Hebrew tongue is Abaddon, but in the
Greek tongue Apollyon " (Revelation, ix, 11).   He is

proud (1 Timothy, iii, 6) ; powerful (Ephesians, vi, 12) ; wicked (1 John, ii, 13) ; subtle (2 Corinthians, xi, 3) ; deceitful (2 Corinthians, xi, 14) ; fierce and cruel (1 Peter, v, 8). He is the father of lies and a murderer from the beginning (St. John, viii, 44) ; one who loves to work lying wonders, that is to say the craft of magic (2 Thessalonians, ii, 9). He is the prince of the power of the air (Ephesians, ii, 2) and a sinner from the beginning (1 John, iii, 8) ; finally he was cast out into the blackness of darkness (St. Jude, 6 ; 13).

It is interesting to note that even so extremely advanced a writer of the modernist school as Dean Inge, when preaching at St. Mark's, North Audley Street, London, W., on Sunday, 6th March, 1932, remarked : " Liberal theologians may jeer and philosophers scoff, but there it is. We cannot get rid of the Devil. ' Deliver us from the Evil One,' is the right translation. I have not the slightest doubt that Christians are enjoined to believe in a positive, malignant spiritual power."

An obvious question which next arises and which has been amply discussed by the fathers and school-men is : What was the nature of the sin of the rebel angels ? This point presents some difficulty for theology has logically formed the highest estimate of the perfection of the angelic nature, the powers and possibilities of the angelic knowledge. Sins of the flesh are certainly impossible to angels, and from many sins which are purely spiritual and intellectual they would seem to be equally debarred. The great offence of Lucifer appears to have been the desire of independence of God and equality with God.

It is theologically certain that Lucifer held a very high place in the celestial hierarchy, and it is evident that he maintains some kind of sovereignty over those who followed him in his rebellion. There can be little doubt too that among their ranks are many mean and petty spirits—to speak comparatively—but even these can influence and betray foolish and arrogant men.

There are many historical examples, indeed, of men so besotted as to cause themselves to be saluted and even worshipped as God—Herod, Caligula, Heliogabalus, the Persian king Khusrau.

To come down to more modern days. About 1830 there appeared in one of the American States bordering upon Kentucky, an impostor who declared himself to be Christ. He threatened the world with immediate judgement, and a number of ill-balanced and hysterical subjects were much affected by his denunciations. One day, when he was addressing a large gathering in his usual strain, a German standing up humbly asked him if he would repeat his warnings in German for the benefit of those present who only knew that tongue. The speaker answered that he had never been able to learn that language, a reply which seemed so ludicrous in one claiming divinity that many of the auditors were convulsed with laughter, and so profane a charlatan soon lost all credit.

John Nichols Tom, the son of a Cornish publican and self-dubbed Knight of Malta, early in 1838 was shot near Blean Wood, Kent, during a riot which he had incited owing to his having persuaded a number of rustics that he was Christ returned to earth. He exhibited the five wounds in his hands, feet, and side, and gained no inconsiderable following. Upon the

tree beneath which he fell some fanatic actually
attached an engraved plate : " Our real true Messiah,
King of the Jews." Henry James Prince, " the
Beloved " founder of the Agapemone, openly claimed
divinity, whilst his successor T. H. Smyth-Pigott in 1902
declared to the congregation of his church at Clapton :
" I am that Lord Jesus come again in my own body
to save those who come to me from death and hell."
Smyth-Pigott died in 1927.

It is apparent then, that although rationally it
should be inconceivable that any sentient creature
could claim divinity, actually the contrary is the case.
The sin of Satan would appear to have been an attempt
to usurp the sovereignty of God. This is further borne
out by the fact that during the Temptation of Our
Lord the Devil, showing Him " all the kingdoms of
the world and the glory of them ", said : " All these
will I give Thee, if Thou wilt fall down and worship me."
Here the Devil is demanding that divine honours
should be paid him. And this claim is perpetuated
throughout the witch trials. The witches believed that
their master, Satan, Lucifer, the fiend, the principle
of evil, was God, and as such they worshipped him
with the supreme honour due to Almighty God alone,
they adored him, they offered him homage, they
addressed prayer to him, they sacrificed.

The Devil, Satan, was and is the god of the witches,
and we may now inquire concerning their practice and
profession, how a novice joins that horrid society,
and what obligations so damnable a state entails.

The first business required of a candidate who
desired to become a witch was to make a formal
compact with Satan. This might be either expressed

or tacit. The expressed pact consisted of a solemn vow of fidelity and homage paid before witnesses, to the devil visibly present in some bodily form, or else to some wizard or magician acting in the devil's stead. The tacit pact involves the offering of a written petition to the devil, and this is not unseldom done by proxy through the medium of a witch when the contracting party is afraid to summon or directly have speech with the fiend.

That a determined man will be able in some way or another to get most intimately into touch with the dark shadow world is not to be denied. The existence of evil discarnate intelligences it is impossible for any thinking man to doubt, whilst it is certainly established that this realm of rebellion and disorder owns one chief, and it is reasonable to suppose, many hierarchies, a kingdom that is at continual warfare with and opposed to all that is good, ever striving to do ill and to bring man into bondage. It is this connexion between man and the demon with its consequences, conditions, and attendant circumstances that is known as Witchcraft. Thus, even so ultra-cautious and indeed frankly sceptical a writer as Father Herbert Thurston, S.J., finds himself bound to acknowledge : " In the face of Holy Scripture and the teaching of the Fathers and theologians the abstract possibility of a pact with the Devil and of a diabolical interference in human affairs can hardly be denied." Plainly, a man who not only firmly believes in a Power of evil but also that this Power can and does meddle with and mar human affections and human destinies, may invoke and devote himself to this Power, may give up his will thereunto, may ask this Power to accomplish his wishes and ends, and so succeed in definitively and explicitly entering into a mysterious contract with evil whose slave and servant he is become.

St. Jerome explains that a contract with Satan is spoken of in plainest terms by the prophet Isaiah : " We have made a covenant with death, and with hell are we at agreement " (xxviii, 15). St. Augustine too discusses such compacts at length. There were few better known histories throughout the Middle Ages than the sixth century legend of Theophilus of Adana, who when bitterly disappointed and wellnigh disgraced, concluded a pact with the devil, to whom he delivered a document he had written and sealed with his own hand. Presently, repenting most heartily of the evil he had done, he besought with fervent prayer and fasting the Mother of all Mercies. Our Lady wrested the fatal parchment from the demon and returned it to the penitent, who cast it into the flames, shortly after passing away in peace.

Stevenote de Audebert, a witch of the Pyrenees, who was executed in 1619, actually showed the judge, Pierre De Lancre, " the contract and agreement she had made with the demon. It was scrawled in blood and feculent matter, enough to turn a man's stomach to see."

Elizabeth Style, a witch of Stoke Trister in Somerset, in 1664 confessed before a magistrate, that the devil who visited her " in the shape of a handsome Man " promised that she should " have the pleasure of the World for Twelve years if she would with her Blood sign his Paper, which was to give her Soul to him . . . and with a drop or two of her Blood she signed the Paper " with her mark. In 1672 a

Nottingham boy inscribed a formal agreement with the powers of evil.

The most famous and most infamous of these written pacts with Satan is probably that made by the arch-magician, Urbain Grandier, a holograph which is preserved in the Bibliothèque Nationale at Paris.

These formal contracts with the fiend are still made to-day, and indeed *Le Petit Dragon Rouge*, one of the vilest and happily one of the scarcest of the grimoires, sets out in explicit terms (although, I am bound to add, not without a note of caution), the precise formula to be most efficaciously employed.

Maître Maurice Garçon, one of the leading French barristers, in the course of an address delivered before the Institut Métaphysique at Paris, September, 1929, affirmed " The first step for novices in sorcery and witchcraft is to make a contract with the devil ". Among ancient French legal documents and records of the courts there are many examples of these pacts, and those which are being written and signed in blood to-day appear practically identical with the older screeds. The substance of all is that the neophyte pledges his soul to the Evil One in return for power, or wealth, or some other object he desires. " I have not only held some of these contracts in my hand," said Maître Garçon, " but I actually witnessed one of these strange businesses quite recently." He proceeded to relate how it had come to his knowledge that a candidate was going to invoke the devil in a wood near Fontainebleau. Maître Garçon and another witness concealed themselves whence they had a clear sight of the appointed spot. The sorcerer arrived at midnight, and proceeded with the dark ritual, tracing a circle on the ground, lighting two candles, and with hideous blasphemies calling upon Satan, from whom he demanded the fulfilment of his quest. At the climax the man raising himself on tiptoes threw out his hands at full stretch proffering the infernal charter scrawled in his own blood, and promising to win the devil a human soul for every wish that he was granted. That the fiend did not appear was doubtless owing to the fact that these ceremonies were being spied upon and overseen by those not of the wizard fraternity. But, as one of the greatest of theologians and profoundest of philosophers, Francisco Suarez, observes, even if no response be obtained from the demon, " either because God does not allow it, or for some other reason we may not know," the guilt of the experimenter in this dark art and his sin are in no wise lightened. Maître Garçon further related that he knew of numerous cases of persons both of poor estate and in the highest social positions who had signed these protocols with Satan, and he instanced (without naming the individual) a leading French banker who openly attributed his worldly success and his immense riches to a diabolical compact.

It is true that the great moral theologians and doctors teach us that such abominations as a contract with the demon are in their essence null and void, a question discussed at length and thus decided with much learning by Jacques D'Autun. Arguing on different lines and from another point of view, the same conclusion was arrived at by so profound a student of occultism as the Marquis Marie-Victor-Stanislas de Guaita.

None the less it is certain that anyone who is cankered

and infect with evil to such a degree as actually to submit himself a bondslave of Satan, and who signs these charters of hell stands in the utmost peril. For, as Jules Bois says, the interior pact of which the written paper is in some sense an outward sign and symbol is not so easily broken. The infernal yoke, the serfdom of Satan, is not lightly cast off; the intellectual sin it is hard to atone.

In the fifteenth century when a novice joined the Waldensians, who are the Vaudois sorcerers, the demon insisted that he should swear implicit obedience to evil and sign a formal document yielding up his soul, without which no business could be done.

The formal contract in fine opens the door to every kind of witchcraft and black magic.

The second point in the profession of a witch follows upon and may be regarded as essentially a part of the impious compact which has been made. At the devil's instigation the neophyte with horrid imprecations and blasphemy abjures the Catholic Faith, explicitly and in set terms withdraws from and denies the obedience due to God, and is therefore, as the older authorities so justly observe, a rebel, guilty of high treason towards the Almighty King.

Mention of these infernal dedications and the ruthless renunciation of all good occurs in almost every witch-trial. Martin Delrio briefly sums up the matter by pointing out that certain articles are common to all these declarations. " The Christian Faith is rejected and denied with contumely; the worship of and the honour due to God are transferred to Satan; the Patronage of Our Lady is repudiated; the Sacraments are scorned and derided; every divine ordinance is profaned." The actual words may be a shortened formula, or they may be delivered at some length and garnished with revolting profanities, but the substance of the matter is in every instance the same.

The Waldensian disciple upon his full profession denied God and Christ, Our Lady and the Saints, in plain set terms. He blasphemed the Sacraments and vowed never to enter a Church, or if indeed he were obliged for safety sake to be present at Mass he muttered a foul curse at the Elevation of the Host, and if bound to take Holy Water he whispered to the demon : " Sire, ne te desplaise," " My Lord, thy pardon."

The witches are required to be active in their profession, for the devil is a hard taskmaster, although indeed it is true that but seldom do they need any spur to wickedness. It is, however, much to be suspected that any person who renders himself notorious by his contempt for and a certain abhorrence of all sacred things has dabbled (and it may be deeply) in black magic. Not very many months ago I was informed by a friend that one afternoon as he found himself by chance near a small church in a London suburb he went in to pay a visit to the Blessed Sacrament. The church was empty, save for one man who was standing at the sanctuary rails, facing the tabernacle. To my friend's surprise he noticed that the stranger was shaking his fist with wild threatening gestures towards the altar, and muttering to himself in tones of horrid menace. When he heard a footstep he turned and hurried from the place. His mouth was writhed in a bestial grimace of derision, his teeth snarled, his eyes were blazing with maniac fury and hate, and it seems plain that this wretch was a Satanist who had entered the church to curse and insult the Sanctissimum, and who perhaps had he not been interrupted would have proceeded to worse indignity and violence.

From time to time the daily papers tell us of some apparently senseless piece of mischief or damage that has been done in a church. In May, 1936, for example, an extraordinary sacrilege was committed at St. Cuthbert's Church, Stanley. The parish priest found that during the night the church had been entered, and the intruder seemed " to have concentrated upon the tabernacle of the high altar ". A Ciborium was lying upon the altar table, and around it the consecrated Hosts were scattered pell-mell. The pix containing the lunette which had held the larger Benediction Host was found on the roof of the school. There can be no doubt that this desecration and many another similar outrage are the work of Satanists, whose vile society is only too rife and too industrious amongst us here in England to-day.

The ordinary man—the man in the street, as the phrase goes—was wont to regard Satanism as incredible, or at any rate a myth of the far-off Dark Ages, but to-day he has been forcibly brought face to face with a tale of horrors that will admit of no other explanation save the potency, the intensely active and purposeful potency of the powers of evil. Who can doubt that the revolution of Russia, the persecution in Mexico, the anarchy and atrocities of Spain, have been fomented, energized, and directed by Satanic agency ? The wholesale carnage of priests and nuns; the torture of innocents ; so deliberate a destruction of most holy and most ancient shrines ; the burning to the ground of churches, convents, and every home of prayer ; all unmistakably betray their ultimate source and author, hell and the devil. It is reported that among the red raving mobs, the dregs of the populace unleashed to slaughter and the most inhuman savagery, there mingle demons under the form of men who urge on and encourage the bloodshed and the fires, nor have I for one any difficulty in believing that this is indeed the case.

As Archbishop Hinsley said in August, 1936 : " The Spanish terror would seem to aim at the wreck of Christianity and the ruin of civilization." *The Universe*, 7th August, 1936, spoke of " Demoniacal Fury in Spain ", and described by an eye-witness fiendish attacks upon the Blessed Sacrament and on priests and nuns. " When the Reds set about the task of destroying practically every church in Barcelona, they went first to the altars. Pulling the vessels out of the Tabernacles, they scattered the sacred Hosts on the floor and in the street, and completed the sacrilege by trampling on the Hosts." The Barcelona Reds were " like maniacs possessed by the devil ", which pregnant phrase in its literal truth sums up the position. " To batter off the head of a dying priest, to outrage a girl little more than a child and then riddle her with machine-gun bullets—these are the pastimes of the beast that roams under the name of Communism "— or Satanism, call it what you will (*Daily Mail*, Monday, 10th August, 1936). Sir Edward Russell wrote : " For the true Communist there is no God . . . Russia sets up a completely atheist state " (*Hibbert Journal*, July, 1936). This may well seem to be the case, but the gist of the matter lies deeper. The Communist denies God, it is true, he is superficially atheist, but he certainly

has a god, for he has set up Satan as his god, who is
worshipped not with prayer and in churches or holy
places, but by violence, by cruelty, and every atrocity,
by anarchy and blood.

We need not in view of the events which have
happened in our own day be at all surprised when we
learn from Bodin that Trois-eschelles du Mayne, a
notorious sorcerer, told King Charles IX that there
were at that time more than three thousand Satanists
in France. It was said that in the fifteenth century so
vast was the army of witches that had a leader arisen
and an international organization the whole of Europe
would have been thrown into chaos, nihilism, and war.
To-day leaders have arisen, an international organization has been formed, and Europe is honeycombed by
the vast society of devil-worshippers whose members
may be found everywhere, in crowded capital and
remotest hamlet, ever busy at their evil work, ever
recruiting, ever flaunting their doctrines now glossed
under some specious name, now hardly disguised in
their native licence and horror, and if unchecked the
result must be universal confusion, discord, red revolution, and the ruin of humanity.

" To worship the Devil is Witchcraft," says Cotton
Mather. Satanism and Witchcraft are one and the
same thing.

From the pact struck by the witch or Satanist with
the fiend and the formally expressed renunciation it
logically follows, that the novices must cast away such
holy things as the Rosary, or the girdle of St. Francis,
the girdle of St. Thomas Aquinas, the leathern cincture
of St. Augustine, the Scapular of the Carmelites, or
any other Scapular. They will also trample under foot

the Cross, the Medals, or other objects of devotion they possess or once carried on their persons.

The Medal of St. Benedict, who was endued with an especial influence over the dark power, is particularly dreaded by witches, and is extremely potent against all evil spells. During a trial for sorcery in 1647 at Nattenburg, near the Abbey of Metten in Bavaria, the necromancers acknowledged that the attempts against the monks were foiled by the holy Medal. The two possessed boys of Illfurt (Alsace), 1864–9, exhibited the utmost dread of St. Benedict's Medal. A wizard, then, would plainly get rid of so sacred an emblem, and cast it from him with hate and fear. The Carmelite Scapular, bestowed by Our Lady on St. Simon as a sure pledge of final grace and salvation, is equally abhorrent and detested by the servants of the devil.

Suspicion was first aroused in the case of Ernest von Ehrenberg, a cousin of the Prince-Bishop of Würzburg, when he was observed to show a strange contempt for holy things, and was one day seen to burn his scapulars and medals.

It was found that the Waldensians did not know the Lord's Prayer, the Ave Mary, or the Creed, but they would secretly make the Sign of the Cross in the dust and spit upon it.

Boguet notes that the demon forbade the witches of the old town of St. Oyan de Joux (now Saint-Claude) to say the creed.

On the 16th April, 1594, died Ferdinando Stanley, the young Earl of Derby, and although he suffered from a bladder complaint it was commonly believed that his sickness had been much aggravated and his end hastened by witchcraft. Rumour, and something more than mere rumour, accused a number of crones of the worst possible reputation, and these were promptly haled before a magistrate : " One of them being bidden to say the Lord's Prayer, said it well, but being conjured, in the Name of Jesus, that if she had bewitched his honour, she should not be able to say the same, she could never repeat that petition, *Forgive us our trespasses*, no not although it was repeated unto her."

Florence Newton, the Irish witch of Youghal, who was arraigned at the Cork Assizes in September, 1661, when put to the test could not say, " and forgive us our trespasses " in the Lord's Prayer, but boggled at the words, and " being oft pressed to utter the words as they were repeated to her, she did not," which left a very ill impression. Julian Cox, the Somerset witch, when asked by Serjeant John Archer to recite the Lord's Prayer, went over it very readily until she said " *And lead us into temptation*," which she repeated again and again, and could not otherwise.

Since the devil is the " ape of God ", whilst Holy Baptism is the " first Sacrament " and in the phrase of Eugenius IV " the door of the spiritual life ", Satan bathes in a new mock baptism, the witch, who is thus fully incorporated (as it were) into the infernal conventicle. Both Bodin and Boguet comment upon this scurril baptism, the latter giving it as his opinion that the fiend thereby seeks to persuade the witch that the first baptism is thus annulled, and that it can be of no more service to him. This accords with what Nicolas Remy states in his *Demonolatry*, for he was astonished to find that many of the Lorraine sorcerers who had fallen into the hands of justice asked to be purged by a second baptism, and it became necessary to explain to them the folly and the futility of such a request, since Holy Baptism impresses an ineffaceable character on the soul, a spiritual and indelible mark.

Jeannette d'Abadie, a witch of the Pyrenees, confessed that she had often witnessed at the sabbat the impious baptism of children, and among the Swedish witches of Mora on Lake Siljan in the years 1669–1670 the rite was regularly practised. They confessed that the devil " caused them to be Baptized too by such Priests as he had there, and made them confirm their Baptism with dreadful Oaths and Imprecations ". The Salem trials of the New England witches supply very ample accounts of baptism, but concerning these it will be sufficient to quote from Cotton Mather's *The Wonders of the Invisible World*, a passage from the trial of Elizabeth How on 30th June, 1692 : " there came in the Confessions of several other (penitent) Witches, which affirmed this *How* to be one of those, who with them had been baptized by the Devil in the River at *Newbury* Falls : before which he made them kneel down by the Brink of the River and worship him."

In some instances at this baptism the witches forswore their old names and were given new, as for example a sorcerer of Cuneo, della Rovere, who was renamed Barbicapra. The author of *A History of the Witches of Renfrewshire* lays particular stress on this, and writes : " Renouncing of baptism is by Delrio made an effect of paction, yet with us it is *per se* relevant, as was found in the former process of Margaret

Hutchinson [1661] . . . and our witches always confess the giving them new names, which are very
ridiculous, as Red-shanks, Sergeant, &c."

Another detail in the profession is that the witches
give the devil either a lock of their hair or some piece
of their clothing in token of their vassalage, for as
Guazzo explains the fiend is eager to make them his
own in every particular, and this gift establishes a
psychic sympathy or copula. Moreover these objects
are often utilized in confecting a charm.

The Waldensian upon his reception into this horrible
company of devil-worshippers was required to offer
the demon a lock of his hair, nail-parings, and a few
drops of his blood.

In January, 1929, intense excitement was caused
in the United States by the trial at York, Pennsylvania,
of John H. Blymyer, a voodoo-man and professed
witch-doctor, for the murder of Nelson Rehmeyer,
who was locally notorious as a practitioner of black
magic. Blymyer and two companions, Wilbert Hess
and John Curry, visited Rehmeyer, who lived at a
lonely farm, in order to secure a lock of his hair which
was required for removing a " hex " or spell he had
cast on the Hess family. The hair had to be buried
eight feet underground, and the charm would be
dissolved. Rehmeyer refused, and in the course of
the fight which followed he was struck on the head
with a billet of wood and killed. Milton Hess and his
wife Alice testified that Blymyer, who was a pow-wow
man, told them they had been " hexed ", and they
firmly believed such was the case. Blymyer, when
examined, stated that for ten years he was under a
" hex " cast by " Old Man Rehmeyer ", and that

Mrs. Noll, a sorceress, instructed him how to free himself by getting a lock of the wizard's hair. When asked by the judge, " What does hexing do to you ? " Blymyer replied : " You can't rest. It takes the appetite away."

Blymyer was sentenced to imprisonment for life. None the less, " The pow-wow doctors and the necromancer who told Blymyer that he was bewitched by Rehmeyer continue to do business in York County to-day, unmolested and unconcerned over Blymyer's fate . . . York's trust in ' medical ' treatment by charms and incantations, based on mysterious rites culled from mediæval books on witchcraft, seems unbreakable " (*Daily Express*, Friday, 11th January, 1929).

An essential part of the profession is that the witch should swear allegiance to the devil, and do homage. " They who swear fealty to the feudal Lord do so by falling on their knees before him, giving the required kiss and placing their joined hands between his hands, thus symbolizing a lowly and willing obedience of spirit, and the Demons must strictly exact a similar homage from their subjects whenever they hold their assemblies, although the ceremony is conducted in the strangest and most degraded manner, as is every-thing else they do." Thus Remy. A witch of Lorraine named Beatrix Bayona described how when this horrid society assembled " one of the Demons always sat on a high throne with a proud and haughty demeanour, and so each in turn approached him with awe and trembling and, in sign of submission, fell prone at his feet and reverently embraced them ". Marion Grant, an Aberdeen witch (1597), confessed that the devil " causit the Kis him in dyvers pairtis, and worship him on thy kneis as thy Lord ". Elizabeth Style and the Somerset witches (1664) were very particular in their mention of the ceremonious salutation when they met the devil. " Alice Duke, Anne Bishop and Mary Penny had their rendezvous about nine of the Clock in the Night, in the Common near Trister Gate [Stoke Trister is some two miles from Wincanton], where they met a Man in black Clothes with a little Band, to whom they did Courtesie and due observance, and the Examinant verily believes that this was the Devil."

The allegiance vowed by the witch to the devil at her profession was renewed at almost every Sabbat, and in fact became part of the ritual observed on these occasions, as is noted by many authors.

" They swear allegiance to the devil," says Guazzo, " within a circle traced upon the ground. Perhaps this is because a circle is the symbol of divinity, and the earth is God's footstool ; and so he wishes to persuade them that he is the God of heaven and earth." Mother Humphrey, an old witch of Maplestead in Essex, instructing Joan Cony in the craft bade her kneel within a circle on the ground and pray to Satan when the spirits would come to her (1569–1570). Jules Bois in his study *Satanism and Magic* speaks of homage rendered to Satan by those who stand within the circle.

A familiar, an attendant spirit or demon to obey the commands and serve the pleasure of the witch, is assigned to the newly-professed upon admission. In Holy Writ we are told that King Saul " had put away those that had familiar spirits, and the wizards, out of the land ", but when on the eve of Gilboa " the Lord answered him not, neither by dreams, nor by Urim, nor by the prophets ", he said to his servants, " Seek me a woman that hath a familiar spirit, that I may go to her and enquire of her. And his servants said to him, Behold there is a woman that hath a familiar spirit at En-dor " (1 Samuel xxviii, 3, 6, 7, *A. V.*). In Leviticus we have the divine injunction : " A man also or woman that hath a familiar spirit, or that is a wizard, shall surely be put to death" (xx, 27).

William Forbes in his *Institute of the Laws of Scotland* writes that " to some [the Devil] gives certain Spirits or Imps to correspond with, and serve them as their Familiars, known to them by some odd Names, to which they answer when called ". The familiar assumed various forms, sometimes human, sometimes animal, most conveniently to suit the business upon which he was employed. Bishop Binsfeld in his *A Complete Review of the Confessions of Warlocks and Witches* lays stress upon these particulars, and (in agreement with all other authorities) shows how the familiar can disguise himself in that form which is most apt for his requirement. Many writers, however, assert that the familiar can never assume a perfect form, whether human or animal, that is to say there will always be some ugly blemish, some deformity, although of course this may be cunningly hidden and disguised.

In his celebrated *A Treatise of Ghosts*, the Capuchin Father Noel Taillepied writes : " Solid historians tell us that the Pagans had their Lares, Penates, and inferior household deities, whom they honoured as the protectors of the family and the home, and who were none other than familiar spirits who manifested themselves and made it their business to interfere in mortal affairs in order that they might induce and entice men to worship them. Thus the account given by Froissart of the demon Orthon is deservedly famous."

Raymond, lord of Corasse, which is about seven leagues from Orthez, Béarn, having affronted a clerk curate of Catalonia, was by the command of this necromancer visited by a familiar, Orthon, who arrived amid a great gale and tempest. Raymond, however, struck a pact with the demon, who was wont daily to bring news from almost all quarters of the globe, but who stoutly refused to say how he travelled to and fro, whether or not he was winged. Being pressed to manifest himself under some visible form he bade Raymond look from his window early in the morning. There was nothing to be seen save two straws twisting and untwisting in a gust of wind. That night Orthon revealed he was one of those straws. He agreed to show himself again, but when Raymond saw a huge sow, very lean and ill-favoured, in the courtyard, he cried to loo the dogs at her, whereon the shape melted into air, and never again did Orthon return to the castle. Raymond died within the twelvemonth.

The witch's familiar or Astral Spirit is a demon, and as such the word will be used here. Other names signifying a familiar are bunn (generally a term of endearment), imp, likeness, spirit, devil, fiend, angel, maumet, puckrel, nigget.

In reference to this connotation of the term "familiar" it is interesting to note what Professor

T. Gwynn Jones tells us in his study *Welsh Folklore and Folk Custom*. Having discussed haunted houses, ghosts, and poltergeists, he continues, " There is in Welsh tradition some uncertainty as to the character of the Familiar Spirit and its relation to the person whom it serves. Codi cythreuliaid, ' to summon devils ' is properly a matter of witchcraft, depending upon certain formulæ which even professed magicians sometimes failed to control. That the familiar spirits in Wales, like those employed by magicians elsewhere in the eighteenth and preceding centuries were mostly ' demons ', there is no reason to doubt. Although they were generally invisible, at least to others, they were also frequently visible in various shapes— those of a fiery ball, a roaring flame, a round bowl, a goose or a gosling, a dog, especially a mastiff, a bull, and a lovely young woman are noted. . . . Persons who had seen such demons refused to describe the sight and often died soon after the occurrence. There seems to have been belief not only in a demon coming when called and doing what he was told to do, but also in a comparatively harmless type of familiar, attaching himself to certain persons without invocation and performing certain duties of their own choice."

Mr. Wirt Sikes, who was the United States Consul for Wales, writes in his *British Goblins* : " The sort of familiar spirit employed by magicians in the eighteenth and preceding centuries was distinctly a demon." Thus the familiar controlled by Sir Dafydd Llwyd is celebrated throughout all Wales. Sir Dafydd Llwyd, who lived in Cardiganshire in the reign of Charles II, had studied black magic at Oxford. He practised as a physician and was far famed for his

skill and the wonderful cures he effected. Originally
he had held a curacy but he was deprived on account
of his abominable sorceries. The chief source of
information concerning this old magician is a work
very seldom to be met with, *A Relation of the Apparition
of Spirits in the County of Monmouth and the Principality of
Wales* by Edmund Jones, who in the first years of the
nineteenth century was Pastor of the congregation of
Protestant Dissenters at the Ebenezer Chapel near
Pontypool. The Rev. Edmund Jones, commonly
known as " Prophet Jones ", was himself a very
extraordinary character. Not only his fervent piety
and eloquence in the pulpit but, as evidenced by his
nickname, his insight into the future made him
remarkable. As he himself often averred, a belief in
ghosts, witches, fairies, and the whole order of supernatural beings was part and parcel of the Christian
faith, and the man who denied the goblin world was
no better than a Sadducee and a rank infidel.

" It was Sir Dafydd Llywd's great wickedness to
make use of a familiar spirit. . . . The bishop did
well in turning him out of the sacred office, though he
was no ill-tempered man, for how unfit was such a
man to read the Sacred Scripture ! With what
conscience could he ask the sponsors in baptism to
undertake for the child to renounce the world, the
flesh, and the devil, who was himself familiar with
one of the spirits of darkness ? . . . Of this Sir Dafydd
I have heard much but chiefly depend upon what was
told to me by the Rev. Mr. Thomas Lewis, the curate
of Landdw and Tolachdy, an excellent preacher of the
gospel ; and not sufficiently esteemed by his people,
(which likely will bring a judgement on them in time

to come). Mr. Lewis knew the young woman who had
been Sir Dafydd's maid servant, and the house where
he lived." The story went that Sir Dafydd kept his
familiar locked up in a book of spells. On one occasion
he accidently left this book behind him, and at once
sent his page home to fetch it, strictly charging him
not to open it. The lad being, as boys use, of an
inquisitive turn of mind, on his way back to his
master bégan to turn over the leaves, and read
although the words were quite unintelligible to him.
Suddenly there issued forth a huge cacodemon who
with a frowning face in a gruff grumbling voice asked
to be set to work. The boy in spite of his terror had
the wit to say : " Fetch me some stones out of the
river Wye." In a few moments stones and pebbles
began to fly through the air, when Sir Dafydd, who
from the delay had a shrewd suspicion of what must
have happened, came hurrying upon the scene, and
conjured the spirit back into the book before any
serious mischief had been done.

Whilst Cornelius Agrippa was lecturing at Louvain
there happened to be lodging in the same house as
this famous occult philosopher and his wife a young
student, who had long been very anxious to pry into
all the secrets of divination and goety. His chance
he thought with glee was now surely come. But
Agrippa when he went abroad invariably double-
locked his study door and carried the keys in his purse.
The youth who was handsome, rash, eloquent, and
of a warm amorous complexion, as a preliminary
began to woo the lady pretty hotly, nor was it long
indeed before she granted him an ample share of her
favours. This wanton was Agrippa's third wife, a

native of Mechlin, who had much beauty but so little honesty that he was at last compelled to divorce her. Nor would she have hesitated to filch her husband's keys had opportunity offered, as her gallant often wheedled and pressed her, but they were too safely guarded for even her nimble fingers to reach, and conscious of her adulteries she shrank from arousing suspicion in any direction. At length urgent business, a wealthy and exacting patient—for Agrippa was practising and highly esteemed as a physician—compelled him to be absent for some days, and meanwhile he entrusted his keys to his wife, most strictly enjoining her that nobody should so much as venture to set foot across the threshold of his study. She promised that he should be obeyed in every particular, and no sooner had he ridden off than she hastened to hand over to her lover the bunch of keys, only begging him not to move anything or displace a single caliper or sphere. He protested that he would use every caution, indeed he desired no more than a peep at the workshop of so great and reverend a master, at the same time in his own mind he had determined to purloin some manuscript or formula which might instruct him in the art of turning metal into gold, perhaps he might even secure a pinch of the powder of transmutation itself. It was late and the house was wrapped in sleep when the adventurous young man crept softly down the stairs and unhasped the door of the mysterious sanctum. As half-daring, half-afraid, he held the flickering lamp high above his head he saw that upon the philosopher's desk there lay open a huge book close written as it seemed in scarlet characters which might be blood. Gently drawing to the door, lest he should be interrupted

at his unhallowed task, he advanced, set down
his light upon the table, and seating himself in the
quaintly carven chair he bent to con that cabalistic
page. What secrets did it hold, what runes of awful
power ? The cipher was strange, in no tongue he
knew, but he made shift as he pored thereon to pronounce some few words. Suddenly he fancies he hears
a sharp knock upon the door. He listened for a
moment, but all was still. He turns to his task. Hardly
has he uttered some half a dozen syllables more than
the knock is repeated with awful force. Leaping to
his feet he tries to speak, but his tongue is parched and
dry and he cannot articulate a sound. His hair bristles,
and his body is cold with the sweat of fear. The door,
slowly turning on its hinges, discloses a stranger of
majestic form upon whose face there sits eternally
a grim black scowl and whose eyes glow with fury
like red coals of fire. Advancing he sternly demands
in threatening tones why he was summoned. " I did
not call you," stammers the wretched youth. " You
did ! " cried the stranger, " and learn that demons are
not invoked by fools in vain ! " His crooked claws
are at the young man's throat, and a moment later
he cast aside his body as it were some empty husk
upon the floor. Not many hours after dawn Agrippa
in silence and with frowning brow comes swiftly back
to his house. He enters the study, and with a glance he
realizes what has happened, even as he guessed whilst
many leagues away. With mighty gestures and
impious charm he recalls the familiar whom he
sharply upbraids for so rash a deed, commanding the
murderous spirit to assume a human form, and then
immediately to reanimate the poor dead body and to

walk forth with it up and down in the market place and crowded streets. With horrid mutterings the demon obeys. He appears as a grave and sober burgher of middle years in rich attire. The student revives, and putting his arm through that of his unearthly companion, they go forth together very friendly in the sight of all the passers-by. They even enter the college courts and quadrangles and are hailed by the dead man's comrades with jest and merry greeting as they bustle to and fro to lecture-rooms and classes. It is noon ; from tall belfry and from lowlier convent gablet rings forth the Angelus. Cold and lifeless the youth falls to the ground ; his companion is nowhere to be seen. At first it is thought he has expired in some apoplexy or fatal fit. But when they examine his body marks of strangulation are found on the neck. The prints of the cruel claw of the demon are only too plain. It is whispered that his companion vanished in a flash of flame. Suspicion is aroused. The magistrates institute inquiries. They visit Agrippa's house, and question those dwelling there. That evening Agrippa and his wife fly from the town.

So the legend runs. Similar stories are related of many warlocks and there is no reason why they should not in effect be substantially true. The ignorant who meddle with magic out of the itch of an idle and wicked curiosity are courting dangers whereof they are wholly unaware.

It was a very ancient and widespread notion, possibly of oriental origin, that a witch might keep and confine his familiar in some one instrument or place. There was a common proverb, for example, in the fifteenth century, " Beware of the devil in Ossiach."

Now Ossiach was a Benedictine monastery in Austria, and the story went that the monks had imprisoned a demon in a crystal or glass vial. Paracelsus was believed to have confined his familiar in the pommel of his sword. There is nothing either theologically or philosophically impossible in the fact that a spiritual body, an angel (either good or evil) can be contained in even a point of space.

In the Canary Isles, before the natives embraced Christianity, familiar spirits who had assumed human forms could be seen walking about, not only at night but in broad day, conversing with and accompanying their wizard masters on various businesses.

A famous Spanish scholar and physician of the sixteenth century, Dr. Eugenio Torralba (who incidentally is mentioned by Cervantes in *Don Quixote*) was for many years ministered to and served by a familiar. Whilst Torralba was still a young man, a student of medicine, he formed, owing to their interest in the same pursuits, an intimacy with a certain Fra Pietro, a Dominican. One day the friar in close confidence imparted to his friend that he was attended by an angel or genius named Zequiel (Ezechiel). He was bound by no pact or vow, however, to this spirit upon whom he merely had to call for help to be relieved in any necessity and advised as to his future undertakings. Fra Pietro promised to present Torralba to Zequiel, and at a fitting opportunity the form of a young man with fair hair and a mild countenance stood before them. Addressing the doctor the spirit said : " I will hold myself at your service so long as you live, and I will follow you faithfully wherever you go." There was no suggestion of any other bond or agreement between the two. Henceforward Zequiel appeared to the doctor at the quarterly changes of the moon, and more often, whenever he was summoned, if there was need of him. Torralba expressly stated that the spirit had never uttered a word contrary to religion, never given him bad counsel, never inspired evil thoughts, and not infrequently even accompanied him to Holy Mass, so that he verily thought an angel was his monitor and guide.

On one important occasion Torralba was consulted by Cardinal Bernadino Lopez de Carvajal, a theologian of acknowledged eminence, concerning a dark and mysterious business. A lady of wealth and position had with great trepidation and alarm informed the Cardinal that she was nightly disturbed by the phantom of a man, completely unknown to her, who declared that he had been murdered and unavailingly sought rest. The Cardinal had directed his body-physician Morales to watch with the lady and report what occurred. Morales for several nights had remained in the chamber but could discern nothing. although at a certain hour he felt a chill as if of the grave, accompanied by a loathly smell of corruption which filled him with no ordinary horror and fear, whilst the lady cried out that the ghost had appeared. Cardinal Carvajal, knowing Torralba's deep studies in occultism, prayed him to join Morales at the next opportunity, and accordingly the two doctors took their station in the haunted room. About one o'clock they heard an anguished cry, the air grew deathly cold and was filled with the stench of human decay. Torralba saw by the bed the figure of a man covered with wounds, the countenance distorted and pale with pain. A little further there lurked an even more terrifying apparition, the half-formed shadow of an evil woman, her vile face leering horribly from the darkness. " What would you ? " demanded the scryer. " The treasure ! the treasure ! " moaned the vision. Upon being questioned, Zequiel informed Torralba that in a cellar long years before had been buried the body of a miser, assassinated, all unshriven and unhouseled, for the vast sums it was known he had concealed in the house. The woman, whose spectre had been seen, was his servant who had admitted the ruffians with whom she was in league, but after the murder they could not find the hiding-place of the money-bags, and so perforce remained unsatisfied. The crime had never been discovered. Zequiel revealed the sliding panel which gave access to the secret room where the wealth was stored, and which actually opened out of the lady's bedchamber. The money being thus recovered, a part was devoted to masses for the dead man's soul, the remainder to other pious and charitable uses, and so the unhappy and unquiet house found rest.

Eventually Torralba was denounced to the Inquisition as a sorcerer. When examined he frankly acknowledged his intercourse with Zequiel, who was, he maintained, a good spirit, perhaps an angel. After a long investigation the lightest of sentences was passed, mainly consisting of a formal and public abjuration of all heresies and magic. He was, however, bound by a solemn oath to hold no further communication with the familiar.

Zequiel, as we have remarked, appeared as a comely fair-haired young man. A Suffolk witch of the reign of Charles II confessed that the demon visited her "in the form of a Pretty handsom Young Man first". More often the familiar is evil-favoured and misshapen, so ugly indeed as to betray his diabolic origin. The late Mrs. Violet Tweedale saw a familiar of this kind at Nice. She noticed that a certain Prince Valori, who frequented the fashionable Riviera, seemed always to be attended and shadowed by a man in grotesque attire. This personage was gaunt and emaciated, "with very long thin legs, and he was dressed entirely in chocolate brown—a sort of close-fitting cowl was drawn over his head, and his curious long, impish face was made more weird by small, sharply pointed ears rising on each side of his head. He appeared to have 'got himself up' to look like a satyr or some such mythical monstrosity." At a fancy-dress ball Mrs. Tweedale saw Prince Valori magnificently costumed as a French courtier of the eighteenth century, and by his side moved the man in brown. They came up to her, and she naturally concluded that he was about to present his friend. The Prince, however, seated himself by her and talked whilst the satyr stood behind them in perfect silence. Mrs. Tweedale says that she felt exceedingly uneasy all the while. Later she took the opportunity of quietly asking a Russian lady, a clairvoyante, who the brown satyr was. "Why don't you know?" was the reply. "It is his familiar who constantly attends him. People say they became attached whilst he was assisting at a Sabbath in the Vosges, and he can't get rid of it. Sabbaths are still held at Lutzei, and each initiate receives a familiar. The familiars have names —Minette, Verdelet, and so forth. One of my ancestors

de Laski, the Polish boyar who patronized Dr. Dee,
owned a familiar called Sainte-Buisson." "Then
the satyr attached to Prince Valori is not flesh and
blood ? Horrible ! " exclaimed Mrs. Tweedale. " Is
he always there ? " " Oh yes. Any one who is
clairvoyant sees him. I myself have seen him in
Paris." A few mornings after, Mrs. Tweedale meeting
Prince Valori on the Promenade des Anglais boldly
asked him, " By the way who is that tall man so
curiously dressed in brown I have seen with you
lately ? " The Prince's face changed : " You also,"
he muttered. " My remark was a thoughtless
impertinence. I am sorry to have hurt you. Pray
don't answer." He shook his head gloomily, and after
a moment's silence, " I am not the only one in the
world so afflicted," he said.

Mrs. Tweedale knew General Elliot, who commanded the forces in Scotland, and was a distinguished
figure in society in the nineties. The General had a
familiar " Wononi ", to whom he actually used to
speak aloud in the middle of a dinner party.

The animal familiar, imp or maumet—" puckrel "
is the old English country name—was quite distinct
from the familiar in human shape. In England, most
frequently in Essex, Suffolk, and the Eastern Counties,
and in Scotland there is abundance of evidence concerning the puckrel. " To some of the baser sorte of
them [witches] he [the devil] oblishes him selfe to
appear at their calling upon him, by such a proper
name which he shewes unto them, either in likenes
of a dog, a Catte, an Ape, or such-like other beast ;
or else to answere by a voyce onlie. The effects are to
answere to such demands, as concernes curing of

diseases, their own particular menagery : or such
other base things as they require of him. But to the
most curious sorte, in the formes he will oblish himself,
to enter in a dead bodie, and there out of to give such
answers, of the event of battels, of maters concerning
the estate of commonwelths, and such like other great
questions : yea, to some he will be a continuall attender,
in forme of a Page : He will permit himselfe to be
conjured, for the space of so many yeres, either in a
tablet or a ring, or such like thing, which they may
easily carrie about with them." Thus concisely King
James VI of Scotland (not to be James I of England for
another half a dozen years) in his famous *Dæmonologie*
summed up the question of familiars.

At Windsor, in 1579, Mother Dutton, who lived at
Clewer kept " a Spirite or Fiende in the likenesse of
a Toade ". Mother Devell, whose cottage was " nigh
the Ponde in Windesore " had a spirit in the shape of a
black cat, called Jill. Mother Margaret, a cripple, who
was in the Windsor almshouses, maintained a
" Kitlyng or Feende by her named Ginnie ". One
notorious witch of that knot " kept a Ratte, beeyng
in very deede a wicked Spirite, naming it Philip ",
and this rat she fed with blood " issuing from her
right hand wrest, the markes whereof evidently
remain ". The Lancashire witch Mother Demdike
entertained a familiar who first appeared in the shape
of a boy, but later in the likeness of a brown dog, and
was called Tibb.

This was in the early seventeenth century, the reign
of James I, but to come down to the present day, a
resident of Horseheath, a village about fourteen miles
from Cambridge, gave the following details regarding

the sorceries of Mother Redcap, a notorious witch who died in 1926. " One day a black man called, produced a book, and asked her to sign her name in it. The woman signed the book, and the mysterious stranger then told her she would be the mistress of five imps who would carry out her orders. Shortly afterwards the woman was seen out accompanied by a rat, a cat, a toad, a ferret, and a mouse. Everybody believed she was a witch and many people visited her to obtain cures " (*The Sunday Chronicle*, 9th September, 1928).

Very frequently the witch did (and for the matter of that does) keep some small animal which is nourished on a diet of milk and bread, and often stimulated with drops of her own blood, in order that she may divine by its means. The details of this particular method of augury are by no means clear. Yet it seems certain that something unhallowed and even diabolical must enter in, and we are bound to regard the medium as magical or ensorcelled. Probably of old the witch observed the gait of the animals, and its actions ; the tones of its voice were easily interpreted to bear some fanciful or likely meaning, whilst no doubt a dog, or such a bird as a raven, a daw, a pie, could be taught tricks to impress the simplicity of inquirers. At the same time it is a very well known fact that most animals are not merely extraordinarily intelligent but also extraordinarily psychic. The dog and the cat and many birds are in close touch with the unknown. Both dogs and cats are aware of any coming misfortune in a house, especially if it be a death. Dogs, moreover, have the faculty of seeing ghosts and are afraid of the supernatural. This is common knowledge.

The witch's familiar might be obtained in various ways. The demon familiar who appears in human form can only be procured at the sabbat, or else by some very explicit covenant with the fiend following upon a direct invocation. Thus, as has been noted, Prince Valori obtained his infernal companion at a sabbat in the Vosges. Virginie, the maidservant of Madame Belloc, a pious lady living at Agen at the beginning of the last century, confessed to her mistress that she was a Satanist and at a Sabbat had been assigned a familiar, an unclean spirit, who appeared as a young man and frequently had commerce with her.

" The Laplanders bequeath their demons as part of their inheritance which is the reason that one family excels another in this magical art." So often the puckrel was presented by the older witch of a family to the younger witches. Alice Hunt and Margery Salmon, two witches of Saint Osyth, were given two familiars apiece by their mother, Mother Barnes. Sometimes too a witch would present a familiar to another member of the society. Mother Waterhouse, a Chelmsford witch, possessed a black cat sent to her by the grandmother of Elizabeth Francis, a fellow witch. The old woman added instructions that the cat must be carefully nourished with blood and bread and milk.

The demon familiar, even in animal form, could converse. The Devil appeared in the size and shape of a dunnish coloured ferret to Joan Prentice, who dwelt in the almshouse at Hinningham Sibble. She was preparing for bed when the ferret, whose eyes glowed red as fire, came out of a corner and cried : " Joan Prentice give me thy soul." " What art thou ? "

stammered the wretched old woman, sore afraid.
" I am Satan," came the reply, " fear me not. I am
here to obtain thy soul." At night a grey shadowy
thing stood by the straw pallet of Elizabeth Clarke in
her miserable hovel at Manningtree and talked with
her, and anon brought her victuals. The imps of
Elizabeth Hubbard, a poor widow of Stowmarket,
were like three children who kept whispering that she
must deny God, Christ, and all good works. By their
aid she wrought fearful mischief throughout the
neighbourhood.

The familiar might also be procured by certain
impious rites or actions involving a profanation of
Holy Communion. As early as the twelfth century
Gerald de Barry, the distinguished Welsh writer, warns
priests against letting the Host by any accident get into
the hands of magicians. In the thirteenth century
Jacques de Vitry has an account of a woman who kept
the wafer in her mouth intending to convey it out of
church for witchcraft. A little later we find Berthold
of Ratisbon, one of the most famous preachers of the
day, denouncing those, " who do witchcraft with
God's Body, for that is the greatest of all sins that
ever the world committed," whilst those who are
guilty of such horrid impiety are " to the devil the
dearest that he hath ever begotten ".

On Spy Wednesday the Waldensians were wont to
attend the confessional with a great outward show of
penitence and devotion, and when they made their
Easter Communion they would secretly let slip the
Host out of their mouths and under cover of their
sleeves hide it in a handkerchief or glove. Then they
would carry it home and throw it to certain toads

THE SABBAT AT NORTH BERWICK CHURCH

Dr. Fian and his Coven

[face p. 40

which they used to keep and nourish in earthen pots and other vessels. Sometimes when the toads had eaten the Host the reptiles were killed and their blood employed to confect a certain charm. Occasionally the wizards were commanded to bring the Host to the Sabbat in order that they might defile the Body of God with every possible circumstance of filth and profanity.

In 1582 the wife of Edward Jones was called upon to prove to the satisfaction of the Archdeacon of Lewes " that she did eat the Communion bread and put yt not in hir glove ".

James Device, one of the Lancashire coven, was bidden by his grandmother old Demdike on Sheare Thursday morning to go to church to receive the Communion (the next day after being Good Friday), but not to eat the Bread the Minister gave him, since he was to deliver it to such a thing as should meet him on his way home. Yet he did eat the Bread, and as he was returning home, not more than a couple of hundred yards away from the church door, there met him a thing in the shape of a hare, and this asked him if he brought the Bread as his grandmother had bidden him. When he replied he had not, the thing threatened to tear him in pieces. Shaking with fear, he made the sign of the Cross, whereupon the thing vanished from his sight.

At the beginning of the eighteenth century two old dames attended the morning service at Llanddewi Brefi Church, and partook of the Holy Communion ; but instead of eating the sacred bread like other communicants, they kept it in their mouths and went out. Then they walked round the church outside nine

times, and at the ninth time the Evil One came out
of the Church wall in the form of a frog, to whom they
gave the bread from their mouths, and by doing this
wicked thing they were supposed to be selling themselves to Satan and become witches.—There was an
old man in North Pembrokeshire who used to say that
he obtained the power of bewitching in the following
manner :   The bread of his first Communion he
pocketed.   He made pretence of eating it first of all,
and then put it in his pocket.   When he went out from
the service there was a dog meeting him by the gate, to
which he gave the bread, thus selling his soul to the
Devil.   Ever after he possessed the power to bewitch.

The same profane practice persisted both in Berk-
shire and in Lincolnshire.   Not fifty years ago in the
latter county an old woman tried to persuade a young
girl to keep at least half the Bread in her mouth at
her first Communion, promising her that thus she
should become a witch.

In July, 1873, Mr. W. H. Gamlen, of Brampford
Spoke, Exeter, read a paper at Sidmouth, which was
afterwards printed in the *Transactions of the Devonshire
Association*.   He exhibited and discussed that curious
talisman, the toad-stone.   The specimen in question
had belonged to a Mr. Blagdon, of Puddington, to
whose house persons from all parts of the county
constantly resorted to borrow it, since it was supposed
to cure complaints that were presumed to be beyond
the skill of regular medical men to aid, such complaints
having been caused by some wicked person having
obtained power from the devil to do mischief.   The
person to obtain the power must be a communicant
of the Church of England or Rome.   " The power was

said to be obtained by keeping such a portion of the elements on receiving the Sacrament, and, after carrying them round the church and using certain incantations, giving them to a toad met with in the churchyard."

A Manx "Obbery" (superstitious sorcery) is "Bringing home some of the Sacramental Bread and making crumbs of it, when a huge black stag-beetle will come and eat it ".

Grotesque names were generally given to the familiar : In France, Lizabet, Verd-Joli, Maître Persil (parsley), Verdelet, Sainte-Buisson, Abrahel (a succubus) ; in Germany, Reicheher, Schwarzburg, Jammer, Helle-krug, Kuhfuss ; and in England, especially to animal familiars, Grissell, Greedigut, Blackman, Jezebel (a succubus), Ilemanzar, Jarmara, Pyewackett, Elva, Jeso, Arouta, Cramega, Panu, Vinegar Tom. Among the imps which Marion Hocket gave Sarah Barton of Harwich were two called Pretty-man and Dainty. So one of the Italian witches named his familiar, Fiorino.

Michael Dalton, the famous legal writer and author of *The Country Justice*, who died about the middle of the seventeenth century, summarizes the following articles from the Rev. Richard Bernard's *Guide to Grand Jurymen* as being (among others) of prime importance in trials for witchcraft.

1. These witches have ordinarily a familiar or spirit, which appeareth to them ; sometimes in one shape, sometimes in another, such as in the shape of a man, woman, boy, dog, cat, foal, fowl, hare, rat, toad, etc. And to these their spirits they give names, and they meet together to christen them (as they speak).

2. Their said familiar hath some big or little teat upon their body, and in some secret place, where he sucketh them. And besides their sucking, the Devil leaveth other marks upon their body, sometimes like a blue spot or red spot, like a flea-biting ; sometimes the flesh sunk in and hollow (all which for a time may be covered, yea taken away, but will come again, to their old form). And these the Devil's marks be insensible, and being pricked will not bleed, and be often in their secretest parts, and therefore require diligent and careful search.

These first two are main points to discover and convict these witches ; for they prove fully that those witches have a familiar, and made a league with the Devil.

The " big or little teat " or pap upon the witch's body, said to secrete milk which nourished the familiar, and which was one of the main points to discern and convict witches, must be carefully distinguished from the insensible devil-mark to be considered later.

In the case of the Witch of Edmonton, Elizabeth Sawyer, who was in spite of her resistance searched upon the express order of the Bench, it was found by Margaret Weaver, a widow of honest reputation, and two other grave matrons, who performed this duty, that there was upon her body " a thing like a Teate the bignesse of the little finger, and the length of half a finger, which was branched at the top like a teate, and seemed as though one had suckt it ". A boy, only nine years old, who lived at Rattesden, a small village in Suffolk, confessed that " he suckled an imp, and commanded it to do mischief ". He came of a bad stock, being the son of a witch, who had been hanged

(1645). John Palmer, of St. Albans (1649), confessed that " upon his compact with the Divel, hee received a flesh brand or mark, upon his side, which gave suck to two familiars ". The Kentish witch, Mary Read, of Lenham (1652), " had a visible Teat, under her Tongue, and did show it to many." At St. Albans about 1660 there was a wizard who " had like a Breast on his side ". There is similar evidence adduced in the accounts of Rose Cullender and Amy Duny, two Suffolk witches, executed in 1665 ; Temperance Lloyd, a Bideford witch, hanged in 1682 ; Widow Coman, an Essex witch, who died in her bed (1699) ; and, indeed, innumerable other examples might be quoted affording a whole catena of pertinent illustrations. The phenomenon, it is observable, seems to be stressed only in the records of England and New England, where, however, it is of exceedingly frequent occurrence. No doubt many of such instances are explicable by the cases of polymastia (*mammæ erraticæ*) and polythelia (supernumerary nipples) of which there are continual records in recent medical works. It must be freely admitted that these anatomical divagations are commoner than is generally supposed ; frequently they are so slight that they may pass almost unnoticed ; admittedly there is exaggeration in many of the inexactly observed seventeenth century narratives. However, it has to be said that when every most generous allowance is made, the facts which remain (and the details are very ample) cannot be covered by physical peculiarities and malformations.

As we know, a number of devils were permitted to enter swine, and certain writers have held (and nothing is more probable) that demons entered into these animal familiars, and that bound by a blood contract with the witch and nourished with human blood by the reeks and vapours of which they are recreated for " her young ones also suck up blood ", they obeyed the commands of the person they served, going forth to do mischief even to the destruction of life. When they thus assumed the form of or entered into an animal they are clearly " not perfectly *abstract* from all *body* and *matter* " wherefore the natural appetite of the animal would persist, and hence it must needs be fed in the ordinary way as well as rewarded with the sip of blood. This seems a simple and satisfactory explanation of various details in the mystery of the familiar that may appear puzzling. Glanvil suggests that further the sucking of blood " may be onely a *diabolical Sacrament* and *Ceremony* to confirm the *hellish Covenant*", whereby the witches become " *mischievously influential* ".

What wonder then that in 1604 there was passed an Act, 1 Jas. I, c. 12, against Conjuration, Witchcraft, and dealing with evil and Wicked Spirits, whereby it was ordered that if " any person or persons . . . shall use practise or exercise any Invocation or Conjuration of any evil and wicked Spirit, or shall consult covenant with entertain employ feed or reward any evil and wicked Spirit to or for any intent or purpose . . . then every such offender or offenders, their Aiders, Abettors and Counsellors being of any the said Offences duly and lawfully convicted and attainted, shall suffer pains of death as a Felon or Felons, and shall lose the privelege and benefit of Clergy and Sanctuary ".

CHAPTER II

Of the Practice of Witchcraft; of the Malice
and Mischief of Witches; of the Devil's Mark;
and of the Grimoire

Then flourish Hell, and mighty Mischief reign!
Dryden, *The Duke of Guise.*
Many of them also which used curious arts brought their books
together, and burned them before all men : and they counted the price
of them, and found it fifty thousand pieces of silver.
The Acts of the Apostles, xix, 19.

The most complete, as it is certainly the most
authoritative, summary of the mischiefs wrought by
witchcraft is that delivered in the famous Bull of
Innocent VIII where the evil is set forth in words of
burning eloquence and conviction : " Many persons
of both sexes unmindful of their own salvation and
straying from the Catholic Faith, have abandoned
themselves to devils, incubi and succubi, and by their
incantations, spells, conjurations, and other accursed
charms and crafts, enormities and horrid offences,
have slain infants yet in the mother's womb, as also
the offspring of cattle, have blasted the produce of
the earth, the grapes of the vine, the fruits of trees,
nay, men and women, beasts of burthen, herd-beasts,
as well as animals of other kinds, vineyards, orchards,
meadows, pasture-land, corn, wheat, and all other
cereals ; these wretches furthermore afflict and torment
men and women, beasts of burthen, herd-beasts, as
well as animals of other kinds, with terrible and piteous
pains and sore diseases, both internal and external ;

47

they hinder men from performing the sexual act and women from conceiving, whence husbands cannot know their wives nor wives receive their husbands ; over and above this they blasphemously renounce that Faith which is theirs by the Sacrament of Baptism, and at the instigation of the Enemy of Mankind they do not shrink from committing and perpetrating the foulest abominations and filthiest excesses to the deadly peril of their souls whereby they outrage the Divine Majesty and are a cause of scandal and danger to very many."

This historical pronouncement carries no mere historical interest. The wisdom of Pope Innocent is speaking to us to-day, and his words are as awfully solemn and as eternally true in the twentieth century as they were four hundred and more years ago. We have in these noble sentences set forth the very essence of witchcraft, that is to say the implacable hate the witch bears all mankind, and the dark power these slaves of Satan have obtained to contrive damage and destruction, ay, even of life, to the glut of their murderous malice and malignity.

The witch is an evil thing, indeed ; a social pest and parasite ; the devotee of a loathly and obscene creed ; an adept at poisoning, blackmail, and other creeping crimes ; a bawd ; an abortionist ; a minister to vice and corruption, battening upon the foulest passions of the age. Witches

raise jars,
Jealousies, strifes, and heart-burning disagreements,
Like a thick scurf o'er life.

Their baneful activities range from domestic annoyances and accidents, singly trivial enough maybe, but in sum horribly fretting and vexatious, to the most serious injuries, the ruin of property, sudden illness and wasting death, and ultimately to the embroiling of nations, to anarchy and red revolution, for the witch is and always has been a political factor. The witch is, in effect, a perpetual menace, a source of instant danger to any ordered society. In the humblest walks of life, in townlets and small villages, witches although almost isolated members of the infernal organization are yet potential murderers, even as the master whom they serve was a murderer from the beginning.

A correspondent in *The Times*, 19th September, 1930, writes : " In 1900 I was living in a small Sussex village between Groombridge and Eastbourne. An old villager one day began to talk about witches. ' The worst on 'em about here's not long dead,' she said. She told me a few of the common tales, injuring children, damaging poultry, &c. Then she warmed up. Pointing to the adjacent cross-roads, she said : ' I was standing just there, one day, and *she* was there. Along come one of Squire ———'s big farm carts, you know, him at the Park.' (Just then ' the Park ' was let to ' furriners '—i.e. non-Sussex people.) ' *She* looked at it, and down went the horses into the road over their knees, and the cart over the axles. ' "

Another correspondent in the same paper, three days later, related that when he was living in a small town in Somerset about 1912–13 he used to visit an old woman who told him that she had had an ulcerated leg ever since she came to the town and that there was no hope of her getting any better, since her ailment was due to a bad woman next door who had come and overlooked her one midnight. She further remarked that Somerset was particularly full of " bad folk ", that is to say witches. I suggest that the secret tradition has been handed down from the days of Julian Cox, Ann Bishop, and Margaret Agar.

In February, 1923, at Gorefield, a small village in Cambridgeshire, Mr. Scrimshaw and his family were bewitched, and much distress ensued in the house. Mrs. Holmes, who lived about a mile away, claimed to be able to break the spell as she had been " born in Chime-hours ". I will do what I can to help neighbour Scrimshaw," she said, " if they are witching him I can stop them." She collected some apple pips ; some locks of hair and nail parings from each member of the family, and these with two black pins she put in a bottle which was thrown on the kitchen fire. As the bottle burst she declared the charm was broken. However, new disturbances took place at the farm, coincident with which Mrs. Holmes died (*The Evening Standard*, 19th March, 1923).

Four peasants were tried at Szeged (Hungary) in January, 1928, for having killed an old woman, alleged to be a witch. The defendants were near relations of Vincent Tokar, who had long been bedridden owing to the malice of this hag. She visited him at night, and by her cantrips drained him dry as hay so that he dwindled, peaked and pined, and was left in so pitiable a state that his cousins resolved even with violence to free him from the evil spell. That evening they waited in the bedchamber, and when the woman entered swiftly dispatched her. The court acquitted the accused since they had acted under irresistible compulsion being compelled to believe in the stated origin of Tokar's illness. Moreover in the circumstances the case indicated the existence of a witch.

Some two years later there was a similar occurrence in a Hungarian village. A well-to-do farmer was seized with a sudden fever. One evening the sick man, raving in delirium, shouted that a witch had seized him by the throat and cast a curse upon him. " Save me from the witch," he cried, " she will appear at midnight." For three nights the family kept vigil, and on the third night as the church clock was striking twelve the door was flung open and a fearful crone hobbled in, but the men of the house sprang on her and a blow laid her dead on the floor. At that very moment the farmer rose from his bed, completely cured. Those concerned were tried for homicide and sentenced to short terms of imprisonment, which were much reduced by the Supreme Court at Vienna.

In September, 1928, Camilla Illasi was convicted at Padua of witchcraft, cruelty to animals, and extortion. She had terrorized the village of Bassanello for years, trafficking in black magic. She kept numbers of birds, dogs, cats, and rabbits which she used for her foul charms and auguries. The peasantry feared and hated the witch, who long cunningly evaded the law, but at last she was caught and reaped the full reward of her iniquities.

Writing in *The Church Times*, 8th May, 1931, and describing the Essex village of Good Easter, Donald Maxwell remarks that the people are still firmly convinced of the power of witchcraft and the evil eye. " There was no doubt whatever that old Mother Blankley was a witch. There was proof of it. What about Farmer Attridge's heifers and the strange litter of pigs in Old Mead's barn? She was a witch right enough."

A tourist in Cardiganshire writing in *The Daily Express*, 27th December, 1932, evinces surprise that in Wales to-day many people believe firmly in the power of witchcraft and the evil eye. " I was positive that my little pig was bewitched when one day he sat up on his haunches in the sty and laughed at me like a woman I know. I went to the wizard about it," one woman told him. Another woman said that when her two pigs refused to eat she consulted a wise man, who instructed her : " After sunset take a few hairs from the pigs' backs. Rub them into a ball of lard. Put the tongs over the fire and place the ball of lard on it. You must be alone. You will see a blue flame and in it the face of the person who bewitched your pigs. Feed the pigs next morning." This was done, the pigs were cured and the following day they ran to their food.

A few years ago a lady who was walking through the market square at Tavistock saw an old woman pilfering small articles from the stalls. She called the attention of one of the sellers to this, whereupon the hag swiftly turning round asked : " With which eye did you see all this ? " " With both my eyes," was the reply. The old woman muttered quickly to herself, and added aloud : " For meddling with what does not concern you, by this and that you shall see no more." So saying she waved her hand swiftly across the lady's face, not touching her, and hobbled away. Within an hour the lady lost her sight, and blind she remained until the day she died, which was in 1931.

A correspondent in *John O'London's Weekly*, November, 1936, observed that " even now belief in witchcraft in the upper parts of the Wye Valley is not quite extinct ". Mr. E. Thomas, writing in the following month, remarked, " when we lived in a small village in Montgomeryshire some years ago we found a widespread belief in witchcraft among the farmers of the district." If the cattle became sick the farmers visited the conjurer at LL—— to inquire who had bewitched their beasts. When two farmers had a serious quarrel, one of them went to the conjurer to procure a charm to injure his neighbour.

Other methods a witch might employ to plague her neighbours were by making the cows go dry, and so stealing the milk ; by enchanting the churn, whence butter would not come ; by burning the bread in the oven or souring it ; by spoiling the ale at brewing time. To us to-day generally these mishaps may not mean so much, for they can at least fairly easily be rectified, they may even appear a trifle ridiculous, not to say comical. But two centuries and less ago (and in some remoter districts now) when a household might depend for its comfort, nay, even for its sustenance, upon the success of these domestic operations things wear a very different face, and such malicious interference would have very disastrous results. Examples of all these mischiefs occur again and again throughout the witch trials. Alice Martin, a Devonshire witch, arraigned in 1565, used to enter houses begging for milk. If refused she would mutter " Give no milk : give no milk ", and from that day they could make no butter nor cheese nor have milk from their kine. About ten years ago there was a notorious witch living in

Caithness who wished to buy a young cow from a neighbouring farm. The owner refused to sell, saying he needed the milk. The witch replied that he would never again get milk from that cow, and her words came true. More recently a Welsh farmer was charged with assault. He had drawn blood from a reputed witch, and had compelled her to come to his house and unspeak the churn. He probably acted under great provocation and was justified in his somewhat rough and ready procedure.

Mother Waterhouse, one of the Chelmsford coven, who was hanged in 1566, confessed that she had sent her familiar to destroy the brewing. Mother Palmer, of Framlingham, came to Robert Waite's house and asked for a draught of beer. She was refused, and answered the goodwife, " You will want a cup o' beer yourself before long." After that they could make no beer which did not sour in a couple of weeks. The demon of Tedworth, who incited by the villainy and witchcrafts of the drummer, so plagued Mr. Mompesson's house, used to spoil the food by filling the porringers with ashes.

In Guernsey, not many years ago, a witch ruined the melons by the blight of a small black fly which the scientists found it impossible to recognize.

A particularly loathly annoyance whereby witches tormented their victims was through an uncouth spell to render them verminous. This filthy cantrip persists to-day. I have known the threat used and the dirty charm employed by sorcerers. In 1617 three Guernsey witches, Collette du Mont, her daughter Marie, and Isebel Becquet, were tried on multiplied charges. The household of James Gallienne, his wife and children had been cursed, and many other depositions of neighbours proved the accusation. Cattle died, mares miscarried, cows could give no milk, sheep sickened and fell, children and women were taken ill, men were lamed and palsied. There was no end to the mischief. Horrible black pimples broke out on the bodies of the afflicted persons ; insects swarmed in their houses, and lice in such abundance that they had to be swept away with brooms. The witches were found guilty by the Royal Court of Guernsey of having practised the damnable art of sorcery and of having thereby caused the deaths of many persons, of having destroyed and injured much cattle, and of many other abominable crimes. They confessed, and were very justly strangled and burned at the stake.

At Bedford, about 1637, old Gammer Rose amongst other charges was accused of making " a man to be alwayes lowsie ". The matter was proved beyond any question.

In 1645 a fearful witch, Elizabeth Fillet, of Witherenden, was put on her trial for various misdeeds. The wife of John Spink having made a slighting remark which was overheard by Mother Fillet, their child sickened and was suddenly covered with lice. In the same year Thomas Monticute refused old widow Thomazine Ratcliffe, of Shelley, some faggots. He became full of strange lice. A very respectable Norwich woman in 1843 made complaint before a magistrate that an old hag had bewitched her by sending her and her children a vast number of vermin. There dwelt as lately as 1874, in a lonely hut hard by the rugged promontory " La Roque du Guet ", Caûbo Bay, Guernsey, a known witch of long continuance, who plagued the whole countryside by her spells. A woman scrupulously clean in her person and attire against whom the witch had a previous grudge chanced to make use of some not very complimentary expressions in speaking of the old hag, and instantaneously her clothes were covered with vermin of the most loathsome description.

A Guernsey lady, Miss E. Le Pelley, in 1896 related that two young fellows, still in their teens, one day happened to chaff an old woman, when suddenly she got furiously angry, and stooping down gathered a handful of dust which she flung in the air, at the same time gabbling a sentence very quickly. The boys went home, and found they were covered with vermin. One was so enraged that he took his gun, ran back to the witch's house, and levelling it at her cried : " Now rid me of the lice, or I will shoot you." The old wretch was really frightened. She took up some dust, scattered it on him, repeated some words, and the vermin disappeared. The other youth was worried for three days.

Mrs. Le Patourel, of St. Martin's, was told the following by the lady to whom it happened, her own mother-in-law, at the time of the incident Miss Mauger, of Saints. Miss Mauger and her sister, who came of a wealthy old family, went to school in England at a new fashionable academy, where they imbibed rather grand notions. On their return home, being very handsome girls and fond of gaiety, they used to go to all the country dances, and were much sought after as partners by the beaux of the Island. But as young ladies sometimes will they held their heads pretty high, and only cared to dance with the most select and most eligible gentlemen. One evening when they were present at a dance with a girl friend and all three happened to be particularly smartly dressed in new frocks, some man whom they did not know came up without any introduction and asked each of them in turn to dance with him. Each, however, refused rather coldly, letting it perhaps be seen a little too plainly that he was hardly the partner for them. He turned away muttering that they would soon repent their rudeness. A minute later one of the girls said to her sister, " Oh, Marie, whatever is that crawling on your lace ? " Red with confusion, the girl killed the insect, only to see swarms more moving over her white satin skirt. The other two girls to their horror found that they also were alive with vermin. In the utmost confusion all three hurriedly left the room, and hastened home. Do what they would they were plagued for three days, when the lice vanished as suddenly as they had appeared. Mrs. Le Patourel says that in telling the story her mother-in-law always concluded : " The shame of it I can never, never forget."

Mr. John de Garis, of Les Rouvets, comments : " I have heard of too many instances of this power of giving vermin being exercised to admit of doubt. The surprising part is the removal. I have not heard of a case for more than thirty years."

Dr. A. N. Symons, of Jersey, notes : " Several times I have heard that the Witches could cover a person with lice by magic. Miss R. V., who formerly lived with her people at Coin Varin, says that one of her brothers was troubled in this way by a witch who lived in the cottage, now ruined, beside Les Luanes Hill. He took a whip and threatened to thrash the witch, whereupon the trouble was removed."

Mr. John L. Amy, the author of *Jersey Folk Lore*, relates the following incident which was told him by his mother, who had it from the widow of the man who was bewitched. Jean L. was a farmer of some wealth and influence in his parish of St. Lawrence, and much respected throughout the whole district. It happened that he had to attend at Court on a certain Saturday to pass a contract which meant £400 to him, a business country folk were wont to complete with considerable preparation and ceremony. To visit the Royal Court on such an occasion was in fact a gala day, and necessitated donning Sunday clothes and every rustic formality. A few days before the great event there came to the farm begging for a pot of cider one Collas D., a shiftless and ill reputed vagabond, to whom incidentally the farmer had always refused alms. " Be off with you," cried the goodman with some vigour on seeing the ragged rascal at his gate. " Cider or Contract," was the reply. " Either you give me the cider or you do not go to the Court on Saturday." Jean L. laughed in the beggar's face. The important morning arrived, and spruced in his smartest toggery, swinging his black malacca cane with the silver head jauntily as he strode along, Maître Jean set out on his way to the Court. All was well until he had reached the top of Mont Cochon Hill, and he had actually forgotten the threat of Collas D. It felt good to be alive with a contract for some hundred pounds in one's pocket. And he was *alive* with a vengeance ! He began to twitch and itch. He halted, tore off his collar and set about scratching his neck and face. As he looked at his clothes he turned sick with horror and dismay. He saw that he was literally swarming with filthy vermin from head to foot. No help for it. He hurried back home by the short cut across the fields keeping in the shadow of the hedges lest anyone should see him. When he opened the door of his house the lice all vanished, not a trace was there to be seen. But it proved far too late to resume his journey.

In Cornwall some half a dozen years ago two men were ill-wished with vermin. The spell was broken by standing in a church porch on Sunday morning and muttering to themselves as the congregation was leaving : " We have lost our flocks, call them home."

The sterile witch-charm known as "Tying the points", or in French *nouer l'aiguilette* :

to starve up generation,
To strike a barrenness in men and women,

so that the sexual functions in either sex were wholly incapacitated and a complete frigidity ensued was always regarded with especial abhorrence as an abomination mortally injurious to the most intimate human relations. Yet Delrio remarks that in his day it was one of the commonest as it was one of the vilest businesses of sorcery.

Bodin adds that there were no less than fifty methods of casting this accursed spell, which indeed is still employed by witches to-day, as a modern French writer, Roland Brévannes, attests.

The bond-slave of a murderer, the witch is also a murderer, a point that has already been touched upon, and one scarcely requiring any further enlargement. In Africa the ju-ju man will " hate " his enemy to

death.   The medicine doctor puts ju-ju on some
person, and that person dies.   He may fall down
suddenly ; he may waste inch by inch.   Only because
the wizard has looked at him, has pointed towards
him, and willed him to die.   That is all.

The German and Italian witches used to disinter
human corpses, especially the bodies of criminals who
had been hanged, to use them for the murderous
slaughter of men.   From such horrid material they
confected charms of especial potency.

In the Navarrese witch-trials of 1610 Juan de
Echelar confessed that a candle had been used made
from the arm of an infant strangled before baptism.
The ends of the fingers were lit, and burned with a
clear flame.

The right hand of a gibbeted felon, severed at the
wrist, was employed for the ghoulish charm known as
the Hand of Glory ; the Dead Man's Candle ; or,
the Corpse Candlestick.   The instructions to fashion
this magical taper are given at length in *Les Secrets
du Petit Albert*.   The ghastly relic of mortality was
mummified by being placed in an earthen pot with
coarse salt, dragon-wort, black pepper, nitre, and
various spices.   It was then bleached in the hottest
noonday sun, or baked over a fire fed with bracken
and vervain.   Certain impious incantations accompanied the process.   A candle having been moulded
from the fat of a hanged murderer together with
virgin wax and Lapland sesame the dead fingers were
twisted so as to hold this horrible taper, which burned
with a blue flame.   Whilst this was alight all those in
the house became entranced in a hypnotic sleep, and rendered incapable of word or movement.   Housebreakers

and assassins would purchase the Hand of Glory from witches at a high rate, and in the days when criminals were hanged in chains by the highway it was by no means impossible to procure the horrid ingredients for such a charm. There were, indeed, several recipes for it, and even to-day such practices are not unknown since it is authoritatively stated that in parts of Russia maidens have been killed in order to obtain the human fat for the manufacture of these necromantic candles. Madame de Baucé bought at a high price a Hand of Glory and a toad from the Parisian witch, La Voisin.

On the night of the 3rd January, 1831, a gang of Irish thieves broke into the house of Mr. Naper, of Loughcrew, Co. Meath. They had with them a dead man's hand with the fingers twisted round a candle. The servants, however, were alarmed and the robbers fled leaving the Hand of Glory behind them. It was suggested that it had not been exactly prepared, in which case the charm would certainly fail.

The witches, it must always be remembered, are adepts in the art of poisons, and no doubt the effect of their spells in many cases was not infrequently aided by a noxious draught. The devil, or Chief Officer of a coven, " delivers unto his *Proselite,* and so to the rest, the *Rules of his Art* instructing them in the manner of *hurting* and *helping.*" Even John Webster whose *Displaying of Supposed Witchcraft* (1677), " utterly denied and disproved " " a *Corporeal League* made betwixt the Devil and the Witch ", is bound to acknowledge " secret poysoning, we grant to be too frequent and common, because those persons commonly accounted Witches are extreamly malicious and

envious, and do secretly and by tradition learn strange
poysons, philters and receipts whereby they do much
hurt and mischief ".

Among the minor, but very active, agents concerned
in the scandals that came to a climax with the notorious
poisoning of Sir Thomas Overbury in 1613 was
" sweet father " Forman, as the Countess of Somerset
used to call him, a professed sorcerer, astrologer, and
necromancer, who vended curious philtres to the more
wanton court ladies, and having obtained a licence
from Cambridge University to practise medicine
almost openly trafficked in poison. Mrs. Anne Turner,
his daughter, who was hanged at Tyburn for her share
in the murder, was at her trial frankly saluted by Sir
Edward Coke as a bawd, a whore, a sorcerer, a witch,
a felon, and a murderer.

Of the same kidney was Dr. John Lambe, " an
absolute witch, a sorcerer, a juggling person given over
to lewd, wicked, and diabolical courses, an invocator
and adorer of impious and wicked spirits." Practising
as a physician, he sold poisonous draughts of such
graduated strength that a speedy or a slow death might
be arranged according to his client's convenience.
There can be little doubt that had it not been for the
all-powerful protection of the Duke of Buckingham the
Doctor would have been brought to Tyburn. He
was so hated indeed that he dare not walk abroad in
the streets of London, save in disguise. One afternoon
in 1628 he ventured to visit the Fortune Theatre in
Golden Lane to see a new play, but being recognized
on his way home, a brutal mob attacked him and with
hideous yells of " Kill the Duke's devil ! Kill the
wizard ! Kill the poisoner ! " they beat him to death.

The Marquise de Brinvilliers and her paramour Sainte-Croix were continually consulting astrologers and warlocks with regard to the efficacy of their drugs and the right times to administer their arsenic and lunar caustic, for there is a propriety in these things. The gangs of witches directed by the Abbé Guibourg and Catherine La Voisin numbered many poisoners of the most approved and widest experience, physicians, chemists, apothecaries, who laid claim to being artists in their profession and were mighty proud of their feats.

In Rome the witch Hieronyma Spara dispensed a wonderful elixir, clear, tasteless, and limpid, which sent those who were obstructive—an aged parent, a cruel husband,—to their long last sleep. She was hanged on 5th July, 1659. Even more famous and more enterprising was her successor La Toffania, a Neapolitan witch, who seems to have distributed her drugs wellnigh all over Europe. By a horribly profane sleight she was wont to label her vials Manna of St. Nicolas of Bari ", so that they passed as the miraculous oil which exudes from the sacred tomb of St. Nicolas, and for reverence sake were unexamined. The *Aqua Toffania* appears to have been crystallized arsenic dissolved in large quantities of water with the addition (for some unexplained reason) of the herb cymbalaria. A few drops were generally poured into coffee, chocolate, or soup, and its effects, although deadly sure, were so slow as to be almost imperceptible.

When some victim is marked for death by the witch there is made of the doomed person an image or effigy of wax, clay, marl, lead, leather, wood, or almost any material, and this being pierced with black pins, nails, thorns, or even struck through with a knife or dagger is burned or slowly melted before a great fire. As the image is pricked so the victim suffers in that part of the body ; as it is crumbled or dissolved, so he languishes ; when it is melted away or pierced to the heart, he expires. Such are the theory and practice of this " sympathetic " or " homœopathic " magic, as it is sometimes known. The image thus fashioned for purposes of sorcery has many names : figurine, puppet, moppet, doll, baby (in the obsolete sense of " doll "), effigy, maumet (the same name as given to a familiar), simulacrum, or even picture, since a painted canvas, a portrait, may be effectually employed. If a lock of hair, a piece of clothing, the nail-parings, or some other substance intimately related to the victim can be secured and moulded in or attached to the poppet the charm acquires so much the more force and propulsion. Sometimes a heart, most frequently the heart of an animal, will be used instead of a figurine. Not very many years ago some new tenants who had taken a house in Somersetshire found hidden in the chimney a big black velvet heart with pins thrust through it. They heard that the house had belonged to a witch. Other substitutes are employed. In Somersetshire, again, a sorcerer will write his enemy's name on a piece of paper and fasten this with as many black pins as possible to an onion, which must be put up the chimney. As the onion shrivels and withers so will the victim languish. An onion treated thus was found in a cottage chimney about 1880. Not long ago in a churchyard at Bradford, Yorks, a lemon was discovered stuck full of pins. The Neapolitan witches pierce a lemon, an orange, a potato, with rusty nails or pins to cast sickness upon or to kill the person who has offended them. The Sicilian *strega* transfixes an egg, an orange, or a lemon to the same end.

Sometimes the malefic charm can be directed against the witch in return, as witness an instance that came to the notice of Lady Peirse, and which happened about ten years ago. In a certain south country village in England a local farmer whose cattle ailed most mysteriously and showed every sign of having been overlooked, whilst things in general went wrong with him in every direction, consulted the witch-doctor, and was told to repeat a certain rhyme last thing at night, to nail a sheep's heart to his front door, to lock and bolt the door, to fasten every window, to sit up alone and whatever might happen on no account so much as to lift the latch until morning. He did exactly as had been prescribed. The family all went to bed, and he commenced his lonely vigil by the kitchen fire. After about half an hour there came a loud knocking at the door, and a voice shouted : " Let me in ! Let me in for a moment." The farmer, although trembling and afraid, made no answer, and did not stir from his place. After a very short interval the knocking was repeated, and a deplorable voice in plaintive accents begged for the door to be opened, but the farmer, although it was all he could do not to rise and unlock the door, remained obdurate as he thought of his suffering beasts. Lastly there was heard a very feeble knocking and a dull moaning sound. The farmer, even more alarmed, stoutly kept his post until sunrise the next morning. When he opened the door a near neighbour lay stretched across his threshold, dead. The doctor pronounced it a case of sudden heart failure. Nobody could explain why the man should have come to the farmer's house, whilst the farmer alone of his family had heard the knocks. The cattle recovered in a most extraordinary way, and all other things too began to go smoothly and well.

Mrs. Carbonell knew a case which happened in Devonshire in 1925. D. had a valuable mare which died suddenly. The veterinary surgeon was frankly puzzled, and could only say that it must have been the heat. D., however, felt sure that the mare had been overlooked, and riding over to the near market town, he decided to consult the white witch. On entering the wise man's house, he was greeted with : " I know the business upon which you have come. Go home, cut out the mare's heart, and fill it as full as you can with pins, and the one who has forspoken you will die." The farmer on his return did as he had been bid, and within a very few weeks a certain neighbour, in the flower of his age, sickened and died, nor did the doctor give his illness any name save a decline.

The magic use of actual figurines, moulded from some plastic material in human form, reaches back to remotest antiquity to Egypt, to Assyria, Babylonia, and India. It has prevailed among all peoples, savage and civilized, and admits of almost infinite variants in preparation and performance.

From ancient Egypt the magic use of wax figures passed to Greece and thence to Rome. The Anglo-Saxon Penitential incorrectly ascribed to Ecgbert, Archbishop of York, punishes this kind of sorcery, and provides for heavier penalties if the victim dies. At the Colchester Summer Assizes of 1580 there were many indictments for witchcraft and conjuration of spirits. Amongst others Nicholas Johnson of Woodham Mortimer was charged with making the portrait in wax of Her Majesty Queen Elizabeth. Elizabeth Device, the Lancashire witch, made a clay picture of John Robinson and crumbled it away, and within a week the man died. In 1900 an Italian burned a wax figure of President McKinley, quilled with pins like a hedgehog, on the steps of the American Embassy in London. Image magic is common enough to-day here in England, and in all countries of the world.

In a sentence passed upon a knot of witches at Avignon in 1582, *A Summary of All the Crimes of Witches*, one article runs thus : " that the Father of Lies should have a care to delete and obliterate you from the Book of Life you did at his direction and command with your own hands write your names in the black book there prepared, the roll of the wicked condemned to eternal death ; and that he might bind you with stouter bonds to so great a perfidy and impiety, he branded each of you with his Mark as belonging to him."

The Devil's Mark to which allusion is here made, or the Witches' Mark, as it is sometimes called, was regarded as perhaps the chief point in the identification of a witch, it was the very sign and seal of Satan upon the actual flesh of his servant and any person who bore such a mark was considered to have been convicted and proven beyond all manner of doubt of being in league with and devoted to the service of the fiend. This mark was said to be entirely insensible to pain, and when pricked, however deeply, it did not bleed. So Mr. John Bell, minister at Gladsmuir, in his tract, *The Trial of Witchcraft; or Witchcraft Arraigned and Condemned*, published early in the eighteenth century, explains : "The witch mark is sometimes like a blew spot, or a little tate, or reid spots, like flea-biting ; sometimes also the flesh is sunk in, and hollow, and this is put in secret places, as among the hair of the head, or eye-brows, within the lips, under the arm-pits, and in the most secret parts of the body." Robert Kirk, minister at Aberfoill, in his *Secret Commonwealth* (1691) writes : "A spot that I have seen, as a small mole, horny, and brown-coloured ; throw which mark when a large pin was thrust (both in buttock, nose, and rooff of the mouth), till it bowed and became crooked, the witches both men and women, nather felt a pain nor did bleed, nor knew the precise time when this was doing to them, (their eyes only being covered)."

Thus in the case of the Guernsey witches who were convicted by the Royal Court in July, 1617, Isebell Le Moigne confessed one night that, when she was at the Sabbath, the Devil marked her on the thigh. "The mark thus made having been examined by women appointed for that purpose, they certified that they had thrust pins deep into it, and that Isebell felt no pain therefrom, nor did any blood follow when the pins were withdrawn."

Whilst the notorious French wizard, Louis Gaufridi, "Lucifer's lieutenant, and Prince of all the hosts of sorcerers from Constantinople to Paris," lay in prison at Marseilles two physicians and two surgeons were directed by the judges to search him for the devil's marks. In their report which is very technical and detailed they speak of having discovered three callous marks, which when probed gave no pain, and which from this and other signs they are bound to pronounce not to be natural.

Inasmuch then as the discovery of the devil-mark was regarded as one of the most convincing indications —if not indeed an infallible proof—that the accused was guilty, it is easy to see how the searching for, the recognition and the probing of, such marks actually grew to be a profession in which not a few ingenious persons came to be recognized as experts and practical authorities. In Scotland, especially, the " prickers ", as they were called, formed a regular gild. They received a good fee for every witch whom they discovered, and, as might be expected, they did not fail to reap a golden harvest. One of the most notorious was John Kincaid of Tranent, who was acknowledged a master in his craft, although he found a serious rival in John Bain, who also showed himself a whole-hearted enthusiast. About 1630 Mr. John Balfour, of Corhouse, was feared all over the country for his exploits, and proved so ardent a publicist that he eventually came under the notice of the Lords of the Privy Council, who finding that his knowledge " has only been conjectural " put an abrupt end to his activities. Yet some twenty years later one John Dick was energetically pursuing the pricker's profession. The regular trade of these " common prickers " came to be a serious nuisance, and confessedly opened the door to all sorts of roguery. There was a Mr. Paterson, " who had run over the kingdom for trial of witches. . . . This villain gained a great deal of money, having two servants ; at last he was discovered to be a woman disguised in man's clothes." In 1649 a Scotch pricker was called in at Newcastle-upon-Tyne, but the experiment hardly proved satisfactory. He charged twenty shillings for each subject, and eventually he turned out to be a mere cheat. In 1662 the Lords of His Majesty's Secret Council forbade any sort of pricking for witchcraft save it were done by special Order in Council, and within a very few months several prickers were sentenced to terms of imprisonment.

The fleeting upon the water, or as it is generally known, the " swimming " of a witch, the water-ordeal, was popularly considered to be so supremely efficacious a test that it was still in use, albeit wholly illegal, of course, among rustics as late as the nineteenth century. The witches tied with " their thumbes and great toes . . . acrosse " and steadied by ropes—(" a roape, tyed about their middles ")—were let down into the water, some running stream, or a pond. If she sank the suspect might be cleared ; if she swam her blackest guilt was evident. For water was a holy element, it had become instinct with life whilst the earth was yet barren and uninhabited ; and as the witch had rejected the sacramental water of Baptism, so the pure lymph would refuse to receive her into its bosom. The analogy is perfectly sound, and King James is quite correct when he writes : " It appeares that God hath apoynted (for a super-naturall signe of the monstrous impietie of the Witches) that the water shall refuse to receive them in her bosome, that have shaken off them the sacred Water of Baptisme, and wilfullie refused the benefite thereof." William Perkins of Cambridge, in his *Discourse of the Damned Art of Witchcraft*, posthumously published in 1608, endeavours to argue against this conclusion, by laying down that " The

element out of the use of the Sacrament is no Sacrament, but returnes again to his common use ", an
opinion which much commends itself to a recent writer,
who thus regards Perkins as having exploded the sacred
character and symbolism of Holy Water. Perkins
was no doubt a very grave and earnest author, but his
theology (as here) is often extremely faulty, and it is
because of this that the inference seems entirely to have
escaped him. Holy Water is a sacramental, and
possesses a particular efficacy of its own. It has, moreover, the virtue to drive away those evil spirits whose
mysterious and baleful operations can do such harm
to man. Baptismal water is especially sacrosanct, for
it has been mixed with the holy chrism in solemn
rite. It is not necessary to labour these points in detail,
sufficient to remark how Perkins and his school have
mistaken and are in error in this respect.

Actually the Ordeal by Swimming was the Judgement
of God, and applied for many crimes. It goes back
to very early days, about the sixth or seventh century,
and it is obviously related to the belief that water (in
particular running water "—A running stream they
darena cross "—) will dissolve all enchantment and
magic glamour. During the seventeenth century
swimming was much favoured in England as a test
for a witch, although it was seldom countenanced by
authority. In 1612 two Bedfordshire witches were
swum in a mill-dam by Master Enger, a " gentleman
of worship ", whom they had harmed, and they
" floated like a plank ". In the same year three
Northamptonshire witches were swum, and could not
sink. Examples might be multiplied. In some very few
instances swimming was directed or at the least

permitted by the local magistracy, but Bernard in his
Guide to Grand-Jury Men insists upon the illegality of
this test, and Hopkins who certainly favoured the
process was soon forced to discontinue it.

There was living in 1931 at the Essex village of
Good Easter, a man who in his youth had been in
trouble with the local magistrates for attempting with
his friends the trial by swimming of an old hag, who
was generally believed to be a witch.   She was, however, rescued from their hands before they had thrown
her in the pool, and the charge brought against them
resolved itself into that of attempting to do grievous
bodily harm.

The *Morning Post* of 28th January, 1780, has an
account of two old women of Beck's Hill (Bexhill),
Sussex, suspected to be witches.   Many of the leading
inhabitants approached the parson, the lawyer, and
the mayor, requesting that these beldames should be
put to the test, " to try by swearing, swimming, or
weighing them if the opinion of the people was well or
ill founded."   As it might have fared badly with the
two women if this deputation had just been scouted,
" the Clerk was dispatched for the Church Bible,
which the two were weighed against, and which they
out-weighed, *a sure proof they were not witches.*"   This is
an old experiment and one that was employed from
time to time in country places, but it has never been
officially recognized and can hardly be regarded as
more than a tradition.

It has always been held that if the victim who is
overlooked can draw blood from the witch the spell
will be broken.   Again and again we find in the records
that in order to obtain relief the witch has been

scratched or blooded. This occurs as early as 1279, when John de Warham was fined 12*d*. by the Leet Court at Lynn, Norfolk, for " blood draught on Fair Alice ", whom he had (it seems) wrongly suspected. Passing down more than six centuries we may note an experience related by Mr. Walter Britten, as happening to a friend of his who was making a stay at Sidmouth in the days when the modern bicycle was still something of a novelty. The visitor, an enthusiastic devotee of the wheel, had a new machine sent down from London, and locally became known as " the flying devil ". One evening, being waylaid in a lane near Sudbury by a number of rustics, he dismounted with no small misgiving. To his surprise the leader of the party ran a sharp pin into one of his legs chanting, " Prickee wi' a pin, and draw his blood, an' ee can't hurt ee ! " After which ceremony the whole company at once appeared quite satisfied and friendly. This, of course, was nothing else than the scratching of the witch, so continually spoken of in the old trials, and recognized by the demonologists as a powerful counter-charm to malefic spells.

Writing from Plympton, on the 1st March, 1821, Lady Callcott (then Mrs. Graham) speaks of a rich baker in Plymouth, who some five years before had to pay five pounds compensation to a reputed witch. One of the baker's children being very sickly it was concluded the poor little creature had been over-looked, " and nothing but blood from the witch who had overlooked it could cure it. Accordingly, the lady of the Oven watched her opportunity ; and when the witch next came for a loaf, she and her maid flew on the old crone scratching her severely with long corking pins. The Mayor fined the baker, but it was considered extremely hard that a woman might not scratch a witch who had overlooked her child."

In August, 1927, an English lady who was walking in a wood near Travnik, in Bosnia, apparently aroused the suspicions of some peasant women, who crying out that she was a sorceress who would bewitch their children, attacked her, beating her and scratching her until the blood flowed. She escaped with difficulty, and found protection in the neighbouring village.

In 1928 a West Country smallholder was convicted of assaulting an old woman, whom he had scratched violently with a pin. The defence was that she had ill-wished him and his pig, so he had drawn blood on her to render her spells powerless to harm him for the future.

The black books or rolls of the witches carrying the names of the members of the coven were kept with great secrecy by the chief officer of the local society, or even by the Grand Master of a wider district. They would obviously have been guarded as something as precious as life itself, seeing that they contained the damning evidence of a full list of the witches of a province or county, and in addition thereto seems to have been added a number of magic formulæ, spells, charms, and probably, from time to time, a record of the doings of the various witches. The signing of such a book is continually referred to in the New England trials. So when Deliverance Hobbs had made a clean breast of her sorceries, " She now testifi'd that this *Bishop* [Bridget Bishop condemned and executed as a long-continued witch] tempted her to sign the *Book* again, and to deny what she had confess'd." The enemies of the notorious Matthew Hopkins made great capital out of the story that by some sleight of sorcery he had got hold of one of these Devil's memorandum-books, whence he copied a list of witches, and this enabled him to be so infallible in his scent.

An old Yarmouth witch in 1645 described how one night she heard a knock at her door, and peeping from her window she saw in the moonlight a tall, black man, whom she admitted. After some parley he promised to help her under certain conditions, and taking a little penknife he scratched her hand so that the blood flowed, with which she wrote her name in his book, and he guided her fingers.

Anne Bodenham, sometime servant to the notorious warlock, Dr. John Lambe, was executed at Salisbury when 80 years old. She had many books of spells, and especially a red one " written half over with blood, being the names of witches that had listed themselves under the Devil's command ". This, however, could not be recovered as it had been sent for safe keeping to a wizard named Withers, who lived near Romsey, Hants, and who absconded.

There is a somewhat vague story, no dates being given, that a Devil's book was carried off by Mr. Williamson of Cardrona (Peebles), who filched it from the witches whilst they were dancing on Minchmoor. But the whole coven at once gave chase, and he was glad to abandon it and escape alive.

Sometimes the catalogue of witches was inscribed on a separate parchment, and the book only used to write down charms and spells. Such a volume was the Red Book of Appin known to have actually been in existence a hundred years ago. Tradition said that it

was stolen from the Devil by a trick. It was in manuscript, and contained a large number of magic runes
and incantations for the cure of cattle diseases, the
increase of flocks, the fertility of fields. This document,
which must be of immense importance and interest,
when last heard of was (I believe) in the possession of
the now extinct Stewarts of Invernahayle. This strange
volume, so the story ran, conferred dark powers on the
owner, who knew what inquiry would be made even
before the question was poised ; and the tome was so
confected with occult arts that he who read it must
wear a circlet of iron around his brow as he turned
those mystic pages.

It is a strange and not very edifying chance which
has popularly attached the names of great Popes and
Saints to books of spells and grimoires, and some
authors such as Father Delrio, Pierre Le Loyer, and
Gabriel Naudé, the learned librarian of Cardinal
Richelieu and Cardinal Mazarin, have been at the
pains to show how absurd and indeed scandalous such
attributions are.   There is no need to labour the
point, for of course nobody imagines that Honorius III
composed an infernal grimoire or that St. Albert the
Great is the author of a manual giving directions how
to prepare cabbalistic talismans and a ring conferring
invisibility, any more than we believe (as was once
seriously asserted) that Abel wrote a treatise on judicial
astrology, which he enclosed in a rock where after the
Deluge it was discovered and published by the patriarch
Noah.

The history with the ancillary bibliography of
grimoires and books of spells is immense and im-
mensely complicated, nor even if it were desirable to

treat so dangerous a subject would it be possible to discuss it save at very considerable length. In order to illustrate the witches' library I will do no more then than mention a very few works which are so notorious that no purpose could be served by ignoring them, whilst no harm can come from so slight and guarded a notice.

Among the oldest and most terrible of the grimoires is the *Sepher Toldos Jeschu*, a Syro-chaldaic work, whose pages are happily sealed save to the very few. A book of conjurations, *Ars Notaria*, was once printed under the name of St. Jerome. Owing to a confusion between St. Cyprian, Bishop of Carthage, and St. Cyprian of Antioch the coverted sorcerer, who was martyred fifty years later, a number of mediæval spells have been ascribed to the former. Thus in Denmark and Scandinavia among the witches to-day almost any grimoire is dubbed the *Book of Cyprianus*. St. Ubald, Bishop of Gubbio in the twelfth century, who was especially famous for his powers in casting out evil spirits, is named on the title-page of a theurgical treatise which cannot be earlier than four centuries after his death. In France in the days of the Valois they were selling all sorts of alchemical and magical opuscules as being from the pen of St. Thomas Aquinas, upon whose venerable preceptor, St. Albert the Great, have been fathered perhaps the most famous, or most infamous, of all printed grimoires, *Les admirables Secrets du Grand Albert*, and the collection known by the running title *Le Petit Albert*, which two are the most extensively employed, and in some ways the most mischievous, grimoires to-day. It must be borne in mind that the numerous editions and reprints, both of

Le Grand Albert and *Le Petit Albert*, vary very widely, so much so, in fact, that a modern copy may be an entirely different book from an eighteenth century duodecimo carrying either name, whilst a third collection in its turn will present something quite new. Thus the 1668 sextodecimo, printed at Lyons, has charts of necromantic figures, talismans and pentacles, which are to be found in no other issue. (There is a facsimile, made about thirty years ago.) Add to this that for the most part the two books were clandestinely given to the Press, often without printer's name, the place incorrectly stated, a fudge imprint in fine, and it will be seen how perplexed the whole story is. Some editions are comparatively harmless ; silly maybe, and even superstitious ; others have deadly and dangerous pages.

The *Grand Albert* (as we know it) was possibly first printed about the middle of the sixteenth century, but the eighteenth century editions (of the last rarity) are considered the most complete. The *Petit Albert* was joined with the *Grand Albert* in one volume and edited (1885) by a well-known French occultist, Marius Decrespe. This is said to be the issue most prized by adepts to-day. Decrespe emphatically discredits the opinions of those who suggest that the dual work originated in any sense with St. Albert the Great, or was compiled by a student of the fifteenth century from an unedited manuscript of the learned Dominican doctor. It is almost certain that the two works as we now have them were an amalgamation of the discoveries of several individuals, and that they appeared at Lyons not earlier than the sixteenth century. Stanislas de Guaita drew attention to the fact that in spite of the many reprints both the *Grand* and the *Petit Albert* are very uncommon books.

In the Channel Islands the *Grand Albert* is known as the " Witches' Bible ", and local dialect terms it *Le Grand Mêlé*. The *Petit Albert* is *Le Petit Mêlé*, the word *Mêlé* signifying nothing more than " book ". Together they are often referred to as *Albins,* and only the sorcerer dare keep such " bad books ". There have been many cases of the two volumes appearing in various libraries which were being catalogued after the owner's decease, and such an accident is always regarded as throwing a strange light upon the character and pursuits of the defunct. The old wives say that once a man has owned the *Grand Albert* he cannot rid himself of it, do what he will. The book invariably returns to its place on the shelf, even if it be cast into a fire, thrown away at sea, torn to pieces and scattered to the winds. The only thing to do is to inter it in a grave, and read the burial service over the place, or else to get a priest to drench the accursed thing with holy water and burn it with litany and prayer.

In Jamaica when Monteul Edmond was arrested for the murder of Rupert Mapp, a boy of 12 years old, for purposes of obeah it was found that the body had been strangely mutilated and a search of the prisoner's person discovered a number of magical formulæ " copied from a work entitled *Petit Albert* the pretended author of which is claimed to be a monkish occultist of the Middle Ages ".

The Daily Gleaner, Kingston, Jamaica, on 30th January, 1934, among the police news reported that at the Sandy Bay Court, Leonard Weakley, of Cold Spring, was sentenced to six months' imprisonment for practising the black art. In his house were found the following books : *The Sixth and Seventh Books of Moses ; Albertus Magnus, or the White and Black Arts for Men and Beasts ; The Great Book of Black Magic ; The Book of Magical Art ; Hindoo Magic and Indian Occultism.*

It was stated during the John H. Blymyer trial (1928) at York, York County, Pennsylvania, that the principal " witchcraft guises " employed by the sorcerers are : The Sixth and Seventh Books of the Magical Spirit ; The Art of Moses, popularly known as The Black Art Bible ; Heaven's Letter (Himmelsbrief) ; and The Long-lost Friend, which contains the necromantic rituals and the creed of pow-wowism. *The Art of Moses* is a translation, or adaptation of the *Magia divino-mosaica . . . cum nigromantia* of the sixteenth century. All these grimoires are very rare and the possession of one or two confers a certain distinction upon the witch.

The *Enchiridion* of Pope Leo III, fabled to have been presented by that great Pontiff to the Emperor Charlemagne in the year 800 is, of course, purely apocryphal. There is an early edition of 1584, and the Mainz edition of 1633 has woodcuts in black and red, but the 16mo edition " *chez le Père Angelo de Rimini* " (Paris, 1847), presents ten coloured plates of pentacles, magic circles, seals engraved with words of power, and other curious matter, such as counter-spells to divert malefic enchantments. Upon the title-page is a triangle in a double circle with Hebrew characters, *Tsabaoth Alchim*, etc., inscribed in the midst.

The grimoires need not for their contents detain us. *The Grimoire of Pope Honorius* is said to be found in manuscript at least as early as the thirteenth century.

It was printed at Rome in 1629, and has several times been reissued. The edition of 1670 has many magical and cabbalistic figures, for this volume of witchcraft is chiefly concerned with the evocation of demons.

The *Grand Grimoire* and the *Grimorium Verum* are both to a large extent derived from the famous *Clavicula Salomonis*, *The Key of Solomon the King*, sometimes known as the *Book of the Pentacles*. The legend of a manual of black magic written by Solomon and confided to his son Rehoboam (Roboam) is very ancient. Mr. S. L. M. Mathers, who translated *The Key of Solomon the King* in 1889, says : " I see no reason to doubt the tradition which assigns the authorship of the *Key* to King Solomon." This view, however, cannot be accepted without very considerable qualification, for it is abundantly evident that the *Key*, in any form as we now have it, must have been altered and amplified (and possibly in some particulars retrenched) by those through whose hands it passed. It is safer to allow that the *Key* is substantially based upon immemorial tradition, much of which may go back to the time of Solomon, but that it has suffered various modifications in the course of the centuries without indeed affecting its essential character and design.

It is true that *The Key of Solomon the King* has been claimed to be a work of white magic, but since (to mention no further examples) it teaches how to describe a pentacle causing ruin, utter destruction, and death, whilst another pentacle is productive of earthquakes and great storms, this pretence—for it is plainly nothing more—cannot be maintained. For obvious reasons the malefic nature of a grimoire would often have been dissembled. Moreover the manuscript grimoires are

in general far more detailed and far more terrible than
the printed volumes, bad enough in all conscience
though the latter may be.   The sorcerer dare not
confide the darker secrets of his evil craft, the more
potent and perilous spells to what is after all—however
limited the number of copies—a certain method of
publication.   The compositors might be heavily bribed,
nay, they might even themselves be members of the
Satanic fraternity, but there would always remain the
chance that by some accident a copy of a printed book
might fall into hostile hands and the mine be sprung.
In past centuries this must have been an even more
imminent risk than to-day.   Very often in the printed
manuals a slight difference has been deliberately made
in an exorcism, some little variant occurs in a
ceremonial, lest the horrid science should be too
plainly betrayed to the uninitiated and the intruder.
The adept who is using the book will appreciate this
policy of reticence and heed the signs of caution ;
from his own training and the oral lessons he has
received he can correct such divergences, and that is
the reason why these mystic manuals are so often
scored with manuscript emendations and so copiously
annotated in their broad margins.

It has been said that wellnigh every witch of long
continuance or standing possessed *The Key of Solomon
the King*, and generally in a manuscript written out by
himself. The advantage of this is obvious, for he could
add any number of incantations and charms which he
had been taught by word of mouth.   In the time of
Louis XIV, Duprat, a Parisian schoolmaster who was
not unconnected with the Guibourg-La Voisin gang,
enjoyed a very pretty living by transcribing and

writing out grimoires. In the eighteenth century the
Marquis de Paulmy, a deep student of occultism, made
a large collection of manuscript grimoires, which are
now preserved in the Bibliothèque de l'Arsenal at
Paris. One of the most complete of these is entitled
*The Great Secret, or the Key of Solomon the King and the
Ancient Grimoire*, being, as indeed is indicated by the
very name, a work combining the *Clavicula* with the
Grimoire of Pope Honorius. Although actually it does not
present a large number of figures and charts of circles
it does describe many ceremonies and charms not to
be found elsewhere. Dating from the early part of
the eighteenth century, it is written in a very legible
and elegant hand, and was evidently penned with the
greatest care throughout. A note initialed by the
Marquis de Paulmy says that no Hebrew manuscript
of *The Key of Solomon* has ever been traced. Moreover Greek manuscripts are of the last rarity. Indeed
only one was certainly known, and that reposed in the
library of Charles Albert of Bavaria. Latin versions
were not altogether infrequent. The manuscript
actually is in French. It commences with a Preface,
which does not occur in any other copy, wherein
Solomon confides his *Key* to his son Rehoboam, in
accordance with the old tradition. The book is supposed
to have been found in Solomon's tomb, and the ivory
coffer in which it was contained hence came into the
possession of a Babylonian mage, who gave it to the
world's philosophers. Leaving all legends aside, there
is at least one salutary cautel added to the foreword.
The author or transcriber, whoever he may be, is very
insistent in his word of warning : " I conjure and I
beseech any man into whose hands this manuscript

may fall, I implore him by all that is holy, by his desire
for good success in all his business and doings, that he
shall never turn this book to any common use, that he
shall neither publish it abroad, nor generally disclose
the secrets hereof, nor translate it into the vulgar
tongue, but to show it only to and to suffer it only
to be seen by men who have understanding and who
are well-tried and knowing in these rare secrets."

The earlier chapters of the *Key* describe in detail
those preliminary ceremonies and rituals which are
necessary for the successful invocation of spirits, a
thing not to be embarked upon lightly or without due
preparation and care. The *Key* will have it that the
spirits who shall appear in these circumstances are
benign influences, and but rarely evil, and these latter
should be approached most circumspectly.   The
Christian Faith admits no such distinctions. However
kindly and plausible they may seem to be we know that
all such conjured spirits are demons of the pit.

As Mr. A. E. Waite has justly observed : " Much
that passed current in the west as White (i.e. permissible) Magic was only a disguised goeticism, and
many of the resplendent angels invoked with divine
rites reveal their cloven hoofs. It is not too much to
say that a large majority of past psychological experiments were conducted to establish communication
with demons, and that for unlawful purposes. The
popular conceptions concerning the diabolical spheres,
which have all been accredited by magic, may have
been gross exaggerations of fact concerning rudi-
mentary and perverse intelligences, but the wilful
viciousness of the communicants is substantially
untouched thereby."

Full details of the vestments which must be donned by the charmer are supplied, and he should even wear a particular kind of buskin or shoe ; he must furnish himself with such accessories as a keen knife or whinger ; a long needle or cobbler's awl ; a ring ; a wand ; fire ; holy water ; lights ; certain sweet perfumes ; virgin parchment and a quill never yet used ; ink, and a phial of blood wherewith to write ; which things are absolutely indispensable for the operation since to summon a familiar spirit is no light and simple business as idle and silly meddling folk might suppose.

The manuscript gives an elaborate plan of the magic circle which is to be found in every manual of sorcery and in which unless he will risk the most imminent peril, even death itself, the experimenter must take his stand. This detail is emphasized in all grimoires, and the manuscript admonishes : " Note well that the mage who invokes the spirits must take his place within the circle, nor let him stir thence."   The circle which was to measure nine feet in diameter, must be traced with the sharp point of the consecrated knife, and (the rubrics direct) : " having drawn this circle describe four Pentacles whereabouts are to be written the Holy Names of God, and without this circle describe yet another circle which shall be bounded by a square. Grave all these with thy knife's point."

Actually both Greek and Hebrew characters are traced about the circle and pentacles. Alpha, Omega, can be clearly distinguished ; as well as the mystic word *Agla*, which was used by the rabbis as signifying *Aieth Gadol Leolam Adonai*, Adonai (God Almighty) endureth throughout all ages. There are also written several of the seventy and two Names of God.

However, in different editions and manuscripts of *The Key of Solomon* the circle is varied, and in one ceremony the hierophant is required to have an attendance of four acolytes. Five circles are then traced, the first being greater than the rest, in which the master takes his position. The disciples stand appropriately in the smaller circles. All must be clothed in ephods of stainless white linen, and the master whilst he draws the circles recites the following psalms : II, (Why do the heathen rage,) ; LIV, (Save, me, O God, by Thy Name) ; CXII, (Praise ye the Lord) ; LXVII, (God be merciful unto us) ; XLVII, (O clap your hands, all ye people) ; and LXVIII, (Let God arise . . .). A number of other circles and pentacles having been described, the Four Great Names of God must be written around and about, to wit in the small circles, Adonai, El, Agla, and Jah, and in the larger circle Eloha, Ehie, Elijon, and the mystic Tetragrammaton, that is the Divine Name, the Name of Yahweh, which no man may pronounce (saith Rabbi Abba Shaul) and live, the separated, the hidden and mysterious Name, inscribed here in such manner as may reverently and fearfully be spoken.

Another manuscript of the *Key of Solomon*, now in the Bibliothèque de l'Arsenal, *The True and Only Key of King Solomon*, said to be translated from the Hebrew in the eighteenth century, instructs the experimenter to draw his circle in quite a different fashion. Similar names, however, are to be written, the central monogram being KIS, which stands for *Kadosh Ieve Sabaoth*, Holy Lord of Hosts.

Although as yet unpublished, there is preserved in a private English collection a manuscript translation of

the *Clavicula Salomonis* by Frederick Hockley, an
astrologer and occultist who died about the middle
of the last century. It is entitled " Solomon's Key, by
Frederick Hockley, 1828 ". Pasted inside the cover is
a paper carrying the following : " Magia de Profundis,
seu Clavicula Salomonis Regis, the Key of Solomon
the King, or a Complete System of Profound Magical
Science with a great number of coloured drawings of
the Characters of the Spirits Seals, Pentacles, etc.,
elegant in brown calf gilt leaves." At the beginning
we have : " Key of Solomon in Four books. These
books were found in the Chaldee and Hebrew tongue
by a Jewish Rabbi at Jerusalem & by him translated
into Greek & from thence into Latin and transcribed
by Fred^k Hockley the first day of Marche 1828."

The Bibliothèque de l'Arsenal has manuscripts of
a yet more profoundly dangerous kind than even the
more extreme examples of the group which conveniently
goes under the name of *The Key of Solomon*. Thus *The
True and Only Key*, to which reference has already been
made, provides a curious rose-form pentacle expressly
to invoke the demons of the pit. The Great Conjuration contained in another manuscript is full of horrible
impiety, and may justly be styled the Dark Secret of
Secrets. *The Evocation of the Seven Planetary Spirits*
prescribes that certain substances, chiefly storax and
benjamin are to be burned in a new censer, and I
remember J. K. Huysmans saying how a devil-
worshipper had once told him that the fume of these
two was " agreeable to Satan our master ".

The Conjuration of Uriel and the Seraphim has the most
elaborate and reticulated plans and pentacles, and
among other spirits honour is paid to Alithael, Cassiel,

Sachiel, and Samael.   The angel St. Uriel " Regent
of the Sun "

The sharpest sighted Spirit of all in Heav'n,
as Milton terms him, is mentioned in the Fourth Book
of Esdras, and other ancient writings, but the names
Cassiel and others too plain betray the cloven hoof.

In Francis Barrett's *The Magus ; or, Celestial
Intelligencer,* 1801, is given a specimen of the Book of
Spirits, being the Conjuration of Saturday in ceremonial magic ; the Ruler, Cassiel.   Here then we are
in the realms of demonism undisguised.

Samael is Satan, the arch-fiend, as Collin de Plancy
explicitly states, whilst Stanislas de Guaita says that
Samael is opposed to and fought with the Archangel,
Saint Michael.

Another manuscript, entitled *Zekerboni,* was written
by Pietro Mora, who describes himself as an " occult
philosopher ".   During the Great Plague which so
fearfully ravaged Milan in 1630 there was dwelling
in an obscure quarter Pietro Mora, a mysterious and
formidable figure, who had long been popularly
accused as a vendor of poisons and a witch. A surprise
visit searched his house, but the *sbirri* could trace
nothing extraordinary or incriminating until almost
by chance there was forced a secret panel masquing
the entrance to cellars of prodigious extent, and in
these vaults were discovered not only the horrid
paraphernalia of sorcery, magic robes and wands,
lamps, swords, tripods, thuribles, braziers, curiously
graven shew-stones and crystals, together with a whole
library of grimoires and Ephesian runes, but also a
vast number of sealed jars and carefully labelled phials
containing liquids and chemical preparations, which

upon being analysed by the physicians were pronounced
to be virus and poisons of the most deadly kind. Mora
confessed that he was the leader of a coven of sorcerers,
who had leagued themselves to spread the scourge and
destroy the entire city. This they did by smearing the
handles of doors and gates with a certain lethal ointment.   They poisoned the springs of water, the
fountains in the squares, and even the benitiers in the
church porches. They distributed under the guise of
charity infected clothing and foul linen from the beds
of those who had died of the disease among the
hospitals and the crowded warrens of the poor so that
the pestilence was fearfully increased. The whole knot
were apprehended and being convicted upon most
plain and detailed evidence, they paid the extreme
penalty of the law. The very house of Mora, as a
criminal of especial atrocity, was razed to the ground,
and a column erected on the spot with an inscription
to commemorate his guilt.

There can be little question that Pietro Mora of
Milan was the author or transcriber of *Zekerboni*,
although it does not necessarily follow that the manuscript which has been preserved is his original. It may
be a copy, and indeed it seems to be in a later hand.
A circumstance which makes the identification more
probable is that *Zekerboni* introduces into many of the
spells certain terms and expressions borrowed from
alchemy, and we know that Mora long sought the
elixir and the philosopher's stone.

Zekerboni has a drawing of the " Great Pentacle "
where four circles enclose a mesh of cryptic designs,
crossing and recrossing, and scattered with Hebrew
and Greek letters punctuated by curious sigils and

points. The ceremony commences thus : " After the
Master is come with his disciples to the appointed
place of evocation he shall strike fire, and he shall
exorcize the new fire wherewith he shall light the
magic candle. This must be set in the lanthorn which
must be held by one of the disciples so that the Master
may most conveniently read the conjurations. Another
disciple shall hold him ready with paper, a pen and
the ink ; a third disciple shall carry the consecrated
sword with naked blade. The Master shall light the
charcoal for the censing and the fumigations. When he
hath taken his stand within the circle, holding a
lighted taper in his left hand, he shall forthwith begin
the conjuration—." The formula which, it is recom-
mended, shall be very legibly inscribed upon a fair
parchment without blot or erasure differs in the various
manuals. Each have certain phrases in common. The
Holy Name of God is called upon, and most spells
require the demon to manifest himself " in a pleasing
form, without any horror of shape or size, without any
loud or thunderous noise or alarum, without seeking
to harm him who summons thee, and without hurting
any who are of his company ".

When the spirit appears the magician must impose
his commands upon him, and then give him licence
to depart. The dismissal of the spirit is a very essential
detail in the ceremony, for unless the demon is sent
away it is possible that he may linger and great
mischief may ensue. One form of concluding the
rite is : " Depart then, gracious and kindly spirit,
return in peace unto thy dwelling-place and unto thine
own habitation, but yet do thou hold thyself ready to
attend and appear before me whensoever I call upon

thee and summon thee in the name of the Great Alpha, the Lord. Amen. Amen. Amen." It will be noticed how cunningly fair-spoken and even pious phrases are employed to masque the impiety of this horrid business.

Occasionally a manuscript grimoire will appear in the sale rooms. In April, 1934, part of the collection of M. Lionel Hauser was put up to auction at Sotheby's. There were many items of exceptional interest. A Treatise of Ceremonial Magic, written on vellum in cypher in French, *circa* 1750, which had belonged to and been used by the Comte de St. Germain, fetched £42 10*s*., whilst a nineteenth century manuscript collection of spells, conjurations, and exorcisms, realized £10.

In their great Catalogue of Medicine, Alchemy, Astrology, published in 1929 (No. 520), Messrs. Maggs, the well-known London booksellers, included " A Manuscript Book of Black Magic written in Shakespeare's England ", which was further very accurately described as " An Elizabethan Devil-worshipper's Prayer-Book ". The date assigned is *circa* 1600, but there seems to be no clue to the identity of the compiler of the manuscript, which is written on twenty-three leaves of vellum and illustrated with thirteen crudely drawn but very powerful drawings, some of which are coloured, of the demon king Vercan, who is pictured under various forms. There are also six other drawings of demons. All of these have their several invocations on the opposite page, inscribed in Latin. The spirits to be summoned or exorcised are : Vercan, Maymon, Suth, Samax, Sarabotres, Mediac or Modiac, and Arcan. King Vercan, who is regarded as the most powerful of the demons, is called upon in thirteen prayers. He is shown as a kind of semi-human monster with a fearfully grotesque human face, horned, having a hairy body, and the feet of a bird of prey. Twice he appears with three heads, and once he is riding a bear. It should be remarked that the invocator is always surrounded by a magic circle, for indeed as a later enchanter has it, " the circles are certain fortresses," and no manifestation has power to break through these boundaries, although often the spirits will endeavour to tempt or force the operator out of the circle.

The other demons of the grimoire are : King Maymon, who appears as a black familiar with two bird-heads, and two human heads at his knees. He rides upon a dragon, and is linked with the planet Saturn. King Suth is brown. Wearing a diadem and flourishing a great sword, he bestrides a stag, and is companioned with Jupiter. King Samax is antlered, and rides a kind of panther. He is linked with Mars. King Sarabotres is green. He rides a roe, and wields a sceptre. His planet is Venus. King Mediac (or Modiac) has huge horns. Clad in red mail, he rides a bear, and is linked with Mercury. King Arcan is a black demon with flaming eyes and grinning fangs. He is hunting with bow and arrows on the back of a roebuck. His planet is the Moon.

It very infrequently happens that there is any mention of a grimoire in a contemporary trial. John Walsh, of Netherbury, Dorset, possessed a book left him by his late master, which had great circles in it, wherein he would set two wax candles and a cross of virgin wax, to raise the familiar spirit of whom he would then ask for anything stolen. When his book

THE DEMON KING MAYMON

[face p. 92

was taken from him he could no longer summon a familiar. Rebecca West, an Essex witch, met with some other witches by appointment at the house of Elizabeth Clarke, where they all spent some time praying to their familiars, and afterwards some read in a book belonging to Elizabeth, whereupon the said familiars did appear.

A Magic book, which formerly belonged to Dr. John Caius, the famous Cambridge scholar, is preserved in the British Museum.

Dr. John Harries (1785–1839), a celebrated Welsh physician and seer who dwelt at Cŵrt-y-Cadno, a hamlet in remotest Carmarthenshire, but who was resorted to by the whole countryside, possessed a great Book of Magic which none but the wizard himself might read with impunity. The Book, indeed, was always kept locked, because (as the thaumaturge was wont to say) if any ignorant person who knew not the mystic mantra were to turn its pages he might let loose unreined influences ready to destroy him. Many wonderful stories are told of Harries, and there seems no reason to doubt that he was an occultist of extraordinary power. He openly avowed that his knowledge of future and distant things was imparted to him by familiar spirits, and his son Henry, who succeeded him, inherited his father's mysterious gifts. Henry died in 1849. He specialized in astrology, having in his youth been apprenticed to the well-known astrologer Raphael of London. Some said that the notorious Book was actually not a book at all, but a number of papers kept in an iron-bound box, which the doctor regarded as of the utmost value. So perhaps it was a manuscript grimoire. One story went that many years after the death of the Welsh wizard and his sons, the book and a magic crystal were bought from his descendants by a London barrister on a walking tour, who having heard of the fame of Harries visited the village. The family parted with the Book and the crystal at a price, but nobody in the house dare touch them or would lend a hand in their removal.

There is to-day (1933) a wise man dwelling near Llangwrig, Montgomeryshire, who is famous throughout all Wales. From near and far people come for his help. He breaks the spells of those bad folk " who have power ", that is to say witches. In a rosewood box he keeps two books, an almanac and another, whereby he can divine and cast a horoscope or map out the planets for his clients.

Upon the black roll of magicians stands no more notorious name than that of Cornelius Agrippa, and there seems little doubt that this terrible accusation is in great part due to his youthful treatise, the *Three Books of Occult Philosophy*. Even Professor Henry Morley when writing his *Life of Henry Cornelius Agrippa von Nettesheim, Doctor and Knight*, added on the title-page " Commonly known as a Magician ". Composed in 1510, not even the First Book was printed until one and twenty years later, and when after about another twelvemonth it was announced that the whole work was in the press at Cologne, Conrad Cöllin, a learned Dominican of Ulm, very justly caused the book to be thoroughly examined by the theologians before it was given to the public. So far from being an obscurantist Cöllin was the most liberal of scholars, and there was no persecution or oppression. Satisfied that it contained no heresies, he gave his formal consent to the issue of the work. " Suffer it to be printed, if they wish," he says in an extant letter. Since the *Occult Philosophy* has been analysed in some detail by Morley it will suffice to say here that the work is a commixture of Neoplatonism and the Cabbala. The last book has a long chapter on demons, and there is a good deal of angelology with some curious matters that skate on very thin ice. Indeed these *Three Books of Occult Philosophy*, or rather of Magic, for Agrippa himself confessed that his title was little more than a subterfuge, " alone constitute him a conjurer "—the phrase is Morley's.

It is all the more unfortunate that after Agrippa's death there should have appeared an abominably superstitious and profane Fourth Book of the *Occult Philosophy*, whilst in the same volume was printed a fitting companion, the *Elements of Magic* by Peter of Abano, that " vilest of vile books ", to which reference has already been made. It is significant that those responsible for seeing these grimoires through the press did not dare to give the place or the printer's name on the title-page.

In spite of his virtuous and emphatic protestations it is impossible to regard Francis Barrett's *The Magus; or, Celestial Intelligencer* as anything other than a particularly elaborate and complete grimoire. Published in 1801 by a well-known firm, James Lackington, Allen and Co., at the " Temple of the Muses ", Finsbury Square, *The Magus*, a fine quarto, is illustrated with a number of detailed designs of magic circles and pentacles, and also with several striking coloured plates, the *Powers of Evil*, being heads of

Demons, Astaroth, Abaddon, Mammon, and *Vessels of Wrath*, Theutus, Asmodeus, and the Incubus. Barrett not only sketched the heads himself with great care, but he supplies a very ample account of the familiar shapes and forms in which the spirits manifest themselves, " likewise the whole perfection of magical ceremonies is here described syllable by syllable." " The Construction and Composition of all Sorts of Magic Seals, Images, Rings, Glasses, etc.," may be found exhibited in these pages. The author, who lived at 99 Norton Street, Marylebone, in an advertisement invites those desiring to delve further into these curious matters to join his school " which will consist of no greater number than Twelve Students ", an extremely significant circumstance. The manuscript of *The Magus*, which is preserved in a private collection, enlarges upon certain particulars not altogether desirable to print, and Barrett stands forth as a magician self-confessed.

The rough woodcuts which embellish such manuals of sorcery as *Le Dragon rouge*, *La Poule Noire*, and *Le Dragon Noir* have little importance. None the less both *Le Dragon rouge* and *La Poule Noire*, which first appeared in print about 1800, have been reissued again and again, and are yet extensively consulted and employed. They are grimoires of the worst type, and even furnish necromantic evocations.

During the Helsingfors Satanist scandals of 1931, when it was discovered that a number of graves had been desecrated and bodies mutilated, upon the arrest of the cemetery caretaker, Sarrenheimo, and the search of his house it was found that he possessed a library of books dealing with the practice of the black art, and one manual in particular (said to have been printed in England) advised the use of human remains in confecting certain foul charms.

There are in use by witches to-day volumes simply entitled *Magick*, which give the full ritual for the celebration of Black Masses, with diabolic litanies, and other infernal ceremonies including the blood sacrifices on the altar. A Gnostic Mass is described, and one rubric runs, " the blood sacrifice is the critical point of the World Ceremony of the Proclamation of Horus, the Crowned and Conquering Child, as Lord of the Aeon." The Gnostics in the second century had books " full of wickedness ", and stripped of its pseudo-mystical verbiage the plain meaning of this rubric is that divine honour must be paid to the devil, Satan-Pantheus, with whom (Stanislas de Guaita says) St. Michael fought victoriously for he it is whom they salute as the Child, the Cosmic serpent who tempted Eve and by whom came death and sin.

One of these grimoires has this warning : " The student, if he attains any success in the following practices, will find himself confronted by things too glorious or too dreadful to be described. It is essential that he remain the master of all that he beholds, hears, or conceives ; otherwise he will be the slave of illusion and the prey of madness."

Éliphas Lévi, whose two great works *Dogme de la Haute Magie* (1855) and *Rituel de la Haute Magie* (1856) were together translated in 1923 as *Transcendental Magic* by Mr. Arthur Edward Waite, lays down five *Conditions of Success in Infernal Evocations* : (1) Invincible obstinacy ; (2) a conscience at once hardened to crime and not subject to remorse and fear; (3) ignorance, affected or natural; (4) blind faith in all that is incredible; (5) a completely false idea of God. If these are understood in the right way they may be regarded as sufficiently summing up the essential characteristics of black magic and all goetic experiments. By *a completely false idea of God* I understand the express renunciation of God, the paying of divine honour to Satan with whom a contract (tacit or explicit) is made and whose will is done by the witch.

It must ever be borne in mind that the practice and profession of black magic are not lightly to be undertaken; the dark mysteries are no jest, no pastime of an idle hour as many fools and empty inquirers seem to suppose. There are no dilettanti in witchcraft.

There are the mountebanks, of course, who give fatuous talks on black magic in Mayfair drawing-rooms; there are the bright young things who try to raise the devil in a circle and do not succeed; there is the fifth-rate novelist who peppers his trashy thrillers with occult episodes borrowed *en bloc* from some standard work. There is and there always will be plenty of humbug, and very paying humbug too, along these lines.

Before the secrets of the grimoire can be unfolded the price must be given, the terrible barter must be exchanged.

Another volume, of which mention is made—one that is often confused with, but should be distinguished from, the grimoire—is what we may term the Devil's Missal. Probably this had its origin far back in the mist of the centuries among the earliest heretics who passed down their evil traditions to their followers, the Albigenses and the Waldenses or Vaudois.

Enough has been said to show that mischief and malice were part and parcel of the witch's profession, and indeed there was required from them at their reception into this dark society a vow that they would devote themselves wholly to evil. They were moreover pledged to carry on an active Satanist propaganda, to win recruits and to use every endeavour to draw other men and women to their detestable practices and the worship of the fiend. Thus in the case of Janet Breadheid, of Auldearne, we find that her husband " enticed her into that craft ". A girl named Bellot, of Madame Bourignon's academy, confessed that her mother had taken her to the Sabbat when she was quite a child. Another girl alleged that all worshippers of the Devil " are constrained to offer him their children ". At Salem, George Burroughs, a minister, was accused by a large number of women as " the person who had Seduc'd and Compell'd them into the snares of Witchcraft ". Elizabeth Francis, of Chelmsford, a witch tried in 1566, was only about twelve years old when her grandmother taught her the art of sorcery. The Pendle beldame, Mother Demdike, " brought up her owne Children, instructed her Graund-children, and tooke great care and paines to bring them to be Witches." It is hardly to be believed that a modern writer of a certain school—fortunately at once negligible and freakish—should characterize this dedication of young children to hell and the lord of hell as " a ceremony, at once simple and touching ".

To-day the Satanists are thoroughly imbued with the missionary spirit, and are ever eager to enlarge their ranks to the destruction of immortal souls. A very general method is for the Satanist to lure his intended proselyte into the most odious debaucheries, even to tempt him to the commission of some crime, and then if he seem laggard to subscribe his service to the demon and join the infernal gang the pressure of blackmail can be brought to bear until the poor wretch is wholly ensnared and lost. Any defection from the ranks, any attempted betrayal, or in many cases, lukewarmness even, is punished by death. Thus the members are terrorized, and many an unexplained, undiscovered murder is in truth the work of Satanists, the vengeance they have wreaked upon some traitor.

It is not necessary to do more than mention in passing the immense sums of money which have been so lavishly poured out by this dark brotherhood to corrupt and destroy whole countries and nations by their anarchy and red revolutions.

It is a commonplace of Catholic teaching that there has been a True Religion in the world ever since the creation of man—" the Universal Church began with Abel the Just "—and when Christ Himself came this existent True Religion received the designation of Christianity. Opposed to the True Religion throughout was the cult of evil, Satanism.

Witchcraft was potent—indeed more potent than ever after—and the devil had his worshippers before the coming of Christ. Not to speak of the Oriental magic of the Egyptians and the Chaldæans; nor of Hebrew necromancies, which the Bible condemns again and again; sorcerers flourished in Greece and Rome, and the whole body of ancient legislation clearly shows that before the dawn of Christianity, in the

paynim era when a multiplicity of heathen cults prevailed throughout the Roman empire, witchcraft was
as uncompromisingly prohibited as ever it was
denounced and punished by the great Pontiffs, by
Innocent VIII and Sixtus V ; in Germany during
the sixteenth and seventeenth centuries ; in England
by the parliaments of Elizabeth and James.

It is an empty and utterly baseless theory to suppose
(as a certain type of imaginative writer has been
indiscreet enough to assert) that witchcraft is the
survival of some primitive cult of which nothing is
known, concerning which nothing can be definitely
discovered, and which is certainly not mentioned
in any record or by any author. The development
of such a fantasy merely leads to a wholesale wresting
of historical facts, to a ludicrous perversion of evidence
—probably quite unconsciously misread—and to
general cheap claptrap all round.

None of the earlier religions existed with the express
design and end of perpetrating evil for evil's sake.
Now this constitutes the very essence of witchcraft,
which is first and foremost the cult of hell. It is surely
permissible to express surprise when one finds Satanism
described as " a joyous religion ".

Bit with the novelty of the thing, some enterprising
folklorist next asks us to look upon witchcraft " in the
light of a fertility cult ", being careful, of course, for
convenience sake to ignore the occult phenomena
lest the issue be confused. It seems superfluous to
remark that not a tittle of sound evidence can be
brought forward to support such a *capriccio*.

That here and there lingered various old harmless
customs and rustic festivities which had come down

from pre-Christian times and which the Church had allowed, nay, had even sanctified by directing them to their right source, the Maypole dances, for example, and the Midsummer fires, which now honour St. John Baptist, is a matter of common knowledge. But there is no continuance of a pagan fertility cult.

Nor will anyone seek to argue from some extraordinary but isolated and infrequent instances of survival. In Easter week, 1282, John, the parish priest of Inverkeithing, celebrated the profane rites of Priapus, collecting young girls from the villages and compelling them to tread a measure in honour of Father Bacchus. When he had led these females forth in a troop, out of sheer wantonness he danced before carrying in front on a pole a representation of the human organs of reproduction, and singing and capering himself like a mime he viewed them all, and stirred them to lust by filthy language. The older men who being scandalized by this shameless performance rebuked him gently because they respected the dignity of his office, he violently abused, and comported himself more madly than ever. He also at dawn in Penance Week insisted that some should prick others who were stripped for penance with sharp goads, and when the graver burgesses protested he sturdily defended these indecencies. One night he was stabbed to death, nor was his assailant discovered.

About a dozen years before these pranks at Inverkeithing a cattle plague had broken out in various districts, which led to the revival of long dead mummeries. Two or three monks, it is said, advised the country folk to erect an image or terminal to Priapus, and through some ritual which involved the lighting of new fire by the friction of wood they prophesied the beasts would be relieved. At Fenton a Cistercian lay-brother actually set up this figure before the hall hearth and sprinkled the byres of the lord of the manor with holy water to which he had added " filthy matters of his own invention ". Here we have an example of a lewd and degraded super-stition no doubt, but to talk of " Priapus-worship " and to describe the Cistercians as " monastic wizards " is not a trifle ridiculous, and betrays an extraordinary confusion of ideas.

In 1749 Girolamo Tartarotti (1702–1761), a minor journalist, one of the many literary *abbati* who swarmed throughout Italy at that time writing with equal elegance facile verse and fluent prose, published at Venice a large quarto volume, which he entitled *A Study of the Midnight Sabbats of Witches* (*Del Congresso Notturno delle Lammie*). His chapters are composed with an immense parade of learning—he quotes from more than three hundred and eighty authors—perhaps no such wonderful task in those days of leisure and large libraries. He shows himself, as the fashion went, a complete sceptic, and the thesis of this " member of the Republic of Letters ", for so he floridly dubs himself, is that there were never any assemblies or rendezvous of Satanists, and indeed summing it up in a few words that witchcraft is imaginary and a sick dream. *A Study of the Midnight Sabbats of Witches* is a very rare book, Tartarotti has been completely for-gotten, and he would not be worth mentioning here were it not for one curious and interesting point. In the course of his excogitations he discusses the famous " Canon Episcopi ", an enactment to be considered in detail later, which speaks of certain women who seduced by the snare of the demon " believe and declare that they ride upon beasts with Diana, goddess of the pagans ", and with multitudes of women flying through the air in service and attendance upon her. From this Tartarotti evoked the fantastic idea of a " Dianic cult ", and he contends that witchcraft was nothing else than this imaginary cult. (Chapter IX : *The identity of the Dianic Cult with modern witchcraft is demonstrated and proven.*) Actually his arguments, if we may dignify unsupported statements and romancing by this name, could convince nobody, and the whole thing fell to the ground and was ignored.

A recent writer chancing upon Tartarotti's book (either, I suppose, at the British Museum or drawing from the notice in the Soldan-Heppe *Geschichte der Hexenprozesse*) promptly borrowed the idea, and came out with a new thesis concerning " the Dianic cult ", " as I propose to call it," which embraced " the religious beliefs and ritual of the people known in late mediæval times as ' Witches ' ". Of course Tartarotti was never so much as mentioned. The theory was at first mightily commended in certain quarters for its novelty, its scientific modernity, but when in the Foreword to a translation of Remy's *Demonolatry* (1930) I happened to show that Tartarotti's crochet had long since been discredited and had fallen into oblivion, the " Dianic cult " was speedily dropped, and very little (I believe) has since been heard of it.

Witchcraft does not belong to the antiquarian past ; it lives and energizes, a monstrous and fearful menace to-day, and it is perhaps only by a clear and understanding view of the history of black magic that we can be aware of the imminent dangers which surround us.

As the Duke of Lauderdale once wrote : " It is impertinent arguing to conclude, that because there have been Cheats in the World, because there are some too credulous, and some have been put to Death for Witches, and were not, therefore all Men are deceived."

CHAPTER III

OF THE WITCH COVENS AND THEIR GRAND MASTERS ;
OF THE WITCHES' JOURNEY TO THE SABBAT ; AND OF
THE SABBAT ORGY

*So vile and pestilent a superstition, whose evil and reprobate
adherents the common consent of society holds as enemies to general
order and, indeed, the foes of the human race.*
POPE JOHN XXII.

*Satan calleth them together into a Devilish Synagogue, and that
he may also understand of them how well and diligently they have
fulfilled their office of intoxicating committed unto them, and whom
they have slain.*
LAMBERT DANEAU.

The dark and secret Society of Witches spreads—
a huge network of evil—over the whole world.
Throughout Europe and America in particular the
organization of Satanists is very thorough and very
complete.   In less than the span of a limited lifetime,
not more than sixty years indeed after the first settlers
had landed at Massachusetts Bay, Cotton Mather
notes as a detail significantly dangerous in itself and
worthy of particular attention the systematic and
methodized federation of the Salem witches. He says,
" 'Tis very Remarkable to see what an Impious and
Impudent *imitation* of Divine Things is Apishly
affected by the Devil," and after showing that in
many striking incidents the sorceries of the native
Indians might be taken to be a burlesque of the
Biblical narrative, he continues : " The Devil which
then thus imitated what was in the Church of the *Old
Testament,* now among *Us* would Imitate the Affairs

of the Church in the *New*. The *Witches* do say, that
they form themselves much after the manner of
Congregational Churches ; and that they have a *Baptism*
and a *Supper*, and *Officers* among them, abominably
Resembling those of our Lord."

There are, it is true, cases upon record and instances
to be met with to-day of the solitary witch, dwelling
apart and alone in some remote and unfrequented
corner, apparently leading an almost isolated and
eremitical life, but this is a rather rare exception.

The members of the witch society in various districts,
large or small, villages, towns, great cities, or even
shires and provinces, are linked up, and a corre-
spondence is maintained between them in many
mysterious ways. There is an active freemasonry
of evil.

One of the oaths demanded from a novice is generally
a pledge to frequent the midnight assemblies. These
conventicles or *covens* are the meetings of bands or
companies of witches summoned and forgathering
under the discipline of an officer, who naturally was
assisted in his work by other functionaries. Obviously
the members of a coven would all belong as nearly
as possible to the same neighbourhood, and especially
was this the case in former years when the means of
transit were far more slow and difficult than at the
present day. It appears from the evidence at numerous
trials, both at home and abroad, that those who
belonged to a coven were bound to attend the weekly
Esbat or rendezvous. The arrest of one member of
a coven often led to the implication of many more
who belonged to the same gang.

The number of witches which constituted and still

constitutes a coven has been much discussed. In a famous Scotch trial of 1662 when the revelations of Isobel Gowdie, of Auldearne, gave the fullest details concerning almost every circumstance of witchcraft, amply describing the Sabbats, the minor meetings, the ceremonies and instructions in malefic charms, she confessed " ther ar threttein persons in ilk Coeven ". In a very exhaustive investigation of this point Mr. Alexander Keiller thus sums up : " To those unaware of the probable organization of what might be termed the Witch Sect in Europe, in at any rate the sixteenth and seventeenth centuries, it may be explained that the Administrative and Executive Unit of Witchcraft customarily consisted of thirteen persons, and was usually termed a ' Coven ' or ' Coeven '." This scholar has explored in great detail " The Territorial Distribution of Witchcraft in Aberdeenshire ", and he has also set forth " The Personnel of the Aberdeenshire Witchcraft Covens in the years 1596–7 " showing that there were five distinct covens each formed of thirteen members, as well as three other covens which owing to the lack of necessary data cannot be precisely completed.

Until at least the latter part of the seventeenth century a well-organized group of witches existed between Shotley Bridge and Corbridge in the county of Northumberland. Ann Armstrong a farm servant at Burtree House, a few miles from Stocksfield-on-Tyne, was for a time partially drawn into the society and when in February, 1672–3, she voluntarily deposed before a number of magistrates her witness was most clear and detailed. Lieut.-Colonel G. R. B. Spain writes : " It is obvious from the evidence that Ann

Armstrong was closely in touch with a witchcraft organization over a large district of some fifty square miles." (" The Witches of Riding Mill, 1673 " : *Cornhill Magazine*, March, 1929.) Ann Armstrong described how the witches were divided into " coveys, consisting of thirteen persons in every covey ".

On the other hand it can be equally well shown that in many cases the local group or coven of witches did not consist of thirteen members. Sixteen witches belonged to the St. Osyth coven in 1582 ; ten witches formed the coven that infested the Waltham and Hedingham countryside five years later. The witches of Warboys who so plagued the Throgmortons and killed Lady Cromwell were three in number. No less than thirty-five witches can be traced in connexion with the famous Pendle Forest trials (1613). To attempt to divide this total into covens of thirteen is singularly futile. In the effort to do so not only has evidence been juggled, but Mother Demdike and Mother Chattox are placed in the same group, upon which Mr. L'Estrange Ewen justly comments : " This is a wild argument. Demdike and Chattox could not have been in the same coven because they were very keen rivals." Some of the London covens of Satanists to-day are composed of as many as thirty or forty men and women ; other circles again are quite small and only comprise ten initiates.

The *Officers* among the witches, of whom Cotton Mather speaks, were in the first place the local Chiefs or Masters of a coven, above whom was the Grand Master of a district.

There is very ample proof that " the Devil " of the Sabbat was not infrequently a human being, none other indeed than the Grand Master of the district, and since his officers and immediate attendants were also termed "Devils" by the witches some confusion has on occasion ensued. In Jersey the Grand Master, the Devil's deputy, was known as "Le Tchéziot". In a few cases where sufficient details are given it is possible actually to identify "the Devil" by name.

During the trial in December, 1481, at Neuchatel, of Rolet Croschet, he confessed that when quite a lad he had been taken to a meeting of witches by Jaquet Duplan. Here he was welcomed by "the Devil", a tall dark man, named Robin, to whom he did homage and who made much of him. The second time Croschet went to a rendezvous of sorcerers the gathering was much smaller, and the president was Captain Hanchement, evidently a well-known figure in the town, by whom he was appointed the local messenger for the society, and he used to go up and down to the various witches' houses giving notice of the assemblies and other bad businesses. At another time he attended a meeting of some other covens than his own belonging to Vauxtravers a few leagues away, and here the Provost was Etienne Goynet.

In 1579 at Windsor there used to meet "within the backside of Master Dodges in the Pittes" a coven presided over by Father Rosimond, of Farnham. It has been too ingeniously suggested that Father Rosimond *alias* Osborne, whom Mother Stiles of the coven named as her "chief", was a priest. But, no, this "wise man" (as he is termed) was a widower with a daughter who proved wellnigh as versed in sorcery as himself.

It is true that sometimes a clergyman stands revealed

as a high official among the witches. The Rev. George Burroughs, pastor at Wells, Maine, was accused by eight of the Salem witches " as being an head Actor at some of their Hellish Rendezvouses, and one who had the promise of being a King in Satan's Kingdom ". He was often heard to brag " that he was a *Conjuror*, above the ordinary Rank of Witches ", whilst several of the Satanists declared that " he was the Person who had Seduc'd, and Compell'd them into the snares of Witchcraft ". Now it is established beyond all question that George Burroughs was the Grand Master of the district. Admittedly in the wave of extreme rationalism which so inexplicably swept over Massachusetts at the beginning of the eighteenth century the General Court reversed George Burroughs' attainder and awarded damages to his heirs, but this does not in the least (as a recent historian appears to think) clear him from the guilt of witchcraft nor yet does it rebut even one particular of the charges which were proven up to the hilt again and again. Cotton Mather, for example, never altered his opinion of Burrough's culpability, and did not spare to express his sternest disapproval of the general *volte-face*.

Among a list of " confederates against Her Majesty Queen Elizabeth, who have diverse and sundry times conspired her life " we have Lord Paget, Sir George Hastings, Sir Thomas Hanmer, " Ould Birtles the great devel, Darnally the sorceror, Maude Two-good enchantresse, the ould witche of Ramsbury, several other ould witches." Full details are lacking but it seems plain that Old Birtles was the Grand Master or " Devil " of a coven of Wiltshire Witches.

The evil William, Lord Soulis, of Hermitage Castle,

often known as " Red Cap ", was " the Devil " of a
coven of sorcerers. He was protected by a terrible
charm against any injury from rope or steel ; cords
could not bind nor sword pierce him. And so when
he was seized by his enemies they rolled him up in
sheets of lead and boiled him to death at a place
called the Nine-Stane Rig.

> On a circle of stones they placed the pot,
>   On a circle of stones but barely nine ;
> They heated it red and fiery hot,
>   And the burnished brass did glimmer and shine.
> They rolled him up in a sheet of lead
>   A sheet of lead for a funeral pall ;
> They plunged him into the cauldron red,
>   And melted him body, lead, bones and all.

The chamberlain and chief counsellor of Philip IV
of France, Enguerrand de Marigny, was a Grand
Master of sorcerers prominent among whom were a
notorious warlock, Jacobus de Lor, his wife and man-
servant. Jacobus killed himself in prison whilst awaiting
trial ; the witch, his wife, perished at the stake. Under
Louis X, on 30th April, 1315, de Marigny was hanged
at Paris.

An even more mysterious figure was Robert III
d'Artois, the Grand Master of a veritable legion of
witches. During the year 1333 he endeavoured to
kill Philip VI, the Queen, and the Dauphin by his
spells and enchantments. The design, before it could
be matured, was betrayed by one of his minions, and
proscription and sentence of perpetual banishment
being pronounced against him, he fled to England
where he proved powerful enough to stir up Edward III
against France, and to his influence may be
immediately ascribed the outbreak of the Hundred

Years War. He was feared and shunned everywhere as a past master of image magic, and it was also whispered that he possessed a number of most impious manuscripts of goety written by Moorish sorcerers.

From these two instances, Enguerrand de Marigny and Robert III d'Artois, we see that the activity of the Witch society was no mere piece of casual mischief wrought by doting village crones, who harmed their neighbours and scattered domestic ills and unhappiness, —bad businesses enough—but it reached further and meddled with the highest politics to the confusion of kingdoms and the ruin of dynasties. Such, as we fearfully realize when we look at the world around us is its chief business, wherein it is fatally energetic and alive to-day. To reduce the world to a chaos of blood and horror ; to stamp out and destroy all that is beautiful, all that has some reflection of God ; such are the aims and object of the Red and the Witch.

One of the most interesting identifications of " the Devil " occurs in the course of the notorious trials of Geillis Duncan, Agnes Sampson, Dr. John Fian, and their associates in 1590–1. As is well known, the whole crew was in league with Francis Stewart, Earl of Bothwell, an incendiary vehemently suspected of the black art. Long after when George Sandys was staying at Naples there came to the inn a Calabrian, an eminent scholar, who insisted on seeing the English traveller. " And he," writes Sandys, " would needs persuade me that I had insight in magick : for that Earle *Bothel* was my countryman, who lives at *Naples*, and is in these parts famous for suspected negromancie." In Scotland, Bothwell, then a young man, was almost overtly aiming at the throne, and the witch covens one and all were frantically attempting the life of King James. Agnes Sampson, "the eldest witch of them all," confessed that she had fashioned a waxen puppet, and baptized it saying : "This is King James the Sixth, ordained to be consumed at the instance of a noble man, Francis, Earl Bothwell." At the next rendezvous of witches the presiding "Devil" anxiously questioned her concerning the moulding of the image, and what effect had followed the melting of the figure at a slow fire and the piercing of it with great black pins. There can be no doubt at all that Bothwell was the moving force who energized and directed the very elaborate and numerous organization of demonolaters who were attacking the King, seeking both his crown and his life. Bothwell was in fine the Grand Master, the "Devil" of the witches, and the centre of a vast political plot.

In the nineteenth century both Albert Pike and his successor Adriano Lemmi have been identified upon abundant authority as being Grand Masters of societies practising Satanism, and as performing the hierarchical functions of "the Devil" at the modern Sabbat.

In his *Displaying of Supposed Witchcraft*, 1677, John Webster had suggested with reference to Margaret Agar and other "*deluded Haggs*" of the Brewham coven, tried at Taunton during the June Assizes of 1665, that the "little Man in black Clothes with a little band" who presided over the meeting at Hussey's Knap, a coppice near the hamlet, and who instructed the crew in moulding wax figurines and pricking them with thorns was the local Grand Master, a man-Devil, and Burns Begg points out that the witches on occasion " seem to have been undoubtedly the victims of unscrupulous and designing knaves, who personated Satan ".   This, however, is no palliation of their crimes, and they are not one whit the less guilty of sorcery and devil-worship if they obey and adore a representative of Satan, rather than the demon himself. Nor do I think that the man who personated Satan at these horrid assemblies was so much an unscrupulous and designing knave as himself a demonist, believing intensely in the reality of his own dark powers, wholly and horribly dedicated and doomed to the service of evil.

Moreover sometimes the demon himself appeared whilst the rites were in full blast, as at the horrible mockery of the Last Supper attended one Good Friday by Madeleine Bavent when Mathurin Picard was the celebrant of those blasphemies, and during this abominable supper a dark familiar walked round the table at which the company were seated, crying aloud : *Not one of you shall betray me !*

God, so far as His ordinary presence and action in Nature are concerned, is hidden behind the veil of secondary causes, and when God's ape, the Demon, can work so successfully and obtain not merely devoted adherents but fervent worshippers by human agency, there is plainly no need for him to manifest himself in person either to particular individuals or at every Sabbat. None the less it is certain that he can do so, that he has done and yet does so very frequently, and the number of cases in the records of trials which are to be explained in no other way, that is to say where the devil manifests himself in some shape, appears to and has most intimate connexions with his besotted worshippers, are extremely numerous, and from what I know I am persuaded that we may safely avouch that to-day the demon is more frequently himself present at the modern sabbats than he functions through a deputy.

In the Caverne des Trois Frères, Ariège, France, there is depicted on the upper wall of the cave by some Palæolithic artist ten thousand years ago the figure of a man clothed in the skin of a stag with a horse's tail and wearing on his head huge branching antlers. This Caverne has a gallery of over four hundred pictures, but this figure " The Sorcerer " at the far end, painted high up on the rock in the " wizard's chamber ", as it has been called, dominates the whole. Here then we have a masked magician, a Grand Master of the Old Stone Age.

A whole catena of evidence from the Fathers and Doctors of the Church might be easily adduced, all sternly denunciatory of those who dress themselves in the hides of animals and don great horns, thus decked out for licentious and profane assemblies and the performance of obscenest rituals. Thus St. Cæsarius of Arles (470–542) more than once anathematizes those who dress themselves in furry pelts and who don horned helmets, completely metamorphosed into animals. He warns the faithful : " If ye abhor any participation in their sins, ye will not suffer these human stags or bull-calves or other monsters to approach you, nay, not so much as to come nigh your dwellings."

Prohibitions of these devilish mummeries and bestial vizardings are to be repeatedly found in the early Penitentials.

We are forcibly reminded, and indeed there is a most intimate and vital connexion between the two, of the fiendish masks and dresses assumed by the witch-doctors and sorcerers of Africa and Tibet.

There is complete evidence that the hierophant at the witches' Sabbat, when a human being played that rôle, generally wore this traditional disguise. Nay more, as regards the British Isles at least—and it seems clear that in other countries the habit was very similar—we possess a pictorial representation of " the Devil " as he appeared to his worshippers. During the famous Fian trials—to which reference has already been made—Agnes Sampson confessed : " The devil was clad in a black gown with a black hat upon his head. . . . His face was terrible, his nose like the beak of an eagle, great burning eyes ; his hands and his legs were hairy, with claws upon his hands and feet like the griffin." In the pamphlet *Newes from Scotland, Declaring the Damnable life and death of Doctor Fian* we have a rough woodcut, repeated twice, which shows " the Devil " preaching from the North Berwick pulpit to the whole coven of witches, and allowing for the crudity of the draughtsman and a few unimportant differences of detail—the black gown and hat are not portrayed—the demon in the picture is exactly like the description Agnes Sampson gave. It must be remembered, too, that at the Sabbat she was in a state of morbid excitation, in part due to deep cups of heady wine, the time was midnight, the place a haunted old church, the only light a few flickering candles that burned with a ghastly blue flame.

Now " the Devil " as he is shown in the *Newes from Scotland* illustration is precisely the Devil who appears upon the title-page of Middleton and Rowley's masque *The World tost at Tennis*, 4to, 1620. This woodcut presents an episode towards the end of the masque, and here the Devil in traditional disguise, a grim black hairy shape with huge beaked nose, monstrous claws, and the cloven hoofs of a griffin, in every particular fits the details so closely observed by Agnes Sampson. I have no doubt that the drawing for this masque was actually made in the theatre, for although this kind of costly and decorative enter-tainment was almost always designed for court or some great nobleman's house, we know that *The World tost at Tennis* was produced with considerable success on the public stage " By the Prince his Servants ". The dress, then, of " the Devil " at the Sabbats seems frequently to have been of the nature of an elaborate theatrical costume, such as might perhaps have been found in the stock wardrobe of a rich playhouse at London, but which would have had no histrionic associations for provincial folk and even simpler rustics.

Lambert Daneau, whose *Les Sorciers* was translated in 1575 by Thomas Taylor as *A Dialogue of Witches*, says that the " witches acknowledge the Devil for their God, call upon him, pray to him, and trust in him ", and when they assemble at their Sabbats, " they repeat the oath which they have given unto him in acknowledging him as their God."

From almost every witch-trial in every land evidence to this effect might be accumulated. The matter is perfectly plain, and it is futile to attempt to conceal or confuse the issue, the God of the witches is and was the Devil, " the wicked one," " that old serpent

A Courtly Masque:

The Deuice called, The VVorld tost at Tennis

As it hath beene diuers times Presented to the
Contentment of many Noble and Worthy
Spectators:

By the PRINCE his Seruants.

Inuented and set
downe, By
{ Tho: Middleton
&
William Rowley } Gent.

The Diuell. Deceit. The World.

THE WORLD TOST AT TENNIS
The First Quarto

called the Devil, and Satan, which deceiveth the
whole world," " the Prince of the power of the air,
the spirit that now worketh in the children of disobedience," who " sinneth from the beginning ", " a
murderer from the beginning," " a liar, and the father
of it." Be it remarked that these phrases are neither
" cheap claptrap " nor " purple patches " nor swayed
by colourful prejudice. I quote the simple unvarnished
words of the Authorized Version of the English Bible.

On those occasions when no visible presence of
discarnate evil, no demon, appeared or presided at
the Sabbat orgy, divine honours were paid to Satan's
deputy, the Grand Master, although it does not follow
that he was in himself and of himself regarded as
absolute God. It is a nice, but none the less an
important distinction, and although essentially true
I am not prepared to say that as such it was apprehended by the majority of the witches, assuredly not
by the poorer and clownish folk from whom, in the
British Isles at any rate, so many of the covens were
recruited.

Among certain primitive peoples and in various
savage tribes the chieftain or King was regarded as
representative of and partaking in deity. He was, in
fact, a man-god, and we find that very often he was
ceremonially put to a violent death. As summed up
by Sir James Frazer : " the motive for slaying a
man-god is a fear lest with the enfeeblement of his
body in sickness or old age his sacred spirit should
suffer a corresponding decay, which might imperil
the general course of nature and with it the existence
of his worshippers who believe the cosmic energies
to be mysteriously knit up with those of their human

divinity." Such in brief is the theory of " The Dying
God " or " The Divine Victim ", as it is conveniently
known.

It is a curious and irresponsible fantasy which
attempts to superimpose the hypothesis of the " Divine
Victim " upon the Grand Masters of the witches.
Such a figment is difficult to be approached in serious
discussion, since it offers no vestige of reality, and
vaguely imaginative conjectures are not easy of
refutation, or rather they carry their own disproof.
Yet we are assured that certain figures, both historical
and legendary, as for example King Edmund, the
" deed-doer ", King Edmund Ironside, King Cnut
" the Great ", Bishop Walcher of Durham, William
Rufus, St. Thomas of Canterbury, St. Joan of Arc,
Gilles de Rais, Robin Hood, Friar Tuck, were not
only Grand Masters of witch societies, but also " the
Incarnate God ". Every one of these personages was
ceremonially put to death, and the sacrifice was
repeatedly consummated. When we venture to
ask what tittle of fact exists to support this amazing
assertion, we are coolly instructed that in the first
place all records, all evidence from history must be
swept aside as useless (a very necessary preliminary
this, I am willing to admit), and " the Christian
inquisitors are unanimous on this point ", which
last statement is, I venture to say, wholly unfounded.
It really is not worth while—even if space allowed
—to enter into all these cases in detail. I would merely
point out that in the instance of St. Joan of Arc these
wild theories have been dealt with by scholars and
historians to be exploded once and for all. Nor would
it be difficult to show how preposterous such fabling

is with regard to the other names. The murder of
William Rufus in the New Forest was due to homo-
sexual jealousy, and although they have been
squeamishly suppressed practically the full details of
the affair can be traced. If anyone likes to consider
that Robin Hood and Friar Tuck were wizards I
hardly suppose that any serious objection will be raised,
but I submit that it is distinctly offensive to very
many when St. Thomas à Becket stands thus defamed.
I am only too well aware that devotion to St. Thomas
is weak and anæmic enough in England. It is a
matter for regret that his holy Feast is not celebrated
amongst us with greater solemnity, that his secondary
Feast of the Translation is observed in only one
diocese. Yet there are still those who visit Canterbury
" The holy blisful martir for to seke ". St. Thomas
still has his clients who keep Tuesday in his honour,
who have kissed the hallowed spot where he fell, who
make pilgrimage and worship at his shrine.

In the case of historical figures the sole argument
to show that such-an-one was a Grand Master of
witches and " the Incarnate God " seems to be a
violent death. I shall not be in the least surprised to
be told that Jack Sheppard, Dick Turpin, Eugene
Aram, George Barnwell and Sweeney Todd were
" Incarnate Gods ", whilst to companion Friar Tuck
lct us have Grindoff the Miller, Bill Sikes, Count
Fosco and Cock Robin.

To quote a shrewd saying of the famous Dr. Henry
More : " *At this pitch of wit . . . is the Reason of our
professed Wit-would-be's of this present Age, who will
catch at any slight occasion or pretence of misbelieving those
things that they cannot endure should be true.*"

The name Sabbat, the derivation of which does not appear to be exactly established, may be held to cover almost every formal assembly of devil-worshippers, and thus ranges from comparative simplicity, the secret rendezvous in the open air or in some poor hut of half-a-dozen witches devoted to the fiend and presided over by the official of the village, to a large and crowded congregation adoring the demon upon his throne and marshalled by incarnate evil intelligences, a mob outvying the angels of the pit in malice, blasphemy, and revolt, the vomit of pandemonium on earth.

The day of the week whereon the Sabbat was held varied in different localities and at several times. There is indeed an accumulation of evidence for every night, although Friday was most generally favoured. Saturday and Sunday were if possible particularly avoided, especially a Saturday. At the trial of Louis Gaufridi in May, 1614, it was proved that the Sabbats were held on every night of the week. Wednesday and Friday were the Sabbats of blasphemy and the Black Mass, whilst to the other nights were allotted the most hideous villainies which humanity can conceive or perform. In England, it was stated during the seventeenth century that the " Solemn appointments and meetings . . . are ordinarily on Tuesday or Wednesday night ". The witches of Burgundy met on Tuesday night, so we may conclude with Boguet " that there is no fixed day for the Sabbat, but that witches go to it whenever Satan so commands ". This is confirmed by Madeleine Bavent who says : " There seemed to be no fixed day for the assembly."

Antide Colas confessed that she was wont to attend

the Sabbat upon each of the greater Festivals of the year, as for example at Christmas, Easter, Corpus Christi, and Boguet gives us the reason for this too—" the wicked one celebrates his assemblies on Holy Days, and thus mockingly seduces the creatures of God from His service."

Thus we hear of Sabbats being held on the vigils of the " nine chief feasts of the year ", namely, Easter, Epiphany, Ascension Day, the Purification, Nativity and Assumption of Our Lady, Corpus Christi, All Saints, and the Nativity of St. John Baptist. In one English village the Sabbat was held on St. Bartholomew's Eve, this apostle being Patron of the Church and parish. Throughout Eastern Europe a Sabbat was held on the Eve of St. George. In Western Europe the day of one of the principal assemblies was on 30th April, the Eve of May Day, famous over all Northern Germany as Die Walpurgis-Nacht, the Night of Saint Walburga.

The Grand Sabbats were convened in a great variety of places, whilst the lesser Sabbats could be easily assembled in an even larger number of spots, as might be most convenient to the Satanists of the district, a field near a village, a wood, a tor, a valley, an open waste beneath some blasted oak, a cemetery, a ruined building, some solitary chapel or deserted church, and often in a house belonging to one of the initiates.

It was advisable that the selected locality should be remote to obviate any chance of espionage or casual interruption, and in many localities some wild ill-omened gully or the lone hill-top was shudderingly marked as the notorious haunt of witches and their fiends.

De Lancre says that in the Basque country the Grand Sabbat was invariably held near a stream, a lake, or water of some kind. Bodin confirms this to some extent, for Antoine Gandillon, a witch of long continuance, told him that there must always be water in the place of the Sabbat, and the little coven of the village of Coirières held their Sabbat near a mill-dam. The Breton witches assembled among the ancient cromlechs and ruined dolmens of their province. The market-crosses of sleepy old towns and English villages were among the favourite rendezvous of our country warlocks and witches. Mother Agar, the Brewham witch, and her company forgathered on Brewham Common, and also at Husseys-knap, a coppice just beyond the hamlet. Dr. Fian and his associates on All Hallows E'en assembled at the lonely and haunted church of North Berwick. Silvain Nevillon, who was executed at Orleans on the 4th February, 1615, confessed " that the Sabbat was celebrated in a house ", and the full details which he gave shows this to have been a large château, no doubt the home of some wealthy local magnate, a Satanist and probably the Grand Master of the district, within whose walls above 200 persons could assemble.

In Jersey the witches' rendezvous was under the shadow of a large rock south of Rocqueberg Point, St. Clement, and it is believed that at their Sabbats they often raised storms which imperilled those at sea and drowned many a fisherman.

The Guernsey witches celebrated " the Feast of the Sabbat " on Friday nights on the hill of Catiôroc, around the cromlech called " Le Trépied ". At the time of the full moon they also met near the mill which stands on the hill at Ville-ès-Pies. Their favourite spot, however, was the sands of Rocquaine Bay, where they used to perform obscene dances chanting a roundelay of which the burden ran " Qué-hou-hou ! Marie Lihou ! " words uttered in impious defiance and mockery of Notre Dame, Sainte Marie de Lihou. This was a spot of such extraordinary sanctity, that although both priory and church are but a heap of shapeless ruins even to-day the French coasting vessels as they pass salute it by lowering their topmast.

One of the most notorious meeting-places for witches was the Brocken, popularly known as the Blocksburg, the highest peak of the Hartz mountains. On Walpurgis Night huge assemblies of Satanists were wont to forgather there, some (it is said) coming from Norway and even from distant Lapland. Local Blocksburgs existed, or rather hills so called, especially in Pomerania which boasted two or three such crags.

Night was almost invariably the time for the Sabbat. Father Delrio aptly observes : " Their assemblies are generally held at dead of night when the Powers of Darkness reign ; or, sometimes, at high noon, even as the Psalmist saith, when he speaks of ' the noonday devil '." The Lancashire witches celebrated their Sabbat " about twelve of the clock in the day time ". The witches of Stoke Trister, near Wincanton, " met about nine of the Clock in the Night, in the Common near *Trister* Gate." Mother Bishop, a Somersetshire witch, confessed " That she hath been at several meetings in *Lie* Common, and at other places in the night ". On one occasion Christian Green of Brewham and other witches met the devil " in *Brewham* Forest about Noon ", but the coven more frequently used to assemble " at a place called *Husseys-knap* in the Forest in the Night time ".

The time at which the Sabbat began was generally upon the stroke of midnight. It lasted until the cock crew, when everything vanished away.

A witch named Babilla Latoma, when minutely questioned by Nicolas Remy about the nightly doing of sorcerers, confessed that nothing was more fatally obstructive to their loathsome businesses than that a cock should crow. Two other witches informed the same judge that when it was time to break up their nocturnal assemblies the officers proclaimed in stentorian voices : " Ho ! make haste and away, all ; for the cock begins to crow." That the crowing of a cock dissolves enchantments is a tradition of remotest antiquity, and the poet Prudentius very beautifully sings how the night-wandering demons, who rejoice in dunnest shades, at the crowing of the cock tremble and scatter in sore affright.

It has been quite confidently and quite erroneously stated that in England the witches' Sabbat was practically unknown, or at most, when the evidence proves overwhelming and such as is impossible to slur or set aside, it is argued that the English Sabbat " was a feeble reflection of its foreign original ", and existed only in an " attenuated " form. It is difficult in the face of facts which certainly cannot be dismissed and which one would have thought could hardly be misinterpreted to appreciate whence this fallacy arose, but since it has been so seriously put forward and maintained it becomes necessary to make specific mention of some few from the many cases in English witchcraft proving the Assemblies or " synagogues " of Satanists—and such gatherings continue very actively to-day—whereat every kind of mischief and devil's craft was hatched and ingeniously propelled.

In 1579 the Windsor coven which was presided over by Father Rosimond of Farnham were wont to assemble for their Sabbats " within the backside of Master Dodges in the Pittes ", and also about eleven o'clock at night at the Pound. They were adepts in making figurines, and having moulded in red wax " pictures " of a neighbouring farmer and his maid-servant, a local butcher, and the Mayor of Windsor, they killed these four persons by sorcery, piercing the figures through and through with sharp hawthorn spines and prickles. A very important Sabbat was held by the Lancashire witches on Good Friday, 1612, at Malking Tower, the abode of old Mother Demdike, where twenty and more indulged in a gluttonous orgy, and plotted no inconsiderable amount of mischief, including the murder of Thomas Lister, of Westly, which they very effectually contrived in less than two or three months. The Salmesbury witches, three of whom were put on their trial in the same year, 1612, used to celebrate their Sabbats on Thursday and Sunday nights on the banks of the Ribble, where they met four tall black men who provided meat and wine, who danced with them and fornicated. Two of the witches who had secretly killed a small child, after the burial of the body dug it up, boiled it in a pot and ate it, seething the bones to obtain fat for the witch's ointment.

Ten years later the witches who plagued the family of that eminent poet and scholar Edward Fairfax of Fewstone, in the Forest of Knaresborough, used to meet at midnight at Timble Gill, where a table was spread with food and flagons, and the Devil sat at the upper end.

In the case of the Second Lancashire witches, 1634, Margaret Johnson confessed that on the Sunday within the octave of All Saints she attended a Sabbat at a house called Hoarestones (which was still standing in 1845) and there were present about forty witches with their familiars. She further stated that Good Friday was " one of their constant days of their general meeting ".

Matthew Hopkins relates that in 1644 when he was living at Manningtree, Essex, a number of witches, both of his own town and from neighbouring villages, " every six weeks in the night (being always on the Friday night) had their meeting close by his house, and had their several solemn sacrifices there offered to the Devil."

About the same year the Leicestershire witches used to forgather at Burton-on-the-Wolds " above four score " at a Sabbat, and at Tilbrooke bushes near Catworth " above twenty at one time " to worship and serve the demon.

In September, 1645, Goodwife Hott, a witch of Faversham, Kent, related how " there was a great meeting at Goodwife Pantery's house, and that Goodwife Dadson was there, and that Goodwife Gardner should have been there, but did not come, and the Devil sat at the upper end of the table ".

Dr. Henry More, the famous Platonist philosopher, learned that a coven of witches held their Sabbats at the house of Mother Lendall of Cambridge, a woman most ill-famed for impiety and evil, and that here late at night the " table was well furnished with guests and meat ", whilst at the head of the board there sat one in black to whom the numerous company louted low with great reverence and did obeisance. Much of the talk among the leaders of the party was carried on in a strange tongue, not understood of the humbler folk present.

The Malmesbury coven in 1671 celebrated their orgies at night in the house of one of the dark fellowship, and here they securely feasted and drank deeply and committed every kind of uncleanness, also plotting evilly enough against their enemies and planning murders with only too speedy and efficacious results.

The very dangerous and extremely well-organized society of witches who infested the Northumbrian woodlands and open moors between Shotley Bridge and Corbridge at the end of the seventeenth century had their general meeting-place at a house called Riding House, near Riding Mill Bridge End, where there was a banquet spread and " their protector whom they called their god " sat at the top of the table in a great gilt chair. One Good Friday no less than sixty-five witches attended a great feast at the house of John Newton, of the Riding, near Riding Mill, where they were served with boiled capons, rich cheeses, butter, white bread, beef, bottles of rare wine, and a vast variety of all meats. Another Sabbat was held at Allensford on the Derwent, when the whole coven danced their ritual measure. Yet another Sabbat was celebrated in the cellar of Master Francis Pye's house at Morpeth.

In Massachusetts whither the foul traditions of witchcraft had been brought from England and there could be no question of continental custom or influence, the Salem witches held their General Meetings and solemn Sabbat—"hellish Randezvouzes," Cotton Mather justly terms them—in a field not far from the village, and sometimes in a house belonging to a warlock who lived there. Here they celebrated a Sabbat on the very day a Public Fast was being kept on account of the sorceries and devilment which were so sorely plaguing the countryside. There were "Meetings, Feastings, Dancings" in other places as well, and a number of novices were baptized into this horrid society in the river at Newbury Falls.

At the risk of some slight repetition I have thought it well to give a catena extending over a century (1579–1692) to show beyond all quibble or question that the English witches assembled at set times and in set places for their formal Sabbats where every species of wickedness and devil-worship prevailed, and that there was in fine amongst them a definite and disciplined organization of the infernal cult of Satanism, which is one and the same the whole world over. It would not be difficult, moreover, to carry on the chain of evidence throughout the eighteenth and nineteenth centuries down to the London Sabbats of the present day.

I believe the point has been raised that the English Sabbats were but small gatherings in comparison with the large assemblies in Germany, in the Pyrenees, at Mohra in Sweden, in the Val Camonica, at Benevento, and other places. It is true that the witches flocked in crowds to certain notorious centres, and when a district was widely infected with Satanism naturally the covens would be more numerous. Yet we hear of no

less than twenty attending a Sabbat in the second
case of the Lancashire witches; sixty-five were
present at the Sabbat in John Newton's house, Riding
Mill; whilst at the notorious Sabbat at North Berwick
church there assembled two hundred devil-worshippers,
although, of course, strictly speaking this is not an
English example. To-day also there are sometimes
as many as twenty-five or thirty at a Sabbat. No
doubt in villages such as Brewham the coven was few,
but the Wincanton society numbered thirteen and
perhaps more. Similar proportions seem to have prevailed (as we might reasonably expect) upon the
continent.

The next detail which presents itself for inquiry is,
how the witches reached the Sabbat? The answer
seems at first glance simple enough : they ride, they
drive, they go on foot, travelling in whatever way is
most convenient. When Agnes Sampson, who lived
at Keith, attended the midnight Sabbat at North
Berwick church, " she passed there on horseback, conveyed by her godson, called John Cooper." When
the Pendle witches assembled at Malking Tower, an
extremely isolated and ancient stronghold which stood
on the further slope of the high conical-shaped hill
which shuts in Rough Lee glen to the north-east, they
" gotten on Horsebacke ", some mounting steeds of
one colour, some of another. When Ann Armstrong,
a servant of the Fowlers at Burtree House, near Stocksfield-on-Tyne, was taken to the Sabbat at Riding Mill
Bridge End she saw the witches arrive on horseback.
Their leader, whom they spoke of as " their protector ",
was " a long black man riding on a bay galloway ",
in other words a garran, a small stout Scotch horse.

When the orgy was over the whole crew took the saddle again for home with their protector leading the party.

Major Thomas Weir, the Edinburgh warlock, and his sister Jean Weir, used to drive to the Sabbats at Musselburgh in a coach, and for more than a hundred years after the execution of these two miserable witches it was said that the rattling and thundering of a heavy coach could be heard at midnight over the cobbles as the phantom equipage whirled along by black steeds of hell passed swiftly down the Bow to halt before Weir's horrible house and then vanish in a flame of fire. It is probable that many hauntings by spectral coaches are to be explained thus, namely that the apparitions are those of wizards who were wont thus to travel to the Sabbat and whose foul ghosts still cling to the route they covered in life on evil bent again and again. A château not far from Morlaix in Brittany is fearfully haunted in this way. On certain anniversaries the windows of the empty house are illuminated from within as by numberless candles, the old cracked bell in the turret clangs harshly, and up the long drive there speeds an ancient coach within which are seated four shadowy figures. These are said to be a certain seigneur, lord of the manor in the early decades of the eighteenth century, his son and two grandsons, all of whom were Satanists, handing down the infernal tradition from scion to scion of their accursed line.

Early in the sixteenth century a gang of Satanists made their headquarters at Yarmouth, and it is plain that they were protected by certain great persons living in that district who belonged to the evil society. In the reign of Elizabeth six Yarmouth witches, including Elizabeth Butcher, a very active devil's agent, were hanged, and under Charles I another five witches were executed. Caister Castle near Yarmouth was formerly visited by a phantom coach which drove round the courtyard of the castle and halted, whereupon a number of dark muffled figures seem to emerge silently from various doorways and corners, and enter the vehicle. The door was slammed to with a horrible noise, the crack of a whip was heard, and the six headless black horses set off at full gallop. No doubt these were the spectres of the wizards doomed endlessly to repeat their journey to the unhallowed orgies of the Sabbat.

A similar coach haunts the roads near Langley Hall, Durham. Although it is true that many cases of witchcraft have not come to light in this district it may be noted that in January, 1651–1652, two notorious warlocks were executed at Durham, and it is more than probable that the organization had secretly taken root there, whilst the boggart coach is the phantom of that which was wont to convey certain sorcerers to their diabolic rendezvous.

Witches sometimes go on foot to the Sabbat, and this usually happens when the place of their assembly is not very distant from their homes. Thus Bernard of Como, a famous Dominican scholar, remarks that when witches are to attend the Sabbat at some spot hard by their dwellings, " they proceed thither on foot conversing as they go." When a Sabbat was celebrated in the field of Longchamois, the witches of Orcieres, about a quarter of a league away, walked thither in a party. The Wincanton witches walked to the Sabbat held on the common near Trister Gate, a bare couple of miles away, whilst for Mother Style of Stoke Trister it can only have been a matter of a few hundred yards.

A young Satanist, Isaac de Queyran, told Pierre De Lancre, the Bordeaux judge, that witches who dwelt at some distance flew home from the Sabbat through the air, whilst those whose houses were not far away returned on foot. De Lancre comments : " It is truly as criminal and abominable for a Sorcerer to go to the Sabbat on foot as to be voluntarily conveyed thither by the Devil."

In all the above cases (save truly in the hints given by de Queyran) the method of proceeding to the Sabbat proves perfectly commonplace and usual, but the witches also employed other means which were extraordinary and indeed preternatural. The popular imagination has seized upon one of these and often exaggerates it into something surpassingly fantastic and bizarre, for although the witch is universally credited with the power to fly through the air mounted upon a besom or some kind of stick it is remarkable in the face of so general and picturesque a belief to find that the confessions avowing this actual mode of aerial transport are comparatively few.

None the less it is significant that the belief in the nocturnal transport through the air of sorcerers, either bent on some malefic business or to attend their assemblies, is practically universal, and exists among savage races as strongly as amongst civilized people. In the Congo, for example, members of the secret society *Bwiti* during certain wizard ceremonies rise from the ground to a height of several feet during the space of a quarter of an hour. The Indians of North America credited their pow-wows with the faculty of raising their bodies from the ground for an appreciable length of time, and a French missionary, Father Papetard told Dr. Imbert-Gourbeyre, that whilst at Oregon he had himself seen more than once native warlocks levitate themselves two or three feet from the ground and walk upon the top of the blades of long pampas grasses without bending the tender panicles. In Australia, too, the native tribes such as the Boandik, West Arunta, Kurnai, and others are perfectly familiar with the aerial transport of magicians, who are said to be conveyed by ghosts, that is to say (as we know) by demons. In one of the tribes of the Wotjobaluk group an ancient seeress not infrequently " went up aloft, being supported, as it was believed, by ghosts [devils], from whom she gleaned information as to the dead ". This is related together with many other striking examples by A. W. Howitt in his work on *The Native Tribes of South-East Australia.*

It stands to reason that Satan, the ape of God, must imitate and caricature the divine phenomenon of mystical levitation.

According to the great *Oxford English Dictionary* the word " levitation " does not date back before 1875. It was first employed in England, and in earliest use with reference to spiritualism (spiritism). Levitation means that the human body is able under certain conditions to be raised from the ground, and to remain for a longer or shorter space of time suspended in the air without any visible support, and not infrequently to move to and fro in the air without the apparent or traceable action of any physical forces.

In hagiography this is a recognized and not infrequent occurrence, and very many instances are noted by the Bollandists in their immense work on the Lives of the Saints. It is not too much to say that some hundreds of such cases have been known. There are the Scriptural examples of Enoch, Elijah, Habakkuk, S. Philip the Deacon, and the transports of Our Lord Himself, Whose earthly life was consummated in that supreme levitation we name the Ascension. There are the cases of early Saints, Saint Mary Magdalene, Saint Antony the Great, Saint Mary of Egypt. There are the modern traditions of such great names as Saint Dominic, Saint Francis, Saint Bonaventura, Saint Thomas Aquinas, Saint Catherine of Siena, Saint Peter of Alcantara, Saint Teresa, Saint Philip Neri— to name almost at random only a very few. In the nineteenth century we have that glorious visionary and mystic Anne Catherine Emmerich ; the Italian Maria Domenica Barbagli ; the Curé d'Ars ; Mary of Jesus who died in 1862, and whose levitations formed the subject of a report in a bulletin of the *Société des Sciences psychiques* ; the Carmelite Sister Mary of Jesus Crucified who died at the Carmel of Bethlehem in 1878 ; an ecstatica living near Nantes, Marie Julie Jahenny, who is still alive.

Perhaps the two most famous examples of levitation are Saint Alphonsus Liguori and Saint Joseph of Copertino. Some of the raptures and upliftings of Saint Alphonsus were experienced in public, as in the church of Foggia in December, 1745, when as he was preaching he was raised to a height from the floor in the presence of a crowded congregation who could not refrain from crying aloud : " A miracle ! a miracle ! "

With regard to the Franciscan Joseph of Copertino, who died at the Conventual house at Osimo in September,

1663, his levitations and ecstatic flights through the air from one place to another were so frequent that the Bull of canonization says no Saint can be compared to him in this respect. His raptures in saying Mass were of daily occurrence, and for no less than thirty-five years his Superiors had to exercise the greatest caution, requiring him on certain feasts, especially those of Our Lady, to say Mass in a private oratory so that the religious " should not be disturbed by the concourse of the vulgar ", many of whom came more from curiosity (it is to be feared) rather than devotion to see this marvellous mystic at the altar.

The evidence for the levitations of Saint Alphonsus and Saint Joseph (as indeed for very many other holy persons) has been sifted with the utmost thoroughness, and there is no room whatsoever left for doubt or question.

In this connexion we cannot neglect to remark upon mediumistic levitations, one of the most famous examples being the case of Daniel Dunglas Home, of whom Sir William Crookes bore witness : " On three separate occasions have I seen him raised completely from the floor of the room. . . . There are at least a hundred recorded instances of Mr. Home's rising from the ground. . . . The accumulated testimony establishing Mr. Home's levitations is overwhelming." In November, 1868, Lord Adare and Lord Lindsay saw Home raised four or five feet from the ground. At Ashley House, Home was carried out at one window and borne in through another at a height of 70 feet from the ground. Once at Adare Abbey, he floated swiftly for a space of twelve yards through the air. In a garden at Stockton he was aerially transported for more than a hundred feet.

William Stainton Moses was levitated six feet;
Eusapia Palladino, on occasion from some inches to
fully five feet; Mrs. French, a couple of feet; Maria
Vollhart, one foot; whilst the Brazilian Carlos Mirabelli even when fastened to an armchair was levitated
in the presence of several acutely observant members
of the Academia Cesare Lombroso, remaining for
several minutes suspended twelve feet from the ground
so that the witnesses could pass and repass under the
body tied to the chair. (It is by no means unusual for
objects in contact with the levitated person to be
similarly influenced by the phenomenon.) At Santos
Mirabelli experienced levitation in the street, being
uplifted from a motor car for about three minutes.

Now angels, be they blessed spirits or demons, have
the power to move matter. The levitation of sorcerers
is effected by the agency of evil forces, devils who
bestow this favour upon an auxiliary and a companion.

Dr. John L. Nevius, of Chefoo, who was for forty
years a missionary to the Chinese, in his study *Demon
Possession* relates how certain Chinese wizards " are
carried by invisible power from place to place. They
ascend to a height of twenty or fifty feet, and are carried
to a distance of four or five *li* ". (A *li* is one-third of a
mile.) The same phenomenon occurs in the case of
European witches, who have been and are borne by the
invisible power of Satan to the Sabbat, or it may be
on some other errand of mischief and destruction.

Paul Grilland in his treatise *On Witchcraft*, published
in 1533, speaks of a trial of a sorceress at Rome seven
years before, at which he was present, and it was
asserted that she flew in the air after she had anointed
her limbs with a certain magic liniment. Some witches,

says Boguet, use a mysterious ointment, and others use none. " Before they go to the Sabbat," writes Guazzo, " the witches anoint themselves on some part of their bodies with an unguent made from various foul and filthy ingredients, but chiefly from murdered children ; and so anointed they are carried away on a cowl-staff, or a broom, or a reed, a cleft stick, or a distaff, or even a shovel, which things they ride."

Dr. Johann Weyer, in his treatise on witches, has transcribed certain formulæ for the magical ointment. He tells how the witches boil the fat of babes in a brazen cauldron. They scum this thickly, and make it into a kind of grease, kneading into it a commixture of hemlock, aconite, poplar leaves, and soot. Another recipe is : Cowbane, sweet flag, cinquefoil, bat's blood, belladonna, and oil. There are, Weyer adds, other ointments, but the essential ingredients remain the same in all.

Collette Dumont, a Guernsey witch, who was executed in 1617, confessed that the Devil had given her a certain black ointment, with which, having stripped, she rubbed her body all over, and then again dressed and went out of doors when she was immediately borne through the air with incredible velocity to the appointed place for the Sabbat. This was sometimes near the Torteval parish churchyard, and sometimes on the seashore hard by Rocquaine Castle.

It is related that a certain Guernsey lady of St. Pierre-du-Bois becoming very suspicious of the long hours of retirement her husband passed in his own apartments was induced by curiosity to watch him. Accordingly one day she concealed herself in the room. He entered, and stripping himself naked anointed his limbs with a certain ointment, repeating the words *va et vient*. He then seemed to disappear from sight. After a while she came forth, and went through the same ceremony, when in a twink she found herself on the summit of Pleinmont in the midst of a large company. A table was spread with costly viands, of which some who were present courteously invited her to partake. Crossing herself for her grace, she said *Au nom de Dieu soit, Amen.* No sooner had she spoken than all had disappeared, and the only signs of any beings having approached the spot were the recent marks of cloven feet which seemed to have scorched and trampled the sward in every direction.

In the *Malleus Maleficarum* it is explained at length how witches having anointed either themselves or some chair or broomstick with the devil's ointment can be and are transported up through the air about their master's business. Sometimes also they are carried on animals, which are not true animals but devils in that form. The witches too not unseldom appear to be metamorphosed into animals, especially cats. And this is merely glamour, a trick of the devil, who, Saint Thomas tells us, can entirely confuse and cheat the senses, so that a witch is persuaded she is changed into a cat, and those of her society see her as a cat, whereas it is all illusion.

" The commonest practice of all witches is to fly up through the chimney. If anyone objects that chimneys are too small and narrow, or raises any other difficulties, he must know that by virtue of that Demonolatry which makes all things monstrous and portentous, they are first bidden to exceed their natural limits ; and moreover the matter becomes more intelligible when it is remembered that the chimneys are square and wide in all peasant's cottages, and it is from this class that the vile rabble of sorcery is mostly derived." In his account of the Swedish witches of 1669–1670, who were conveyed to Blockula, the place of the Sabbat, by diabolic agencies, Anthony Horneck says that, " Being asked how they could go with their Bodies through Chimneys and broken panes of Glass, they said, that the Devil did first remove all that might hinder them in their flight, and so they had room enough to go."

During the trial of the Somersetshire witch, Julian Cox, at the Taunton assizes, 1663, a " Witness swore that she had seen *Julian Cox* fly into her own Chamber Window in her full proportion, and that she very well knew her, and was sure it was she."

From these cases it is certain that witches are levitated and carried in this way to the Sabbat. The ointment is actually of no effect *per se*, and the devil can (and often will) transport sorcerers to the Sabbat without any smearing with unguent or lotions. The ointment is employed as a sort of ceremonial subterfuge, since the demon by means of this empty ritual impresses a sense of his own power upon his worshippers, and thus he ministers to his accursed pride. Moreover the ointment is a mockery of the Holy Chrism which is used in certain Sacraments as well as at the Coronation of a King. In the same way the staff or broom is just an empty adjuvant, a common object which the devil causes to be utilized in these mysterious locomotions as a dark and infernal symbol, infusing as it were something of a ritual and liturgical nature into his beastly orgies.

In connexion with, and actually as an argument

against, the levitation and aerial journeys of witches
there is often cited a document conveniently known
as the Canon Episcopi, which is found in the collec-
tions *On Ecclesiastical Discipline*, a manual for the use
of the bishop in the course of diocesan visitations, put
together by the famous Benedictine Abbot Regino of
Prüm about the year 906, but which although doubtless
very much older than Regino's own day certainly does
not date back to the First orthodox plenary Synod of
Ancyra (now Angora, Asia Minor), which was held in
314, and to which body it was rather unaccountably
referred by many older commentators and legists.

The text of this much debated and highly debatable
section runs as follows : " This too must by no
means be passed over that certain utterly abandoned
women, turning aside to follow Satan, being seduced
by the illusions and phantasmical shows of demons
firmly believe and openly profess that in the dead of
night they ride upon certain beasts along with the
pagan goddess Diana and a countless horde of women,
and that in those silent hours they fly over vast tracts
of country and obey her as their mistress, whilst on
certain other nights they are summoned to do her
homage and pay her service." For some reason
Burchard added Herodias to Diana, and the two
names were maintained in later recensions. The canon
continues to say that an immense number of people,
deluded by this false opinion, take these things to be
very true, and thus fall away from the Christian faith
since they are persuaded that something having a
divine nature and ineffable power exists other than the
one true God. In fine they lapse into paganism.

We must not read more into the Canon Episcopi

than it precisely states. The "abandoned women" whom it so sternly censures are not witches flying to a Sabbat, but poor self-deceived creatures whose guilt consists in honouring, trusting to, obeying, and (so they deem) accompanying as her handmaids a heathen goddess in her nightly coursing through the air. They sin, moreover, in stubbornly maintaining that these evil fantasies and fables, inspired by the Father of Lies, are actual experiences and events. These delusions, no doubt, are very bad and even idolatrous. But there is no sorcery. There has been no pact with Satan. There is no working of Black Magic, no casting of malefic spells, no killing men and cattle.

Bishop Peter Binsfield treats the whole question of the Canon Episcopi at length and clearly shows that it is not aimed at witches and the midnight transvections of sorcerers to the Sabbat, but that quite another sect of deluded women is intended. His arguments are too lengthy to recapitulate here, but they are conclusive.

Later in the seventeenth century when discussing the levitation of witches the learned Jacques D'Autun openly challenged the authority of the Canon Episcopi. He pertinently inquired at what Council of Ancyra was this law laid down ? He quoted the authority of Saint Augustine to show that the historical Councils of Ancyra must be deemed irregular if they are to be regarded as having any higher status than a Synod, and some even lie under the suspicion of Arianism. In any case it was not a General Council of the Church assembled under Papal Authority, and accordingly it could not promulgate a dogma. This Canon has in fact, he concludes, come to serve as a shield for the scoffer and agnostic.

The actual ceremonies of the Sabbat at which the members of the coven have now arrived vary so much (as has indeed already been pointed out) that although the essential features of Satan's synagogue are intrinsically the same at all times and in all countries it is no easy matter to give a general account of assemblies which were marked by such confessed and multitudinous details. This has been commented upon by all the demonologists, and is especially emphasized by De Lancre who made a particular study of the Sabbat as it was held in the South of France at the beginning of the seventeenth century, and who obtained his information at first-hand from the scores of witches he examined.

The liturgy of darkness, indeed, is of its very essence opposed to the comely worship of God, wherein, as the Apostle bids, all things are to be done " decently and in order ".

The Sabbat is always conducted by a President or Chief, who is at the more important and larger meetings the Grand Master of the Satanists, at lesser assemblies the coven-master (who may, of course, be also the Grand Master) or some other official. Not infrequently an intelligence of evil, a demon, assumes corporeal form and presents himself for the adoration of his besotted followers.

The proceedings commence with the ceremonial homage paid to the President by the company, for as the witches told Remy there was always one who was invested with the chief authority on the night of their assembly.

The witches worship him by genuflections and kneeling ; by bowing the body ; by holding up their hands as in prayer ; by grotesque and ridiculous gestures ; by uttering aloud the most horrid blasphemies and imprecations ; by calling upon the demon as god.

When they approach to adore him " Sometimes they bend their knees as suppliants, and sometimes stand with their backs turned, and sometimes kick their legs high up so that their heads are bent back and their chins point to the sky ".

At the trial of Louis Gaufridi at Aix in 1611 amplest details concerning this homage were forthcoming. " The hagges and witches, who are people of a sordid and base condition, are the first that come to adore the Prince of the Synagogue, who is Lucifer's lieutenant, and he that now holdeth that place is Lewes Gaufridy," that is to say he was Grand Master of the district. " Next they goe and worship the Divell who is seated in a Throne like a Prince." This shows that not unseldom a demon in corporeal form was present at these Sabbats.

Collette Dumont, a Guernsey witch, confessed that the Sabbat commenced with the adoration of the Devil, and Isebell Le Moigne, a member of the same coven, described how the demon compelled his votaries to go down on their knees before him, adoring him and calling upon him with the words " Our great Master, help us ! "

Mention of the obscene ritual kiss, " the kiss of shame," the gage of fealty, is universal, and it is clear that this ceremony was invariably insisted upon and most scrupulously exacted. Delrio writes how the orgies are governed by a demon, Lord of the Sabbat, who often appears in some monstrous form as a great he-goat with flaming eyes and the whole company in token of abject submission kiss his fundament. As a sign of completest servitude, remarks Ludwig Elich, at their meetings the witches kiss the devil's posterior. Shadwell puts it bluntly enough : *All kiss the Devil's Arse.* Upon this he glosses : " Kissing the Devil's Buttocks is part of the homage they pay the Devil, as *Bodin* says Doctor *Edlin* did, a *Sorbon* Doctor." Guillaume Edeline, Prior of St. Germain-en-Laye, was executed in 1453 as a wizard. He confessed that he had done homage to Satan who appeared in the shape of a ram by kissing his buttocks with great reverence.

In 1393 Walter Langton, Bishop of Coventry and treasurer of Edward I, was accused of sorcery and of paying homage to Satan in this way. Amongst other accusations he was commonly defamed and delated for the crime of worshipping the Devil by kissing his posterior, and also " it is reported that he hath had frequent colloquies with evil spirits ". A sentence passed upon a coven of exceptionally evil and dangerous sorcerers at Avignon in 1582 details their crimes, when amongst other charges it is said : " You did worship the Prince of Devils in deed and word as very God, and (fie, for very shame !) with the greatest reverence you did kiss with sacrilegious mouth his most foul and beastly posterior." When the Sabbat was held at the haunted church of North Berwick in 1590 the Devil awaited the arrival of the witches " in the habit or likeness of a man, and seeing that they tarried overlong he at their coming enjoined them all to a penance which was that they should kiss his Buttocks in sign of duty to him, which being put over the Pulpit bare, every one did as he had enjoined them ". Another

account has it : " Now efter that the devil had endit
his admonitions he cam down out of the pulpit, and
caused all the company to come and kiss his ers quhilk
they said was cauld lyk yce." A French witch, Jeanne
Bosdeau, in 1594, confessed to the Bordeaux judges,
how at a rendezvous of more than sixty Satanists
at Puy-de-Dôme a black goatish form presided.
" They kiss'd his Backside, and pray'd that he would
help them." A very rare tract of the fourteenth century
tells how the Waldenses in their secret synagogues
adored a demon cat, whom they kissed under his tail.

The ceremonial offering and burning of candles
at the Sabbat is often met with, and indeed these
candles were something more than symbolic and a
parody of the candles blessed by the Church since
they were required for the very practical purpose of
affording light at these midnight rendezvous. Guazzo
tells us how the witches of North Italy presented
" pitch black candles " to the devil ; and Barthélemy
Minguet, a French warlock, in his description of the
Sabbat says that when the company went forward to
adore their Master all of them were holding a pitch
candle of black wax in their hands. These burned
with a blue flame on account of the sulphurous material
with which they were compounded. At the meeting
of the Scotch witches at North Berwick round the
pulpit whence the devil addressed his followers were
set numbers of black tapers which burned smokily
and with a blue light. Old Mother Styles told the
Somersetshire magistrates that when she and her sister
hags met the Man in Black " he delivers some Wax
Candles like little Torches, which they give back
again at parting ".

It has already been pointed out that the devil-worshippers are greedy to draw others into the snare, and ever ready by most treacherous and foulest means to proselytize and betray others to their own damnation, activities which commend them mightily in the eyes of their master. When neophytes were received into this horrid society at the Sabbat the performance was conducted with much grotesque ritual and blasphemy. There was the formal pact; the repudiation of all good; the mock baptism with the infernal sponsors; the acceptance of the duties to be engaged in all mischief; the vows of silence and secrecy; the promise to recruit with diligence.

Instructions were also given to the society; death and destruction were plotted; plans were discussed and developed. Thus we find the North Berwick devil (the Grand Master) harangues his covens from the pulpit; the Pendle witches assemble at Malking Tower to contrive the deaths of their enemies; Alice Duke, Ann Bishop, Mother Penny, and the rest of the Somersetshire gang are instructed in the art of moulding wax pictures and transfixing them with thorns and pins; spells were taught orally; sometimes drugs and poisons were confected; the witch midwives learned the practice of abortion and the quality of emmenagogic savin. If these failed they resorted to surer swifter means. A witch who was executed at Dann in Switzerland " confessed that she had killed more than forty children, by sticking a needle through the crown of their heads into their brains, as they came out of the womb." Another witch-midwife of Strassburg said that she had killed more children than she could count.

Not infrequently high politics were the question at these Sabbats, and the more powerful witches strove to decide the fate of countries and the lot of kings. It is undeniable that many of the wars which have convulsed nations, the broils and unrest, the revolutions that trouble and vex the world to-day, are in the first place organized by and energetically assisted by Satanists. For " rebellion is as the sin of witchcraft ".

Lambert Daneau writes that Satan assembles his subjects at these devilish synagogues in order that he may examine them and understand with what diligence and success they have carried out their duties of harm and hurt to man and beast, whom they have injured, and what deaths they have contrived. The witch whose deeds are vilest and most abominable is the most highly honoured and applauded. Those, on the contrary, who have done no evil, are beaten and punished.

Thus Isobel Gowdie, the Scotch witch, gave a very ample account of how the devil or Grand Master tyrannized over the local coven. " He would beat and buffet us very sore," she complained. " We were beaten if we were absent from any gathering, or if we neglected to do anything he had commanded us." When Isebell Le Moigne, the Guernsey witch, on one occasion refused to accompany the familiar to James Gallienne's house, he returned to her in the shape of a man and bruised her severely about the face and head.

Strict discipline was observed among the Vaudois witches of Arras, and when one of the coven, Jean Tacquet, a rich eschevin, was minded to withdraw his allegiance from Satan, the demon forced him to continue it by thrashing him most cruelly with a bull's pizzle. As in the days of Remy, the Satanists even now bind themselves by a solemn oath never to betray their confederates. Any possible treachery to the infernal society constitutes, of course, the gravest offence in their eyes, and the modern Satanists stop at nothing to silence a traitor. To-day many members of these hellish leagues are only prevented from breaking away through fear. It is, as we might expect, a system of terrorism. Death is the penalty for any defection from their ranks, for naturally they are extremely reluctant that any hint of their dark secrets shall be revealed to the world. Nor are those whose aim it is to engineer universal anarchy and red revolution likely to shrink from a mere casual murder.

The business (so to speak) of the Sabbat having been dispatched, there followed the pleasures, which, as may well be supposed, were of the foulest and grossest kind. They mainly consisted in dancing and feasting. Sometimes they dance before eating and sometimes after the repast. The dances are generally performed in a circle and always round to the left, withershins, nor are they graceful and elegant movements, but the most erratic and ungainly caperings, jiggings and leapings, which prove wearisome beyond words, so what is ordinarily a pastime and a source of lawful amusement becomes a labour and a toil. Nor will the demon excuse any from the dance; those who are old and torpid he drives on until perforce they endeavour to stir their limbs, awkwardly and painfully enough, no doubt. So the notorious warlock parson, Mr. Gideon Penman, showed himself particularly active during the Sabbat rites, and " was in the rear in all their dances, and beat up all those that were slow ".

The witches, according to Boguet, dance in a ring back to back, and he adds : " Sometimes too, although seldom, they dance in couples, and then one partner is here, another there, for always everything is higgledy-piggledy, in rank riot and confusion." De Lancre writes of the witches' revels that they "only dance three kinds of brawls. . . . The first is *à la Bohémienne* . . . the second with quick trippings : these are the round dances ". In the third the dancers were placed one behind another in a long straight line. The brawls (French *le bransle*) was an old French dance resembling a cotillion.

In Belgium this witches' dance was known as *Pavana*.

During the Fian trial Agnes Sampson confessed that at North Berwick church above a hundred persons " danced along the *Kirk-yard*, *Geillis Duncan* playing on a Trump [Jew's harp], and *John Fian* mussiled [masked] led the *Ring* ". As they danced, hand in hand, they were all singing with one voice,

Cummer, go ye before, cummer, go ye,
Gif ye will not go before, cummer, let me.

" These confessions made the King [James I, then James VI of Scotland] in a wonderful admiration, and he sent for the said Geillis Duncan, who, upon the like trump, did play the said dance before the King's Majesty."

The Capuchin Jacques D'Autun in his encyclopædic treatise on magic (*The Folly of the Wise and the Wisdom of the Simple*) speaks of sorcerers who gyrate hand in hand in a circle as if inspired by maniac frenzy.

He further remarks that whereas a dance should be distinguished by propriety and decorum, by a certain stateliness or it may be by lively frolic, the dances of witches are uncouth and ugly, extravagant and lewd. Such are the dances of savages, and it is worth remark that among the North American Indians there is but one word to express both dancing and coitus. Meanwhile the whole company are whooping and howling, hissing and yelling, in an access of horrid rage that is akin to an absolute frenzy.

There is evidence that various instruments accompanied the dance. Violins, flutes, tambourines, citterns, hautboys, and in Scotland the pipes made music at the Sabbat. Those of the witches who had any skill were called upon to perform, and very often they obliged the company with favourite airs of a vulgar kind, but the concert always ended in hideous cacophony and bestial clamour. In North Italy the covens were wont to " sing in honour of the devil the most obscene songs to the sound of a bawdy pipe and tabor played by one seated in the fork of a tree ". George Sinclar in his *Satan's Invisible World Discovered* says : " A reverend Minister told me, that one who was the Devils Piper, a wizzard confest to him, that at a Ball of dancing, the Foul spirit taught him a Baudy song to sing and play, as it were this night, and ere two days past all the Lads and Lasses of the town were lilting it throw the street. It were abomination to rehearse it." At Tranent in 1659 one man witch and eight women witches confessed that they had merry meetings with Satan, enlivened with music and dancing. John Douglas, the warlock, was the piper, and the two favourite airs of the Grand

Master were "Kilt thy coat, Maggie, and come thy way with me", and "Hulie the bed will fa'".

At Aix the witches danced "at the sound of Viols and other instruments, which are brought thither by those that were skilled to play upon them". None the less the sorcerers and hags joined in a kind of howling music with raucous cries imitating song. The Somerset witches of the Wincanton covens said that "The Man in black, sometimes playes on a Pipe or Cittern, and the company dance".

The music in fine was of many kinds, varying from harmonies "softly sweet, in Lydian measures", voluptuous and venereal, to the most horrid cacophony resembling the modern jazz, wherein (be it noted) some acute observers have shrewdly scented the devil's own orchestra. Fr. Philip De Ternant, writing in *The Universe*, 18th August, 1933, justly and in good time condemns the "Voodoo Cult imported into our Dance Halls without protest", and points out how young people are being corrupted by "the roll and the thump of the Voodoo Drum" which "responsive to subtle manipulation not far removed from black magic, plays a most hypnotic part" in the obscene, murderous, and wholly diabolical Voodoo cult. Quite unwittingly, no doubt, to-day many dancers are exercising their steps to the music of the witches. "Dreary pushing and pulling about the floor with almost aimless steps have now taken the place of dancing."

It was not without sound reason that Toussaint l'Ouverture when declaring the independence of Haiti and giving the Island a constitution forbade the Voodoo drum with its syncopation and sub-human appeal. The accursed thing has found a most profligate

and tortuous entry in our midst, and unless recognized and sternly checked the poison will infect, rot,
and fester, for such is its deliberate and appointed
aim.

As the music of the witches, always evil, always
unclean, varied in many modes so the feasts and
banquetings of the witches were very dissimilar and
differed widely both in their meats, their appointments, and also as regards the actual spots where they
took place. According to the climate and customs of
the country and the seasons of the year the Sabbat
with its feast might be held under cover or in the open.
Thus, as we should expect, in Italy and in France the
Sabbat was frequently celebrated out of doors ; in
Guernsey the feast was usually spread on the sea-shore
near Rocquaine Castle ; in Sweden the witches met
at a " place or house " under a roof; the Scotch
covens assembled for the junketings in outbuildings,
farms, in remote and deserted chapels ; in warm
weather the Riding Mill witches forgathered at the
bridge end and on the moors, in colder seasons at
Riding House, in a cellar or a barn ; the Somersetshire witches made their rendezvous at Anne Bishop's
cottage, and in the summer on the common hard by
the village, or in a clearing of Selwood Forest.

In the etching of the Sabbat orgies by Jan Ziarnko,
which illustrates De Lancre's great work (1612),
witches and familiars are grouped round a table, and
Spranger (1710) presents the Sabbat in very similar
detail. In both these the horrid banqueters are seen
eagerly devouring the limbs of a roasted babe. An old
woodcut (1489) shows three witches seated at a board
replenished with food and wine, whilst Guazzo depicts

a numerous company at tables duly covered with neat napery and heaped with all sorts of dishes, which are busily served by a retinue of inferior demons. Sometimes, indeed, the cloths appear to have been spread on the ground, picnic fashion.

The accounts of the feast vary from one extreme to the other. The Milanese witches said that " all who have sat down to such tables are bound to allow that the feasts are foul and stinking, so that they nauseate the most ravenously hungry stomach. All sorts of food may be seen, but so vile and dirty and ill-dressed that the plates were not worth eating ". Nicolas Morèle said that the taste was so dry and bad that he was fain spue out the bits he had taken. " Their wine also is black like stale blood, and is given to the company in some filthy sort of drinking horn. There is plenty of everything save only white bread and salt ".

This is all very concisely summed up in the great work of the theological school of the University of Salamanca, usually quoted as " the Salamanca doctors " : " The witches make a meal from food either furnished by themselves or by the Devil. It is sometimes most delicious and delicate, and sometimes a pie baked from babies they have slain, or disinterred corpses. A suitable grace is said before such a table". Thus when Isobel Gowdie, of Auldearne (1662), described the feast of her society which took place in Grangehill she gave fullest details : " The Devil sat at the head of the table, and all the Coven about. That night he desired Alexander Elder in Earlseat to say the grace before meat, which he did ; and is this :—

We eat this meat in the Devil's name,
With sorrow, and sighing, and mickle shame ;
We shall destroy house and hold,
Both sheep and beeves within the fold.
Little good shall come to the fore
Of all the rest of the little store.

And then we began to eat. And when we had ended eating, we looked steadfastly to the Devil, and bowing ourselves to him, we said to the Devil, We thank thee, our Lord, for this." The giving thanks to the Devil at the finish of the banquet appears to be practically a universal custom. Delrio remarks that he had actually seen and read the formulas for the " devil's grace " before and after meat. They were written out on parchment by a sorcerer constant in his attendance at Sabbats. " The grace said at this table is worthy of the infernal crew. In phrases of hideous profanity they acknowledge Beelzebub as the creator and giver and preserver of all the gifts they receive, and in the same strain do they return thanks to the foul spirit when they arise after having eaten and the tables are removed."

It has been already noticed that Ziarnko and Spranger depict the covens as feasting in cannibal fashion on human limbs, and Dominique Isabelle, a witch of Rogeville, confessed to Remy that she had seen and tasted the flesh of babes at the devil's table. At the trial of Louis Gaufridi in 1610 it came to light that the flesh of young children " which they cook and make ready in the Synagogue " was served to the witches. Madeleine Bavent also describes how on a Good Friday " the assembly performed a horrible

MAGIC, GHOSTS AND PHANTOMS
" Magica de Spectris " by Hennig Grösse

[face p. 156

mockery of the Last Supper. They brought the body of an infant who had been roasted, and this was eaten by them all ". Sometimes human meat was eaten for magical purposes. The witches were adepts at child-stealing, or if they failed to kidnap they would not hesitate to kill their own infants. The flesh was often seethed in a caldron until it became potable, when it was regarded as a charm of surpassing power. Hence a witch busy at her caldron, confecting these horrible ingredients, so often appears in illustrations, as for example the engraved frontispiece to the rare 1656 edition (often called an Elzevir) of a work on *Magic, Ghosts, and Apparitions of all kinds*, issued by Hennig Grösse, a well-known publisher of Leipzig. Thus the Parisian witches of the Guibourg and La Voisin covens in the days of Louis XIV murdered from first to last literally hundreds of " unwanted " babies at their devilish rites, and were supplying at a high price philtres and potions of these horrible ingredients to a vast number of eager clients. A Moorish sorceress will dig up a newly-buried corpse, set it before her between her legs, and guiding the clay-cold hands stirs with them *cousscouss* (granulated flour steamed over broth) which thus acquires certain magical properties, as a love-charm, or more often when mixed with earth from a grave and certain filthy ingredients becomes the *taam*, or " accursed food ", a slow but certain poison if only but a few grains be swallowed.

Nicolas Remy and very many other authorities emphasize the fact that salt never appears at the witches' table. Bodin says that salt as an emblem of eternity is hateful to the demon ; and a German

writer, Philip Ludwig Elich, is most careful to point
out that salt is never seen at these evil banquets.
It were easy to accumulate a mass of evidence from
the witches' confessions in reference to this detail, but
it will suffice to observe that in England and Scotland
this taboo does not appear, the reason being that in
Catholic countries salt is sanctified in solemn sacrament
and ceremonial, since the ritual employs two kinds
of salt for liturgical purposes, the baptismal salt and
the blessed salt exorcized in the preparation of holy
water from which devils flee. Salt is blessed again for
the use of animals, and in honour of St. Hubert.
It is used in the consecration of a church. From the
earliest days indeed it has had a sacred and religious
character. Protestant England knew nothing of all
this.

The food furnished at Sabbats in the British Isles
was for the most part seemingly of good quality and
satisfying, but seldom of any extraordinary kind. The
Forfar coven in 1661 at Mary Rynd's house made
themselves merry with strong March ale and brandy.
The Auldearne society met at a house where they had
beef in plenty, ale and other good drink. The Somersetshire witches who met on Lie Common, " all sate down,
a white Cloth being spread on the ground, and did
drink Wine, and eat Cakes and Meat." Some ten
years later the Riding Mill company were sumptuously
regaled with boiled capons, cheeses, butter, flour, beef,
bottles of wine and " a variety of meat". The
devil enticed the poorer sort of Swedish witches
" by presenting them with Meat and Drink ",
and at their rendezvous, Blockula, which was
evidently a large country house, they sat down

at a very long table whereon were " Broth with Colworts and Bacon in it, Oatmeal, Bread spread with Butter, Milk and Cheese. And they added that sometimes it tasted very well, and sometimes very ill ".

CHAPTER IV

OF THE BLACK MASS; AND OF THE LOVES OF THE INCUBI AND SUCCUBI

They ate the sacrifices of the dead. Yea, they sacrificed their sons and daughters unto devils. Thus were they defiled with their own works, and went a whoring with their own inventions.
Psalm CVI (Douai CV), 28, 37, 39.

It is so rash and foolish to deny the fact of these horrible connexions between the demon and human beings that in order to maintain such a position you must be prepared obstinately to reject and spurn the most weighty and carefully considered judgements of the acutest and liveliest intellects, of Saints and philosophers alike, nay, you must wage open war upon experience and common sense, whilst at the same time you are fatally exposing your ignorance of the power of the devil and the empery evil spirits can obtain over man.
FATHER PETER THYRAEUS, S.J.

"Diabolical Mysticism" includes witchcraft, diabolical possession, and the hideous stories of incubi and succubæ.
DEAN INGE.

The essential feature and climax of the Sabbat orgies was the celebration of the devil's liturgy, the Black Mass. I am of opinion that being present at a Black Mass is to join in the witches' Sabbat, and accordingly the Satanists who perform the Black Mass to-day and all who attend these vile and impious rites are actually holding a Sabbat.

A curious parallel is noted by Dr. Françoise Legey. On the night of the *Achoura*, the tenth day of Ramadan, in order to renew their magic powers, at the bidding of Eblis (the devil) the Moorish sorcerers secretly penetrate into the mosques and pollute the mat of the Imam. They make their ablutions with sour milk and urinate upon the Koran. They also foul the *tafedna*, the reservoirs of warm water in the public baths. They then hold their Sabbat with vile rites in a cemetery.

In 1324 when the Bishop of Ossory was investigating the sorceries of Dame Alice Kyteler of Kilkenny, " in rifling the closet of the ladie, they found a wafer of sacramental bread, having the divels name stamped thereon in stead of Jesus Christ, and a pipe of ointment, wherewith she greased a staffe, upon which she ambled and gallopped through thick and thin." This sacramental bread has been consecrated at a Black Mass, and it was also proved that Dame Alice, a past-mistress of goety, had sacrificed at the cross-ways nine red cocks to her familiar, Robin, son of Art. It may be observed that the sacrifice of a black cock to the demon is not infrequently mentioned in witch-trials.

The Devil's wafer of grotesque shape or impressed with strange characters was often employed by the witches. Gentien le Clerc, condemned at Orleans in 1614, frequented Sabbats, " and he had often seen the devil's priest elevate the host and the chalice, of which both were black." Thomas Boullé and l'abbé Picard were accused by Madeleine Bavent of employing blood-red hosts at their foul celebrations ; in the Mass of St. Sécaire the host is triangular with three sharp points, and black. Similar abominations are usual among the Satanists to-day, so the tradition prevails and Dame Alice Kyteler is closely linked with the twentieth century.

The Neapolitan theologian and legist, Paul Grilland, who wrote on sorcery towards the end of the sixteenth century, describes how unconsecrated wafers are inscribed with letters of blood and amorous devices and thus used at Mass, after which they are crumbled or kneaded into a paste and mingled with food or drink which is given as a love comfit or philtre. One wealthy warlock drew blood from his finger and writing therewith certain obscenities on an altar bread bribed a priest to lay it on the altar-stone under the linen cloths, so that Mass was said over it, with the addition of some secret collects and ceremonies. It may be observed that this practice is not unknown to-day. At Rome there were discovered in a prostitute's house two Hosts inscribed with curious uncials in blood, and these wafers the woman confessed she was going to give secretly to a gallant, beloved by a noble lady, who had furnished the charm. Grilland further discusses in detail the celebrations over unconsecrated breads destined for magical purposes, and also how some interpolate the very Canon of the Mass with lewd and wicked prayers to an evil end. In 1460 at a French trial it came to light that a priest seduced by a witch had actually baptized a toad, fed it with the consecrated Host, and allowed his paramour to use it for the destruction of their personal enemies. The abomination of the Black Mass is performed by some apostate or renegade priest who has abandoned himself to the service of evil and is shamefully prominent amongst the congregation of witches. It should be remarked from this fact that it is plain the witches are as profoundly convinced of the doctrines of Transubstantiation, the Totality, Permanence, and Adorableness of the Eucharistic Christ, as is the most orthodox Catholic. Indeed, unless such were the case, their revolt would be empty and meaningless, void at any rate of its material malice.

Gilles de Sillé of the diocese of St. Malo, and above all the Florentine, Antonio Francesco Prelati, who had been ordained by dispensation at an early age in the Cathedral of Pistoia by the Bishop of Arezzo, served as devil's chaplains to Gilles de Rais, and celebrated black masses in the vaults of the Chapel of St. Vincent at the Château of Tiffauges, when children were sacrificed in scores to the demon.

At Tiffauges to-day from the lonely broken arches of the Chapel one may pass through a cellar door into the crypt below, which dates from the eleventh century. Of no great size and low-sprung the solid roof is transversed by heavy yet not ungraceful semicircular arches supported by massy pillars whose capitals are relieved with carved lozenges and croziers. The place is gloomy, and but a wan watery daylight seems to filter in, showing the rough broken floor in one corner of which gapes the naked opening of some oubliette or little well, down which no doubt were thrown the dead bodies of the children whom Prelati offered upon the altar-stone.

One can well picture the scene illumined only by two black candles, reeking of bitumen and pitch, and by the faint flicker of the rushlight set upon the ground. The silence is broken but by the hoarse blasphemy of the acolyte as he responds in a low tone to the hurried mutter of the young priest clad in the strange vestments of his infernal cult, the mock chasuble of murrey, the hue of dank clotted gore, marked with the inverse cross. The sacred words of power are spoken with a sneer. The golden chalice is raised in hideous parody; the keen knife flashes with swift light, a moment more and the fresh blood gushes from the gaping throat of the youth lying fettered there into the sacramental cup, poor blood commingles with the saving Blood of God, and as the film of death closes over the agonizing eyes of his victim the Italian calls aloud upon Apollyon, the prince of darkness, to accept the sacrifice, to manifest himself and show himself gracious unto his faithful worshippers granting their desire.

It was commonly rumoured that Charles IX of France employed an apostate monk to celebrate the eucharist of hell before himself and his intimates. Bodin at any rate describes how he summoned to his presence a condemned sorcerer named Trois-eschelles du Mayne, who was pardoned on condition that he should give the king an ample account of the Sabbat orgies and all the horrid mystery of witchcraft. This the warlock proved very ready to do, and not only vividly painted Satan's bacchanalia in glowing phrase, but had no scruples about naming a large number of those whom he had recognized at these infernal synagogues.

That the assassination of Henri III, the younger brother and successor of Charles IX, was largely the outcome of constant reports which were assiduously circulating throughout the north of France accusing him of Satanism is now fairly well established. The murder of the Cardinal of Lorraine on the 23rd December, 1588, and the subsequent denunciation of the king from a hundred flaming pulpits as a heretic, deposed, excommunicate, had so incensed popular feeling that a mere mob revolt blazed forth in civil war, but the charges of devil worship determined his death. A contemporary pamphlet of fifteen pages, octavo, published at Paris in 1589 and entitled *The Horrid Sorceries of Henry de Valois, and the Oblations which he offered to the Demon in the Wood of Vincennes. Together with an engraving of the figures of two devils in silver gilt to whom he sacrificed* openly arraigns the monarch's homosexuality and sorceries in terms of sternest condemnation. It is said that in a grove of the forest of Vincennes there were discovered two silver statues of satyrs, curiously gilded, and about four feet high. In his left hand each held a stout club upon which he leaned, in his right was a small bowl of purest shining crystal. Each stood upon a round base, richly wrought, and supported by four feet chased in the baroque fashion. In the crystal bowls were thin grey ashes, as if a handful of unknown herbs or some sort of incense had been burned. What proved more significant than all was that the satyrs had their back turned to a golden cross, some $3\frac{1}{2}$ feet in length, in the midst of which was set a piece of wood, believed to be a Relic of the True Cross.

The enemies of the king created a resounding scandal out of this mysterious discovery, whilst his friends laughed at the whole business, lightly remarking that the two satyrs were nothing more or less than candlesticks of the antique form. To this it was answered that the figures had no sort of pricket to hold a candle, and the fact that they were placed with their backs to the Holy Cross smelt of sorcery. Nor might this be considered an accidental gesture, since the obscenity of the satyrs betrayed them, and if two tapers should be lit to honour the Relic were not angel-bearers or at any rate plain sconces more appropriate and more decent than lewd heathen goat-men?

Yet another contemporary pamphlet *A Sharp Remonstrance addressed to Henri de Valois* gives fantastic stories of schools for necromancy being established at the Louvre, of the celebration of Black Masses, of the invocation of demons, and how the King maintained a familiar, named Terragon, to whose embraces he compelled a public prostitute to submit herself. Whether Henri III dabbled in occult arts or no can only be regarded as " not proven ", for it must be remembered that the evidence is violently prejudiced and inimical, and it is well known that at the very time these and other equally ribald pasquils were pouring from the press and rabid accusations of black magic filled the air the prominent Leaguers were attempting the king's death by fashioning his image in wax and piercing it to the heart with long pins and bodkins, whilst scarcely a day went by that they did not call to consultation some astrologer to read the heavens' face for the royal doom or some foul diviner to cast the runes.

Pierre De Lancre describes in some detail the Black Mass as it was celebrated by the witch covens of the Pyrenees at the beginning of the seventeenth century. The demon or the Grand Master vests himself in the usual robes to say Mass, which is to say (one supposes) he wears the amice, alb, girdle, stole, maniple and chasuble. The words are spoken with a thousand glib sneers and mocking accents. The altar was erected on four supports, sometimes under a sheltering tree, at others upon a flat rock or some naturally convenient place. No *Confiteor* was said, and *Alleluia* was strictly avoided, but the officiant who held in his hand a book of which he frequently turned the leaves began to mutter in a low voice prayers, epistle and gospel, so that it was hardly in this respect to be distinguished from the Mass itself. At the Offertory he drew back a little from the altar and on occasion seated himself, whilst the assembly approached in order, kissed his left hand and presented each one a candle. When the Queen of the Sabbat—the witch who ranked first after the Grand Master, the oldest and vilest of the crew—was present she sat on the left of the altar and received the offerings, loaves, eggs, any meat or country produce, and money, so long as the coins were not stamped with a cross. In her hand she held a small flat disc or plate, technically known as the " pax " or " pax-brede ". This was engraved with a figure of the demon, which the whole congregation devoutly kissed.

At this point the Grand Master or some warlock appointed for that purpose preached a sermon, haranguing the assembly in a strain of the most rancid blasphemy and inciting them to every crime.

The ceremonies continued, and the Host which was elevated was seen to be round and black, stamped with a figure of the demon in red. The words, *Hoc est enim corpus meum*, were spoken. The chalice was also elevated. The congregation prostrated themselves upon the earth, and with loud clamours adored. A second discourse or sermon was pronounced and then the mock communion followed. All present were given a particle of the Host, and they drank twice of the chalice, a brew so infect, so stinking, so cold that it seemed to freeze the very marrow of their bones. None the less each one was compelled to swallow the nauseous draught however ill they might stomach it.

This description appears to point to some potent drug being mingled in Satan's chalice.

It may be remarked that the use of incense at the Black Mass is very rarely noticed, but Silvain Nevillon, a French witch, spoke of a fume which "smelled abominably foul, not sweet and odorous as is the incense burned in churches". At the modern Black Mass the rough tang of acrid herbs often fills the air, for the Satanists to-day during their hellish liturgy burn in braziers, chafing-dishes and thuribles rue, henbane, deadly nightshade, lumps of resin and rotting leaves, a smoke and stench which, as one of the gang declared, " is fragrant and grateful to the nostrils of our Master." Boguet speaks of the Black Mass as sung by a priest vested in an old and dirty black cope with no cross on it. " And to make Holy Water the Devil urinates in a hole in the ground, and the worshippers are sprinkled with his filthy stale by the celebrant who has a black asperge."

When Louis Gaufridi, the wizard-priest of Accoules (Marseilles) was brought to trial in February, 1611, a tale of almost unheard-of abomination was ripped open, and Madeleine de la Palud described in amplest detail the countless Sabbats she had attended, where Lucifer's lieutenant, the Prince of the Synagogue (in effect Gaufridi himself), was worshipped with divine honours. The Black Mass was said in Satan's name, either by Gaufridi or by some other miserable wretch, when " the Host was really and truly consecrated and offered to the demon ", whilst the Precious Blood was sprinkled from the chalice over the vile crew who shouted and yelled : " His Blood be on us, and on our children ! "

Horrible as is the story of Madeleine de la Palud it may be paralleled, and is indeed exceeded, by the narrative of Madeleine Bavent, a Franciscan sister of the Third Order, attached to the convent of St. Louis and St. Elizabeth at Louviers, a little old-world Norman town some twenty-six miles from Rouen.

Mathurin Picard, the evil chaplain of the community, a warlock deeply versed in black magic, was wont to celebrate the infernal eucharist in a midnight vault. Around the altar in this den of devils were set great candelabra, and these alone gave the required light. Mass from the " Book of Blasphemy " was said by Picard, by his assistant Thomas Boullé, and by other wizard-priests who often brought with them Hosts and chalices to be fearfully defiled by the coven. The Host used at these celebrations is described as resembling the usual Altar Bread, but of a slightly reddish hue. At the elevation the whole gang shrieked out the vilest profanities. It was customary for all present to communicate at the eucharist of hell. " Every action I saw performed at the Sabbat," says Madeleine Bavent, " was indescribably loathsome."

In addition to the Black Mass other rites took place —processions, renunciations, liturgical cursings and maledictions, the stabbing and lancing with knives of consecrated Hosts, the throttling of little babes who were sacrificed to the demon. On one Good Friday a woman brought her new-born infant to the Sabbat, and it was decided the child should be crucified, which was done under conditions of peculiar horror. Part of the bleeding body was employed to confect their charms, and the rest they buried.

During the reign of Louis XIV a veritable epidemic

of sacrilege seemed to rage through Paris, and indeed the investigations conducted by the Lieutenant of Police, Gabriel-Nicolas de la Reynie, let loose such an avalanche of scandal and crime implicating not only persons of low degree but the highest and most powerful names in France that at the last the King in his absolute authority was of necessity compelled to quash the whole business. Poisons had been brewed, Black Masses said, necromancy practised, abortions procured, murders contrived, plots laid for the death of court favourite and political foe, and all these abominations seemed to centre round two figures of the blackest underworld of Paris, the abbé Guibourg and La Voisin.

Catherine Montvoisin—La Voisin as she was commonly called—had long been known to the criminal and the curious as midwife, poisoner, bawd and witch. There was no infamy which might not be purchased in the secret chambers of her house, No. 25 Rue Beauregard. She was assisted in the many branches of her mysterious and obscene profession by numerous satellites and lovers, chief amongst whom Romani, a handsome young Italian boy and an actor of great talent, filled many a curious rôle. The two executioners of Paris, M. Guillaume and M. Larivière, contended for her favours, gallants who could bring her fine presents of the limbs and fat of murderers who had swung on the gibbet or been broken on the wheel, whence she made tall black tapers for her secret ceremonies. A wanton hermaphrodite, exotic and perverse, La Trianon dwelt in that awful house, to which also daily resorted some curious old women, whose calling no one rightly knew, La Gallet,

La Lepère, La Joly, La Filastre, La Bosse, La Thomas. As a matter of fact they were one and all, and a score beside, adepts in the art of poisoning and abortionists of no mean skill and practice. A wit called 25 Rue Beauregard " the centre of the city ", and it is no exaggeration to say that all Paris from duchess to drab, from marshal to muckman, crowded La Voisin's doors.

The Abbé Guibourg, known among the witches as M. le Prieur, the illegitimate son of Henri de Montmorency, was a man of some seventy years, who is described as tall and heavy-limbed with a malign and sensual face. " He can be compared with no one else," wrote de la Reynie, " for the tale of his poisonings, and his traffic in drugs and witchcraft. He is familiar with every form of villainy, guilty of a large number of horrible crimes and suspected of complicity in many more." It was M. le Prieur who celebrated innumerable Satanic Masses at the instance of Madame de Montespan in order to secure for her supreme power and the eternal fidelity of the King. Even before Louis had separated from de La Vallière the vicar of St.-Séverin, the Abbé Mariette, had been reciting erotic charms over the hearts of two pigeons consecrated during Mass in the names of Louis de Bourbon and Athénais de Montespan, and apparently the spell had succeeded. But Louis was fickle and apt to be promiscuous in his amours, so his love must be fixed on her alone and the aid of the Abbé Guibourg was requested. In the chapel of the Château de Villebousin near Montlhéry, at Saint-Denis, a long black velvet pall was spread over the altar, and upon this the royal mistress laid herself in a state of perfect nudity. Six black candles were lit, the celebrant robed himself in a chasuble thickly embroidered with esoteric characters wrought in silver, the gold paten and chalice were placed upon the naked belly of the living altar to whose warm flesh the horrible old priest pressed his bloated lips each time the rubrics directed him to kiss the place of sacrifice. All was hushed save for the low monotonous murmur of the blasphemous liturgy. The Host was consecrated, and then the Precious Blood. An assistant crept forward bearing an infant in her arms. The child was held over the altar, a sharp swift gash across the neck, a stifled cry, and warm red drops fell into the chalice whilst the full tide streamed upon the white figure beneath. The corpse was handed to La Voisin, who flung it callously into an oven fashioned for that purpose, which glowed white-hot.

It was proved that a regular traffic had been carried on for years with beggar-women and the lowest prostitutes, who sold their children for this purpose. At her trial La Voisin confessed that no less than 2,500 babies had been disposed of in this manner, for the Black Mass was continually being celebrated not only by Guibourg but by other priests. The figures are so startling that some incredulity has been expressed by those who do not know the Paris of Louis XIV, but there appears no reason to doubt the sum. We may bear in mind that a whole pack of venal and utterly unscrupulous midwives was actively at work ; that when the impostume of filth and crime was ripe to bursting no less than 319 warrants were issued, whilst there were very many more whose names were suppressed so deeply did they implicate the highest in the land, nay, the very Throne itself ; that six and thirty witches, poisoners and abortionists were executed ; that 147, Guibourg, Lesage, Romani, De Vanens, and others were sentenced to close confinement in the remotest fortresses ; that many, such as the magician Blessis, went to the galleys for life ; and many, again, were conducted by the police over the frontier, condemned to perpetual exile. Several persons died in prison, and others again (of noble and unblemished lineage) committed suicide in agonies of shame lest they should be involved, however remotely, or even as witnesses, in such scandalous and abominable proceedings.

Perhaps the most sad circumstance that came to light during the investigation of these orgies of witchcraft was the large number of priests concerned. Not to mention the mere panders and poisoners—and Éliphas Lévi says that Black Magic is " above all the science of poisoning "—amongst those who habitually celebrated the Black Mass were the Abbé Brigallier, almoner to Mlle de Montpensier, who married the Duc de Lauzun ; the Abbé Cotton who offered in sacrifice to Satan a child baptized with Holy Oils used in the Sacrament of Extreme Unction, and then strangled, and whose speciality was " La Messe du Saint Esprit ", which is said over a piece of goat's skin sprinkled with holy water and which is intended to cure certain illnesses, to induce love or hate, even to conjure up the demon, all of which Dr. Jean-Baptiste Thiers in his great work denounces as a most pestilent superstition, nay, more, he roundly condemns this practice as a " Witch's Mass ", and profane in the highest degree ; the Abbé Davot, assistant priest at Notre Dame de Bonne-Nouvelle only a few doors from La Voisin's house, whose custom it was to lay under the corporal at Mass a piece of paper inscribed with the name of the person who should be brought to love, or if hated, damned to die, a practice eagerly pursued to-day—if a priest may be found ; the Abbé Deshayes, who demanded exorbitant fees for his Black Masses and who was also a most skilful coiner ; Father Gabriel, a Capuchin, who with the Abbé Seysson, was wont to say Masses at La Voisin's house over women's after-births and children's cauls to confect charms of particular potency ; the Abbé Lepreux, a school-master, deep in the most shameful court secrets, who dedicated infants to the demon, and consecrated snakes and toads to mingle with poisons for their greater efficacy ; the Abbé Mabile, who celebrated the sacrifice of the Death's Head ; the Abbé Maléscot, who had entered into a sort of partnership with the witch and abortionist, La Gallet, for whom he touted with very considerable success ; the Abbé Mariette, who whilst still young had been banished from Paris for his sorceries (it is clear that he was only saved from the stake owing to family interest, for he was of a wealthy and good house), but who returned almost openly to place himself at the service of Madame de Montespan ; the Abbé Olivier, who consecrated an altar for Black Masses in a brothel ; the Abbé Rebours, who said Black Masses on the body of his mistress ; the Abbé Tournet, who said Masses in order to kill the child in the womb, and who was in great request among the evil sisterhood. This catalogue of a dozen wizard-priests drawn from the archives of the Bastille could easily be multiplied four or five times. There was also Jean-Baptiste Sébault, of the diocese of Bourges, who whilst lodging in Paris at the house of a doctor, named

Charmillon, seduced Marianne Charmillon, a girl of twenty-two, his host's daughter, and continually brought her to the Black Mass. The Abbé Guignard celebrated a Satanic Mass in a cellar over her body, and was served by Sébault in a state of complete nudity. An aphrodisiac was brewed at this orgy. The Abbé Lemaignan sacrificed young children, and possessed whole sets of rich vestments in which to celebrate the eucharist of hell.

It is only too much to be feared that the evil science of Guibourg and his company was handed down throughout the eighteenth century. The Duc de Richelieu, who was born in 1696 and died at the age of ninety-two in 1788, was much suspected of studying goety and the worst kinds of occult science. It was said that whilst quite a young man he had formed too close an intimacy with an Austrian noble whose tastes lay in the same direction, and whose wealth enabled him to purchase the secrets of those who had known the Abbé Guibourg and had been instructed by him in every dark secret of magic. Two Capuchins, who were his chaplains, celebrated Black Masses, at which the devotees assisted, in the old deserted chapel of a lone country-house. After this the Duke and his friend defiled the Hosts, in the hope that thereon Satan would appear to crown and reward their blasphemy.

Under the Regency, necromancers and wizards and traffickers in Satanic eucharists abounded, for Philippe d'Orléans was notoriously addicted to occultism of every kind. As might be expected there are revolting pictures of the Black Mass in the lewd pages of de Sade. In *Justine* such a Mass celebrated in a cloister is described in filthy detail. When Juliette is initiated into the " Society of the Friends of Crime " the Host and Crucifix are desecrated. Again, a little later, two Satanic orgies are exhibited, when the High Altar is the scene of every defilement. There are other and even more obscene descriptions of the Black Mass in the work, but these it is unnecessary to particularize.

Upon the night of the execution of King Louis XVI, 21st January, 1793, a number of French devil-worshippers formed themselves into a definite society to foster revolution and propagate their cult of evil. The third chief of this organization died at Florence about 1905. He was believed to be nearly a hundred years old. This particular Society of Satanists spread very rapidly into Italy and soon penetrated Germany. A little later it had established itself very secretly in England, and there can be no question that it has proved one of the most potent forces for evil since its very inception. It has developed and flourished exceedingly and flung out its poisonous tentacles in all directions. It would be no exaggeration to say that much of the world's misery and unrest is due to this foul conspiracy against God and humanity.

Nowhere in France during the first half of the nine-teenth century was religious life more fervent and more zealous than throughout the diocese of Agen. Under such saintly Bishops as de Bonnac (the first to refuse the constitutional oath of 1792), and Jean Aimé de Levezon de Vezins pious associations, communities and confraternities were warmly encouraged, not the least of these devout fellowships being the Children of Mary founded by Adèle de Trenquelléon and the widow of a physician, Madame Belloc. This latter

THE WITCHES' SYNAGOGUE
Goya

[*face p.* 176

lady employed a housekeeper, Virginie (whose sur-
name curiously has not been recorded), and to her
horror this woman one day revealed to her pious
mistress that she was a Satanist of long continuance,
the member of an infernal society which had its headquarters under the very shadow of St. Caprasius, the
pro-cathedral. Virginie stated that when about twelve
years old she had been taken to a house in the
city were was an altar dedicated to the devil, at which
an aged priest celebrated a Mass of blasphemy during
which there occurred a fearful manifestation of
corporeal evil. Moreover she was taught that each
Communion she must retain the Host in her mouth,
and then eject it secretly so that she might bring it
to the midnight Sabbats to be horribly profaned by
the impious crew, whose necromancies and conjurations were of the vilest and most abominable
description. Madame Belloc hastened to call in the
assistance of the Abbé Degans, to whom Virginie confessed that she would sometimes attend as many as
five or six early Masses in different churches to obtain
the Host. Upon her resolution to repent she fell a
prey to an unclean spirit which the Abbé Degans
expelled with difficulty and after many exorcisms.
One curious feature of the case was the continual
apports of Hosts, many of which were marked with
bloody characters. Much scandal ensued, and an
ecclesiastical inquiry followed. Many suspicious
circumstances came to light concerning Virginie when
she formed a connexion with the pseudo-prophet
Eugène Vintras and his followers, in whose private
chapel at Tilly-sur-Seulles (as one of the sect, Gozzoli,
quite unequivocally testified) the most horrible

obscenities were practised during the celebration of
sacrilegious eucharists.   It is significant that in 1845
Vintras came to England and established himself in
London as the Master of a dark and evil cult which
has never died.

Virginie declared that the Grand Master of the
Agen Satanists became truly penitent, and made his
peace with Heaven.   There can be little doubt, however, that many of the latter statements she made were
untrue.   It is probable that after her first revelations
the Satanists so threatened and terrified her that she
lied freely to conceal their identities and their
rendezvous.   That their chapel was never discovered
is no occasion for surprise.   They very well know how
to cover their tracks.

About the same time 1830–1850 a band of devil
worshippers were carrying on their foul witchcrafts at
Bordeaux, and numberless Hosts were stolen from the
churches, especially from Saint-André and Sainte-
Eulalie.   In 1852 there burst forth a resounding scandal
owing to the celebration of Black Masses in Paris by a
band of most impious and malevolent Satanists.

To retail the sacrilege of Black Masses down the
years would be weary repetition.   Suffice that Satanism
in every country yet has its votaries and is extensively
practised.   It is a matter of notoriety that in 1924
two ciboria, containing 100 consecrated Hosts, were
carried off by an old woman from Notre Dame in
circumstances which clearly indicated that the holy
vessels were not the objects of the larceny.   In 1895
a particularly revolting instance of defilement of the
Host occurred in the Island of Mauritius.   Rome,
Salerno, Naples, Florence, Lyons, London, York,

Brighton, Brussels, Bruges, and many other towns have all suffered from these abominations. In more than one quarter of London—on the northern heights, in a south-west suburb, in the East End, in the City, by the riverside—have the Satanists made a den, a chapel and altar to the demon they worship with rites of the most horrid lewdness and impiety.

It is very well known that the terrible picture of the black mass drawn by Jorris Karl Huysmans in his masterpiece *Là-Bas* (1891) is true in every detail, and all the characters are taken from life, and have indeed been precisely identified. Thus Madame Chantelouve is (in large part at least) Madame Berthe Courrière, and Docre is named by Mons. Léon Deffoux and other authorities as l'abbé Roca, although Mons. Pierre Dufay, whose opinion carries weight, argues that he is rather Canon Van Ecke (or Van Arche), sometime a chaplain of the sanctuary of the Precious Blood at Bruges.

That extraordinary and erratic visionary the Abbé J.-A. Boullan in a letter to Huysmans, dated 10th February, 1890, says : "Amongst ecclesiastics Satanism is more widely practised and ardently pursued than even in the Middle Ages. It is to be found at Rome ; and above all at Paris, Lyons, and Châlons, so far as France is concerned ; in Belgium Bruges is their headquarters." Perhaps it should not be forgotten that the orthodoxy of Boullan himself was more than suspect, and whilst there was much open gossip of strange masses by which evil charms and enchantments were dissolved,—the Eucharist of Glory,—there were also darker hints which pointed to plain Satanism. Boullan asserted that he employed White Magic ;

his opponents—and he had many enemies—declared
that he was an adept in Black Magic.

In May, 1895, when the legal representatives of the
Borghese family visited the Palazzo Borghese, which
had been rented for some time in separate floors or
suites, they found some difficulty in obtaining admission to certain apartments on the first floor, the occu-
pant of which seemed unaware that the lease was
about to expire. By virtue of the terms of the agreement,
however, he was obliged to allow them to inspect the
premises to see if any structural repairs or alterations
were necessary, as Prince Scipione Borghese, who was
about to be married, intended immediately to take
up his residence in the ancestral home with his bride.
One door the tenant obstinately refused to unlock,
and when pressed he betrayed the greatest confusion.
The agents finally pointed out that they were within
their rights to employ actual force, and that if access
was longer denied they would not hesitate to do so
forthwith.   When the keys had been produced, the
cause of the reluctance was soon plain.   The room
within was inscribed with the words *Templum Palla-
dicum*.   The walls were hung all round from ceiling
to floor with heavy curtains of silk damask, scarlet
and black, excluding the light ;   at the further end
there stretched a large tapestry upon which was
woven in more than life-size a figure of Lucifer,
colossal, triumphant, dominating the whole.   Exactly
beneath an altar had been built, amply furnished for
the liturgy of hell ;   candles, vessels, rituals, missal,
nothing was lacking.   Cushioned prie-dieus and
luxurious chairs, crimson and gold, were set in order
for the assistants ;   the chamber being lit by electricity,

fantastically arrayed so as to glare from an enormous human eye. The visitors soon quitted the accursed spot, the scene of devil-worship and blasphemy, nor had they any desire more nearly to examine the appointments of this infernal chapel.

A writer of authority has said : "Turning to English accounts, little or nothing of the Black Mass is to be traced," and we find this echoed more than once. The point of the matter lies here. In 1559 Queen Elizabeth initiated her religious settlement by the enactment of Penal Laws, which in a very few years were greatly increased in severity, and since the Act of Uniformity of this year was designed to compel the use of the Anglican Book of Common Prayer it punished by deprivation and imprisonment all clerics who followed any other service. A little later the Mass was prohibited, and in effect the punishment for saying Mass was death. Even in the reign of George III, in 1767, upon the delation of a common informer, the Rev. Mr. Maloney was tried at Croydon for having said Mass and condemned to perpetual imprisonment, but after three or four years the Government commuted the sentence to perpetual banishment. In 1769 the Hon. James Talbot, a brother of the fourteenth Earl of Shrewsbury, and Bishop of Birtha, was tried for his life at the Old Bailey and only escaped owing to a conflict of evidence as the informers obviously did not know what a Mass was and it was urged that the Bishop might have been conducting some other service. The famous Lord Mansfield utilized every technicality and loop-hole (not to say quibble) of the law to prevent the conviction of priests accused of saying Mass. One point he was wont to urge turned on the fact that the Protestant informers could not be aware in what a Mass consisted and that even if a man were in vestments at an altar using certain ceremonies this might not be the Mass. At any rate it is clear that in Protestant England the Mass had no place, although in certain villages the tradition of the sanctity of the Sacrifice and its mysterious power lingered until the very time of the Oxford Movement. It can, however, be clearly shown, both in England and in Scotland, that the witches celebrated a mock-sacrament.

Before the upheaval under Henry VIII the Black Mass was certainly known in the British Isles. In the twelfth century Gerald de Barry laments those wizard-priests who corrupt the very Sacrament of the Altar to black magic by celebrating Masses over wax images in order to lay a spell on some person, as also others who sing a Solemn Requiem ten times and apply it to some living man that he may die on the tenth day or very soon after, and go down to the tomb. In 1286 an apostate monk, a Cistercian of Rievaulx Abbey, Godfrey Darel, was commonly defamed as a celebrant of Black Masses, and reported to the Archbishop of York.

There is very definite evidence for a mock-sacrament in Scotland as late as the end of the seventeenth century. In August, 1678, the devil convened " a great meeting of witches in Lothian ", where amongst others appeared a hideous figure who had once been admitted to the ministry, and had served the parish of Crichton, about six miles from Dalkeith. This warlock parson, Mr. Gideon Penman, was of notoriously evil life and stood in high favour with the devil who spoke of him as " Mr. Gideon, my chaplain ". He had turned under the devil a preacher of hellish sermons, for he was reputed very eloquent in the pulpit. In mockery of Christ and His holy ordinance of the Sacrament of His Supper, the devil gave a sacrament to the witches, bidding them eat it, and to drink in remembrance of himself. The villain, Penman, used very readily to assist Satan in these ceremonies, and in preaching. Lord Fountainhall, the famous Scottish lawyer (who was incidentally an extreme Protestant), when describing the same assembly of witches says that the Devil "adventured to give them the communion or holy sacrament, the bread was like wafers, the drink was sometimes blood, sometimes black moss-water. He preached, and most blasphemously ".

In New England we find the same tradition of what may be termed the Protestant equivalent of a black mass. The Rev. George Burroughs, a pastor at Wells, Maine, and Grand Master of the coven, preached to the witches at their meetings, " and there they had a Sacrament " with a woman, Martha Carrier, as Deacon. One member of the gang confessed how " the Witches had a *Sacrament* that day at an house in the Village, and they had *Red Bread* and *Red Drink* ". According to Madeleine Bavent the Host at the Mass of blasphemies was red, and there are many references to the Red Drink in the chalice with which the Abbé Guibourg even mingled blood. At Salem the traditional rites of this foul travesty of worship were strictly observed, and these practices must have been carefully handed down and exactly taught to the New England representatives of the witch society.

During the reign of George I the riots of the " Hell-Fire Clubs ", which were simply Sabbats of Satanists, had grown to such a height that in 1721 a proclamation was issued for the suppression of " certain scandalous Clubs or Societies of young persons who meet together, and in the most impious and blasphemous manner insult the most sacred principles of our Holy Religion, affront Almighty God Himself, and corrupt the minds and morals of one another ". The inquiry was strict, and for a time these Clubs or covens were driven underground. Generally they met in the lowest taverns, where the Satanists of to-day are often wont to forgather to celebrate the Black Mass.

In 1745 the well-known wit, George Selwyn, was sent down from Oxford for celebrating (or at least participating in—the details are not clear) a mock-communion. A terrific scandal ensued, which Selwyn's friend attempted to meet by swearing that the whole business was but a drunken orgy. It is pretty plain, however, that there was a good more in it than that, and the fact that we find Selwyn enrolled a member of the " Monks of Medmenham " is doubly significant.

Medmenham Abbey, a Cistercian foundation, is near Marlow, Bucks, on the banks of the River Thames. It was occupied by a notorious profligate, Sir Francis Dashwood, who having converted it into a most luxurious retreat, built or restored a chapel on the model he had seen of the monasteries in France and Italy, and in 1732 here inaugurated " the Order of St. Francis ", so dubbed after his own name, also termed " the Franciscans " or " the Franciscan Monks ". (It may be remarked that there is an inexactitude here. A Franciscan is a friar, and cannot be a monk.) It

seems that only later was this Society known as the
" Hell-Fire Club ". The original number of members,
besides the Superior, was twelve—a witch's coven,
and each was baptized with the name of an apostle.
It is hardly necessary to give the list in full, more
especially as from time to time the numbers varied,
but many of the " Order " were in their day famous
and influential names, as for example John Wilkes,
Charles Churchill, Paul Whitehead, Robert Lloyd,
the Earl of Sandwich, George Bubb-Dodington, and
Selwyn. A certain young Sir John d'Aubrey also
attended the secret meetings. The " monks " or
rather Satanists met twice a year for the space of a
week. " The cellars were stored with the choicest wines;
the larders with the delicacies of every climate ; and
the *cells* were fitted up, for all the purposes of lascivious-
ness, for which proper objects were also provided."

There were novices, whose probationary office " was
to attend upon their superiours in the celebration of
their mysteries, which were all performed in the chapel
of the monastery, when no other servants were ever
permitted to enter, on the most common occasion, as
the very *decorations* of it would in a great measure have
betrayed their secrets ". The various members of this
company were bound to secrecy by oaths and imprecations, since " so outrageous an insult upon the laws was
liable to punishment from the secular power ".

The initiate clad in a robe of white linen was led
to the Chapel at the tolling of a bell, and when at his
knock the door opened to the sound of soft and solemn
music he had to advance to the communion rails and
there make a profession of his principles " nearly in
the words, but with the most gross perversion of the

sense of the articles of faith of the religion established in the country ". The brotherhood knelt round the altar whilst the superior repeated a prayer in the same strain and manner with the *profession* of the candidate *to the Being whom they served.* The novice was elected with mimic ceremonial, and next in a manner not proper to be described, followed their eucharist, every most sacred rite and observance of Religion being profaned, and all the prayers and hymns of praise appointed for the worship of the Deity burlesqued by a perversion to the horrid occasion.

Little wonder that " a formal story was propagated over the whole country, that the end of their meeting was to worship the Devil, to whom this chapel was dedicated, and who had *often* been seen among them, in variety of shapes ".

The truth had leaked out, for it is plain from this contemporary account that the Monks of Medmenham were Satanists, who at their Sabbats carried on and perpetuated the foul and blasphemous traditions of the witch.

I have been quoting from Charles Johnstone's key-novel " *Chrysal* : or the Adventures of a Guinea, wherein are exhibited Views of several striking Scenes with Curious and interesting Anecdotes, of the most Noted Persons in every Rank of Life, whose Hands it passed through, in America, England, Holland, Germany, and Portugal", 1760–65. Johnstone in this remarkable book has painted contemporary life with unflinching exactness, and it is certain that either in some way he managed to be present at the mysteries of Medmenham, or else he gained most detailed information from one of the members of that horrid society.

About the middle of the eighteenth century, on the borderland of Germany and the Low Countries, the devil-worshippers joined themselves into a body, a vast secret organization called " Buxen ". This grew to be a most formidable gang, terrorizing the whole of the Limburg district and the province of Treves, until a state of appalling anarchy ensued. The custom of the Buxen was to meet after nightfall in some lonely spot and to commence proceedings by the celebration of the Black Mass when Hosts, stolen from the tabernacle were foully desecrated. This was the time for the initiation of recruits. It is said that their obscene ceremonies were generally conducted in one of three ruined sanctuaries, the church of St. Rose near Sittardt, the oratory of St. Leonard hard by Roldyck, and a haunted chapel at Oermond on the Meuse. Afterwards, hideously masqued and disguised, they sallied forth— sometimes to the number of two or three hundred— and raided farms, small holdings, country houses, even attacking villages. If they passed a church on the way they invariably burst open the doors, robbed the tabernacle, and gutted the whole building leaving it in flames. A veritable reign of terror ruled, for so carefully was the secret of membership guarded that no man knew whether his neighbour, nay, his brother or his son might not be a Bux. Any attempt at resistance, any suspicion of treachery, met with the most terrible reprisals. The society was only broken up and crushed after the sternest measures had been taken, a permanent gallows being set up in many places, and some hamlets having two gibbets apiece. Leopold Leeuwerk, dubbed their chaplain, a Satanist who had offered hundreds of Black Masses to the demon, was caught at last, whilst another of their leaders was hanged in 1772 on the moor of Graed, and a few years later the Buxen had come to an end.

Closely connected with the Black Mass of the Satanists and a plain survival from the Middle Ages is that grim superstition of the Gascon peasant, the Mass of St. Sécaire. Few priests know the awful ritual, and of those who are learned in such dark lore fewer yet would dare to perform the monstrous ceremonies and utter the prayer of blasphemy. No confessor, no bishop, not even the Archbishop of Auch, may shrive the celebrant ; he can only be absolved at Rome by the Holy Father himself. The Mass is said upon a broken and desecrated altar in some ruined or deserted church where owls hoot and mope and bats flit through the crumbling windows, where toads spit their venom upon the sacred stone. The priest must make his way thither late attended only by an acolyte of impure and evil life. At the first stroke of eleven he begins ; the liturgy of hell is mumbled backward, the canon said with a mow and a sneer ; he ends just as midnight tolls. The Host is triangular, with three sharp points and black. No wine is consecrated but foul brackish water drawn from a well wherein has been cast the body of an unbaptized babe. The holy sign of the cross is made with the left foot upon the ground. And the man for whom that mass is said will slowly pine away, nor doctor's skill nor physic will avail him aught, but he will suffer, and dwindle, and surely drop into the grave.

When the blasphemous liturgy of the Sabbat was done all present gave themselves up to the most promiscuous debauchery without respect of age, dignity, relationship, or sex. There is no obscenity, says Boguet, which is not practised and eagerly pursued in these assemblies. It is true that the sworn confessions of such witches as Madeleine de la Palud and Madeleine Bavent reveal a veritable abysm of turpitude. Gentien le Clerc, a young Satanist of Orleans, whose mother presented him to the devil when he was but three years old, related how he had assisted at innumerable Sabbats held in a meadow near, or sometimes even in the very market square of Olivet, a village on the left bank of the Loiret, about two and a half miles from Orleans.

The ceremony commenced with an asperges of filthy water or even urine. After this the Devil (the Grand Master) celebrated the Mass. He wore a chasuble of the usual form but embroidered with a broken cross, and after he had elevated the Host and the Chalice, both of which were black, he turned his back to the altar in contempt, as is done in the Satanists' liturgy to-day. The infamous Marie de Sains spoke of a diabolical litany, which commenced—

Lucifer, miserere nobis,
Belzebuth, miserere nobis.

The Mass was read from a great book, which seemed to have scarlet letters on the white vellum, and some pages of which appeared all black. It had a rough, furry cover as though made of a wild beast's pelt. The pax was given in the accustomed place, but all present kissed some obscene or grotesque object. After this was done, Gentien avowed that the worshippers, one and all, abandoned themselves to a very riot of lust and spintrian pollutions. To accumulate details were superfluous. The same story is told throughout the centuries. In *Chrysal* Johnstone writes how the Monks of Mendenham after their mock communion service sat down to a banquet " at which nothing that the most refined luxury, the most lascivious imagination could suggest to kindle loose desire, and provoke and gratify appetite was wanting both the superiours and the inferiours vying with each other in loose songs and dissertations of such gross lewdness, and daring impiety, as despair may be supposed to dictate to the damn'd ". To-day the meetings of Satanists invariably end in unspeakable orgies of filth and the most hideous debauchery.

The learned authors of the *Malleus Maleficarum* write at length " *Concerning Witches who copulate with Devils* ", and it is obvious that there is no question here of animal familiars, but rather of evil intelligences who are, it is believed, able to assume a body of flesh. As Saint Augustine says, it is beyond all doubt proven that certain devils do continually practise this uncleanness, and tempt others to it, which is affirmed by such grave persons and with such confidence that it were impudence to deny it. A whole catena of authorities from the earliest times until the present day might be cited, but the matter may be summed up as by Delrio who writes : " So many sound authors and theologians have upheld this belief that to differ from them is mere obstinacy and foolhardiness ; for the Saints, the Fathers and Doctors, and all the wisest writers on philosophy agree upon this matter, the truth of which is furthermore proved by the experience of all ages and people."

Above all sounds the solemn thunder of the Bull of Innocent VIII announcing in no ambiguous phrase :

" It has indeed come to our knowledge and deeply grieved are we to hear it that many persons of both sexes, utterly forgetful of their souls' salvation and straying far from the Catholic Faith have (had commerce) with evil spirits, both incubi and succubi."

The incubus (the word derives from post-classical Latin and literally means *one who lies upon* anything) is the demon who assumes a male form, the succubus or succuba (from late Latin, literally meaning *one who lies under* anything, a harlot) is the demon when assuming a female form, and the famous Dominican Charles Réné Billuart in his *Treatise upon the Angelic Hosts* explicitly informs us : " The same evil spirit may serve as a succubus to a man, and as an incubus to a woman."

Commenting upon the passage in the Book of Genesis (vi, 4), " the sons of God came in unto the daughters of men, and they bare children to them," Pope Benedict XIV explains : " This passage has reference to those Demons who are known as incubi and succubi."

Dom Dominic Schram, a celebrated Benedictine theologian, emphatically lays down : " It is certain that—whatever doubters may say—there exist such demons, incubi and succubi. . . . Wherefore the men or women who suffer these impudicities are sinners who either invite demons . . . or who freely consent to demons when the evil spirits tempt them to commit such abominations."

From these great names, and it were an easy matter to quote a hundred more, it will be seen that the Fathers and Saints, and all scholars and theologians of importance affirm the possibility of commerce with incarnate evil intelligences. The question rises and must be briefly answered how demons or familiars, seeing that they are pure spiritual beings, can not only assume human flesh but thus perform the peculiarly carnal acts of coition and generation.

Following the opinion of Guazzo, who is supported not only by Plato, Philo, Josephus, and other ancient writers, but also by St. Augustine, St. Jerome, and the consensus of all theologians, Lodovico Maria Sinistrari, in his famous treatise *Demoniality* answers that the Demon assumes the corpse of another human being, male or female, as the case may be, or else that from a commixture of other materials he shapes for himself a body endowed with motion by means of which it is possible for the evil spirit to have sexual intercourse with human beings. In this latter instance advantage might be taken, no question, of a person in a mediumistic trance or hypnotic sleep. Jacopo de Voragine relates how once when a priest was sorely tempted by a beautiful woman who entered his chamber in a state of nudity he took his stole and threw it round her neck. With a shriek she fell to the ground, and there lay the rotting corpse of a harlot who had been many days dead.

There is yet another explanation which seems equally possible. Can we not look to the phenomena observed in connexion with ectoplasm as an explanation of this ? Again and again in materializing séances physical forms which may be touched and freely handled are built up and presently disintegrate in a few moments of time. In a symposium *Survival* Miss Felicia Scatcherd relates certain of her own experiences that go far to prove the partial re-materialization of the dead by the utilizing of the material substance and ectoplasmic emanations of the living. Mr. Godfrey Raupert in his *Modern Spiritism* describes in considerable detail how at these experiments and sittings an entire human form " is fully and immediately ' materialized ', . . . The solidity and life-likeness of these forms would seem to depend very largely upon the sensitive and the sitters. If the conditions are very favourable they may have all the characteristics of real human beings with all the functions of a human body in full working order. The pulse or the heart may be felt to be beating, and the organs of sight or of speech or of hearing to be acting to perfection. . . . The forms have been known to remain materialized for a considerable time, to have apported flowers and other light articles, to have carried on prolonged and interesting conversations, and to have acted in other respects like ordinary human beings, possessing and operating in an ordinary human body ".

Here then we have an ample solution of the activities of the incubi and succubi, and although neither of these explanations precludes the other, I take this latter to be the more general from the fact that the incubus can assume the shape of some person whose embraces the witch may desire. There are many recorded instances of this, and it is alluded to by the dramatist Middleton in his play *The Witch* when Hecate says :—

> What young man can we wish to pleasure us,
> But we enjoy him in an incubus ?

Thus when the young gallant Almachildes visits her abode, she exclaims :—

> 'Tis Almachildes—the fresh blood stirs in me—
> The man that I have lusted to enjoy :
> I've had him thrice in incubus already.

That is the early seventeenth century, and at the end of the nineteenth we find that Huysmans in *Là-Bas* introduces the occultist Ledos under the name Gévingey who discusses in some detail the question of incubi and succubi, relating instances which have come under his own knowledge. I do not hesitate to refer to the pages of Huysmans as it is well known that he had deeply studied the whole subject and he has actual documentation for what he relates. The following conversation takes place between Durtal, who is Huysmans himself, and Madame Chantelouve. This demoniacal woman in a scene of closest intimacy cries to her lover : " You must know then that I can possess you when and how I please, in the same way as I have possessed Byron, Baudelaire, Gérard de Nerval, all the men I love . . ." " What can you mean ? " " I tell you that I only have to desire their embrace, as you are longing for me at this moment, and then before I fall asleep . . ." " Well, what then ? " " You, your real self, will—I know it—prove a mere weakling to the Durtal who visits me at nights, whom I adore, and whose burning kisses drive me mad ! " He looked at her in amaze. Then in a flash he realized the truth of those foul incubus lusts of which Ledos had spoken.

We have seen that the Grand Master of a district often presided over and directed the Sabbat orgies, and then it was he, an apostate priest, who celebrated the Black Mass. Sometimes also the familiar assigned to a new witch was in the first place and under certain conditions a man, one of the assembly, who either approached her in some infernal disguise or else embraced her without any attempt at concealment of his individuality, some lusty varlet who would afterwards minister to her pleasure. For we must bear in mind that throughout these witch-trials there is often much in the evidence which may be explained by the agency of human beings, not that this essentially meliorates their offences, for the whole band of sorcerers are acting under Satanic inspiration and are the slaves of the devil. At the same time too we meet those connexions and other dark businesses which admit of no explanation save that of the materialization of evil intelligences of power. Detailed and full as is the evidence we possess, it frequently becomes a most difficult matter when we are studying a particular case to decide whether it be an instance of a witch having had actual commerce and communion with the fiend, or whether she was herself cheated by devils, who mocked her, and persuading her to deem herself in overt union with them, thus led the wretch on to misery and death, duped as she was by the father of lies, sold for a delusion and by profitless endeavour in evil.

It is probable too that a witch would sometimes be served by an incubus or succubus as the case might be, and sometimes by another member of the coven. There are, doubtless, also many cases which stand on the border-line, half hallucination, half reality.

The confessions of the pupils who were in the charge of Antoinette Bourignon afford extraordinary details of these matters. They " declared that they had daily carnal Cohabitation with the Devil ; that they went to the Sabbaths or Meetings, where they Eat, Drank, Danc'd, and committed other Whoredom and Sensualities ". To repeat the several particular accounts were superfluous. One may suffice for the rest, that of a girl, named Bellot, then aged fifteen. She said that her mother had taken her to a Sabbat whilst she was still very young, " and that being a little Wench, this Man-Devil was then a little Boy too, and grew up as she did, having been always her Love, and Caressed her Day and Night." A young sorcerer from Lorraine, Dominic Petrone, was only twelve years old when his mother enticed him into an abominable marriage of this kind, in which he had much delight.

Remy observes that the demons and witches even simulate marriages, and he records the avowals of sorcerers who had been present at such ceremonies. De Lancre describes how at the Sabbats the Devil performs marriages between warlocks and witches, joining their hands with a sneering benediction. Colette Fischer of Mainz acknowledged that it was no unusual thing for witches to wed demons, who (it is related) feign hot jealousy and carefully watch over their spouses. The Rev. John Gaule in his *Select Cases of Conscience touching Witches and Witchcraft*, published in 1646, mentions that the same customs prevailed in England : " Oft times he marries them ere they part, either to himself, or their Familiar, or to one another ; and that by the Book of Common Prayer (as a pretender to Witch finding lately told me in the Audience of Many)." The Capuchin, Jacques D'Autun, writing in 1678, has a chapter upon " The horrid blasphemy and beastliness of these mock-marriages which are celebrated at the witches' Sabbat ".

Rebecca West, a witch of Lawford, Essex, and the daughter of a witch, related how the devil came to her " as she was going to bed, and told her, he would marry her, and that she could not deny him ; she said he kissed her, but was as cold as clay, and married her that night ". He promised to be her loving husband, and swore that her enemies were thenceforth his enemies. " Then she promised him to be his obedient wife till death, and to deny God and Christ Jesus." A young sorcerer, Pétrone of Armentières, declared that when he approached a succuba so intensely cold and gelid did she appear that his own limbs seemed frozen and nipped as with arctic snows. Another warlock, Hennezel, acknowledged that he could not accomplish any venereal act with his succuba, Schwartz-burg, who was he verily believed hewn from ice. A Suffolk witch, the widow Bush of Barton, said that the Devil, who appeared to her as a dark swarthy youth, " was colder than man." Isobel Gowdie and Janet Breadheid of the Auldearne coven, 1662, both asserted that the Devil was " a meikle, blak, roch man, werie cold ; and I fand his nature als cold within me as spring-well-water ".

This unnatural physical coldness of the Demon is commented upon again and again by witches at their trials in every country in Europe throughout the centuries. Now ectoplasm is described as being to the touch a cold and viscous mass comparable to contact with a reptile, and it may be that here we have the solution to the whole mystery.

It is extremely significant too as the pages of Boguet, Remy, De Lancre, and many other demonologists show this coupling with the demon was not accomplished without physical pain. Thus Thievenne Paget declared that the act caused her as keen agony as if she had been in travail. Jeanne Bosdeau who was tried by the

Parliament of Bordeaux in 1594 said that the demon
" had carnal knowledge of her which was with great
pain ". The Pyrenean witches acknowledged that this
fornication with the devil caused them untold sufferings.
Temperance Lloyd, a Devonshire witch, confessed
that the Devil had carnal knowledge of her body
thrice, and always with great pain.

Moreover it is evident from the several accounts of
the Sabbat which agree in various countries that the
Devil or President of the assembly was wont to have
connexion with every one or at least with very many
of the women present. The Grand Master and Officer
also exercised the right to select first for his own
pleasure such witches as he chose, as appears from a
passage in De Lancre who writes that after sorcerer
and sorceress had been joined in mock marriage by
the Devil he first took the bride's maidenhead.

Obviously no one human being could serve so many
women, and it follows that use must have been made
of an instrument ; the artificial phallus was employed.
This is quite clear too from the extremely detailed
description of the genital organs of the President of
the Sabbat given by the Lorraine witches to Nicolas
Remy. Nicole Morèle, Claude Fellet, Alexée Drigie,
and indeed the whole infernal sisterhood spoke of
these as monstrous beyond all conception. It will not
escape notice either that the Devil as drawn from the
life—for the sketch was doubtless made at the actual
performance—on the title-page of Middleton and
Rowley's masque *The World tost at Tennis* is abundantly
and indeed grotesquely supplied in this respect. He is
pictured in exactly similar fashion in more than one old
chap-book, whilst a phallus, to which reference is made

THE DEVIL CHASTISING THE WITCHES
George Cruikshank

[*face p.* 198

in the text, was worn by the actor dressed up as the monkey (*Bavian*) in the May-dance scene in Shakespeare and Fletcher's *The Two Noble Kinsmen*. Troops of phallic demons formed a standing characteristic of the old German carnival comedy. Moreover, several of the fantastic types of the Commedia dell'arte in the second decade of the seventeenth century were traditionally equipped in like manner.

The artificial penis was a commonplace among the erotica of ancient civilizations ; it was very generally utilized in Egypt, Assyria, India, Mexico, all over the world. It has been found in tombs ; frequently was it to be seen as an ex-voto ; in a slightly modified form it is yet the favourite mascot of Southern Italy. Often enough they do not even trouble to disguise the thing. It is mentioned by the Greek writers, by Aristophanes, Herodas, and others. Among the Latins it is spoken of by Petronius and Tibullus. It was familiar in the brothels of Byzantium. It was employed by the Galli, priests of Cybele ; in the worship of Bacchus ; in the debauched ritual of Priapus. A later historian speaks of phallic ceremonies and the use of ithyphalli in the tenth century. "A sterile lust, common in the earliest times," says the *Erotic Glossary of the Latin Tongue*. The Councils, the Fathers, the Doctors of the Church ; Clement of Alexandria, Arnobius, Nicetas, Theodoret, Lactantius, the great St. Augustine, and many a prohibition of West and East have spoken of these practices in terms of severest condemnation. It is demonstrable then that artificial methods of coition, common in pagan antiquity, have been unblushingly practised throughout all the ages, as indeed they are at the present day, and that they have been repeatedly, ay and vehemently, banned and reprobated by the voice of the Church, a malison and an injunction which would doubtless recommend them to the favour of the Satanists, whose dark debaucheries of lust take an additional thrill, a new glamour if they can add to obscenity disobedience. Yet we have also to face the fact that there are darker and fouler mysteries still, hideous copulations of hell, which neither human intercourse nor the employ of a mechanical property can explain.

It is the universal opinion that children are born of these horrible unions. These are either demoniac monsters or prodigies of wickedness. They are always in some way hideously deformed, although of course the blemish may be concealed from sight. In any case their odious and malignant nature inevitably betrays the fiendish origin. At Toulouse in 1275, Angèle de la Barthe, a hag of some sixty, was condemned for having had intercourse with an evil spirit from which conjunction she brought forth a vilely misshapen creature whom she nourished with the flesh of infants, slain by her or dug up from their graves in remote churchyards. Towards the end of the seventeenth century an Essex witch, Sarah Smith, from her commerce with a familiar " was brought to Bed of a Strange Monster, the Body of it like a Fish with Scales thereon, it had no Legs but a pair of great Claws. . . . Which eat and fed for some time. Which Monster . . . was by Command of the Magistrates knock'd on the Head, and several Surgeons were there to dissect it ". Sinistrari gives the names of several persons who made a noise in the world and were shrewdly suspected of being the offspring of the demon and a witch. Thomas Malvenda, a famous Dominican writer, says that children thus begotten are often tall, very hardy and bloodily bold, arrogant beyond words, and desperately wicked. Both Malvenda and St. Robert Bellarmine hold that Antichrist will be the progeny of a demon and a witch. Others indeed have it that Antichrist will be the Devil in the flesh in awful mockery of the Incarnation. Be that as it may, the appalling wickedness, the power and infinite capacity for evil of certain prominent figures to-day can only be explained if we realize that such must verily be the children of Satan and witches.

A candid consideration will show that for every detail of the Sabbat, however fantastically presented and exaggerated in the witch-trials of so many centuries, there is amplest warrant and unimpeachable evidence. There is some hallucination no doubt ; there is lurid imagination, and coarse vanity which paints the colours thick ; but there is a solid stratum of fact, and very terrible fact throughout. And to-day the Satanist is as tirelessly active in our midst as ever he was in bygone ages. Nay, actually the Devil is massing his forces on every side.

Generally the Sabbat orgies lasted till cock-crow, before which time none of the assembly was suffered to withdraw. It is true that in the avowal of Louis Gaufridi, executed at Aix in 1610, he speaks of remaining at the Sabbat two or three hours, just as he felt inclined, but this seems altogether exceptional, and he was moreover the Grand Master of the coven. That the crowing of a cock dissolves enchantments is a tradition of extremest antiquity. The Jews believed that the clapping of a cock's wings will render the power of demons ineffectual and dissolve all magic spells. The poet Prudentius sang : " They say that the foul night-wandering spirits, who rejoice in dunnest night, at the crowing of the cock tremble and scatter in sore dismay." In the time of St. Benedict Matins and Lauds were recited at dawn, and were often known as *Gallicinium*, Cock-crow. The rites of Satan ceased when the Office of Holy Church began.

At the hour of the Nativity, that most blessed time, the cocks crew all night long. A cock crew lustily at the Resurrection. A witch named Babilla Latoma confessed to Nicolas Remy that the cock was the most hateful of all birds to sorcerers. Johann Bulmer and his wife Desirée, who belonged to a coven of Le Mans district, said that the synagogue of sorcerers was usually disbanded by the President and the familiars proclaiming : " Ho ! Speed all and away—away ! For the cocks begin to crow ! "

The sound of bells also is most detested by the hellish crew, and Bishop Binsfeld in a fine passage compares the music of church bells to the hoisting of the royal standard of our King. Not only can they subdue tempests but they put to instant flight devils and witches, they breathe benediction and peace. It is recorded by an Italian writer that on a certain occasion when the debauchery of the Sabbat had been prolonged the horrid crew were surprised to hear the Angelus ringing out its early salutation to the Virgin Mother from a village steeple hard by. The demons fled howling and disappeared with a most noisome stench abandoning their besotted worshippers to fare as best they might. Bishop Peter Binsfeld says that the charm was broken, the glamour dissipated, and the Sabbat vanished if one pronounced with devotion the Sacred Names of Jesus or Mary.

The Sabbat ends. As the dawn breaks the unhallowed crew separate in haste, and hurry each one on his way homewards, pale, weary, and haggard after the night of taut hysteria, of frenzied evil, hate, and vilest excess.

The cock crows ; the Sabbat ends ; the sorcerers scatter and flee away.

CHAPTER V

Thou shalt not suffer a witch to live.
Exodus, xxii, 18.

The word Witchcraft itself belongs to Anglo-Saxon days, and even if we possessed no other evidence of the fearful prevalence in the centuries before the Norman Conquest of wellnigh every kind of traffic with the darker powers throughout all England the fact that these horrid businesses were only too widespread might indeed be considered amply proven when we are able to recognize and enumerate no less than some forty native terms denoting all kinds of black magic and the various professors of that evil craft. Actually the wealth of witness from laws, both ecclesiastical and secular, from sermons and homilies, from leechdoms, chronicles and legend, is overwhelming.

It was in the spring of the year 597 that the Apostle of the English, Saint Augustine, with his little company landed on the Isle of Thanet, presently to be welcomed by King Æthelbert, himself still a pagan, although his wife and dear queen, Bertha of Paris, enjoyed the free exercise of her religion. It will be readily remembered how the King fearing some possible incantations on the part of the strangers insisted that their first interview should take place in the open air under the shadow of a sacred oak, the tree worshipped by the Druids, by the ancient Celts and Teutons, by Slavs and Lithuanians, at Nemi, in Syria, the tree whose majesty was revered by the whole Aryan race. The King's apprehensions, however, were speedily set at rest, and he forthwith invited the missionaries to his royal city of Canterbury, a barbarous and squalid place enough, to which, however, they gladly came, as the Venerable Bede describes, bearing the Holy Cross together with a picture of the Sovereign King, Our Lord Jesus Christ, and chanting in unison sweet psalms and litanies as they went on their way.

After the death of Æthelbert in 616 great reverses befell Christianity, and witchcraft notably increased throughout the land. The dark opposing powers were not easily to be driven from the fair realm of Britain, and in 633 it seemed as if the Faith would be wholly extinguished throughout the North of England on account of the fierce persecutions of Penda, the pagan King of Mercia, whose court was thronged with wizards, diviners, and cunning women.

Rædwald, King of the East-Angles, a most powerful monarch who died about 627, and was fourth Bretwalda, erected (as the Venerable Bede tells us) in one and the same temple a high altar at which Mass was said, and a side altar at which sacrifices were offered to the devil.

In 747 was convened at the behest of Pope Zachary the Second Council of Clovesho, which forbade all abominations and vain pagan practices, "wizardry, sorcery, divinings, fortune-telling, periapts, spells, conjurations, and incantations, which are the very filth of the wicked, yea, heathen falsehood and deceit."

Continuous legislation, the codes of Ælfred, of

Edward and Guthrum, of Æthelstan, and many more
ban witchcraft, demanding the supreme penalty for
those who slay others by their spells. The Secular
Laws of Cnut denounce those who " love witchcrafts
to ensue them, or contrive secret murder in anywise ;
or offer evil sacrifice or by soothsaying, or perform
anything pertaining to such abominable illusions ".
By secret murder is intended any killing through a
charm or some kind of witchcraft. The " evil sacrifice "
is the Black Mass.

The Christian Council of the Gold Coast, of which
the Anglican Bishop of Accra is chairman, published
in January, 1932, a lengthy memorandum dealing
with African sorceries. Among the powers which a
wizard is supposed to possess is " The power to inflict
disease and death upon a human victim without
physical contact or physical medium (popular belief
distinguishes between witchcraft and poisoning) ". The
Christian Council includes representatives of the
English Church Mission, of the Methodist and Presby-
terian bodies. It appears that some of the members
were disinclined to believe in witchcraft, but be that
as it may the warning of the *Vox Populi* of Accra
which commented adversely upon the documents is
soundest of all : " Our sincere advice to the churches
of the Gold Coast is to leave the Devil alone . . . Of
some meek strangers in Palestine it was once reported,
' We would see Jesus '. A Christian Council to-day
would see the Devil and his works and pay for it."

Writing in the *Daily Express* on 3rd June, 1933,
Mr. Arthur Hudson, K.C., former Attorney-General
of the Gold Coast, mentions several instances of
homicide by witchcraft. One of the earliest complaints

that came before him was that of a man whose father had been killed by a wizard. The wizard had been angry with the deceased, had declared that he should die on a certain day, and on that day the victim died. In the present sad state of the law the murderer could not be convicted, and Mr. Hudson wisely attempted to frighten him by threats of punishment if any more complaints were made concerning his activities. In another instance a warlock told a man who had given offence that as he walked home to his farm a snake would come out of the bush and bite him, and that he would die. The man was bitten exactly in this way, and died. Here again the warlock could only be intimidated in hopes that he would for the future for very fear eschew his sorceries.

It would be easy to give many more quotations from and references to Anglo-Saxon and pre-Norman documents and writings of all kinds, but enough has been said to show that witchcraft, known in all its aspects throughout England long before the Conquest, was ever forbidden by the Law and banned by the Church.

After the Conquest the Anglo-Saxon statutes against witchcraft and all ecclesiastical censures and excommunications were in practice continued. William I in a summary of his legislation assigns perpetual exile as the punishment for any murder by black magic. (The technical word in the first instance implies the use of poison, but poison and spells were so invariably intermingled that the terms became synonymous.) It was soon found necessary to make the penalty more severe. Thus the code known as the Laws of Henry I, which may be dated about 1110, decrees that any murder, whether it be by poisoning or by witchcraft, is punishable with death. If, however, the victim has not been killed but has been injured in body or lies sick the offender may make compensation by payment of a heavy fine. The code specifies one particular form of malefic magic which was regarded as especially heinous, the piercing of an image or poppet to slay the man in whose likeness it was moulded.

In 1071 when William I was attacking Hereward the Wake and had abandoned all hope of capturing the Isle of Ely, a Norman knight ventured to suggest that as a last resource they should avail themselves of the help of an old woman, who (as he said) by her mysterious art was able to sap the defenders of their manhood and drive them pell-mell in a panic from their strongholds. The crone was brought to the camp under cover of darkness, but not so secretly that the news reached Hereward by means of a spy. The Saxon chief, disguising himself very adroitly in rags, obtained a lodging at the cottage of a widow where the witch dwelt. He overheard the two hags conversing in French, a language they, of course, deemed a vagrom wayfarer could not understand. At midnight the women went down to a spring of water which ran at the end of the garden, and concealed among the trees he watched whilst they invoked the " guardian of the springs ", a demon who answered in a hoarse and horrible voice. In consequence he was able to employ a counter-spell. When the enemy with great confidence made their next sally, the witch was stationed in a high chariot in their midst to ply her art whilst they fought. The Normans, however, were routed with heavy loss, and the sorceress being cast to the ground was slain in the *mêlée*.

That such foul creatures, ever ready to work harm, literally swarmed throughout England in those centuries cannot be doubted, even as it is certain that Satanists infest the country in our own time. Again and again the laws—silent to-day—forbade and penalized sorcery and enchantments. Nor can we be surprised that on occasion persons tormented by some sorceress have suddenly and violently avenged themselves, as when John of Kerneslawe was surprised one evening by a hideous hag who entering his cottage struck him smartly with her staff, and in a moment all his limbs were writhen and racked with pain. In self-defence, as against the devil, he snatched up a javelin and struck her through so that she died. But John fell into a delirium and ran lunatic, nor did he recover his wits until the clergy of the district very properly ordered that the body of the witch should be burned to ashes.

There was a terrific scandal in 1303 when one of the chief men in the realm, Walter Langton, Bishop of Coventry and treasurer of Edward I, was delated before Pope Boniface VIII as a notorious warlock and of worshipping the Demon with obscene ceremonies. After a most searching inquiry the incriminated prelate proved able successfully to clear himself of the crime.

There seems little doubt that politics were mixed up in this case, as they most certainly were the motive of the famous trials of 1324 when no less than twenty-seven defendants were brought before the King's Bench for murder by fashioning and tormenting a wax image. Upon All Hallows E'en, 1323, a number of Coventry men went privately to the house of a notorious " nigro-

mauncer ", John of Nottingham, who was then living
in their town, and having bound him and his man,
Robert Marshall from Leicester, to closest secrecy,
paid him a large sum of money to undertake the slaying
of King Edward II, the royal favourite young Hugh
le Despenser, and other great men of quality. The old
warlock and his servant forthwith set to work. A remote
and ancient manor, some half a league from Coventry,
was the scene of their operations. In this horrible
haunted house they set about their work. They were
well feed, and provided with seven pounds of fair
white wax and two ells of superfine canvas to fashion
the mommets, the King with a gilded crown on his
head, Monsieur Hugh, and the rest. Long and
thoroughly they laboured at their modelling. It was
resolved that first they would make an experiment
upon Richard de Sowe, a courtier whom they hated.
Accordingly they moulded their figurine, and at
midnight on the Friday before the Feast of Holy Rood
(3rd May) Master John gave Marshall a long leaden
pin bidding him thrust boldly two inches deep into
the forehead of the doll. The next morning the
servant went to de Sowe's house upon some casual
errand to learn that he was writhing on his bed in
agony, uttering piercing cries with burning pains in
the head and frantically delirious whilst the physicians
were at their wits' end to diagnose the mysterious
malady. And so he lingered until some days later
the warlock drew the pin from the brow and struck
it featly into the heart of the image. Whereupon de
Sowe expired, and Marshall panicky and dithering
with fear rushed off to the Sheriff, one Simon Crozier,
before whom he confessed all that had been going on,

which immediately resulted in the arrest of Master John
and the whole gang of conspirators. Shame to say
the wealthy burgesses greased the palm of justice and
escaped, but Master John was not so lucky for he died
in durance on the very eve of the trial, whilst the
unfortunate wight who blabbed was sent back to prison
to abide there.

In the forty-fifth year of Edward III, that is to say
1371, a Southwark man was brought before the King's
Bench upon a charge of sorcery. He was found to have
in his wallet the mummified head and embalmed hands
of a dead man, a skull, and a grimoire. In spite of
such damning evidence the Chief Justice, Sir John
Knyvet, only required him to take solemn oath that
he would never practise any kind of witchcraft nor
cast a spell for good or ill, whilst the book and the
loathly relics of mortality were burned in Tothill Fields.

In 1376 the so-called " Good Parliament " openly
charged Alice Perrers, the fascinating mistress of
Edward III with witchcraft, and declared that she
maintained in her house a mysterious Dominican, " who
in outward show professed physic " but by whose
experiments Alice had allured the King to her unlawful
love. He had fashioned a rare ring of memory the
virtue whereof was to keep the doting monarch ever
mindful of the lady.

Under Richard II and Henry IV there were constant
prosecutions of conjurors and traffickers in black magic,
whilst Henry V was plainly very much perturbed
about the increase of sorcerers in his realms. He even
prosecuted his stepmother, Joan of Navarre, for attempting his life by witchcraft, and her confessor, a Franciscan, John Randolf, an admitted adept, was lodged

in the Tower. There seems little doubt that the friar had moulded wax figurines after the traditional manner.

Dames of high degree indeed seem to have been particularly implicated in accusations of witchcraft employed for political motives, and we frequently have very full details of such cases chronicled of course owing to their notoriety and importance, hundreds of similar instances in the lower walks of life passing unrecorded. Thus in 1441 Eleanor Cobham, Duchess of Gloucester, wife of " the Good Duke Humphrey ", " sometime Protector of England," was " arrested and put in hold, for she was suspect of treason ". It was found that she was deeply implicated in the witchcrafts and sorceries of a learned astrologer, Roger Bolingbroke, with whom also were concerned Thomas Southwell, a canon of St. Stephen's ; Sir John Hume a priest ; William Woodham ; and Margery Jourdemain, a witch of the vilest antecedents. Bolingbroke asserted that he had " wrought the said necromancy " at the duchess' command but it was with a view to ascertain " to what estate she should come ", (in other words her chance of succeeding to the throne) and not to plot any treason against the king. There can be little doubt, however, that the death of Henry VI was being attempted according to the orthodox mode of piercing and melting wax images. Bolingbroke was hanged at Tyburn, beheaded and quartered ; Canon Southwell died in prison ; whilst Mother Jourdemain, " the Witch of Eye " (the Manor of Eye-next-Westminster), who had been imprisoned on a charge of sorcery eleven years before but afterwards discharged, was burned at the stake in Smithfield, since she was guilty of high treason as well as malefic magic. The Duchess of Gloucester was compelled to do public penance, walking the streets of London barefoot and bareheaded, in a white shift, and carrying a lighted taper of two pounds weight. She was then confined for life at Peel Castle in the Isle of Man, a fastness yet horribly haunted by her unquiet ghost.

Before his execution Bolingbroke was set on a high platform outside St. Paul's, whilst a rousing sermon was preached to the crowd. He was dressed in his magic robes, holding a huge scimitar in his right hand and a great gilt sceptre in his left, " arrayed in that marvellous array he was wont to don when about his magic." Upon the scaffold was also placed his necromantic throne, a chair of subtle wizardry, curiously painted, wherein he used to sit when he wrought his dark craft, and on the four corners of the chair stood four swords and from every sword there hung an image of a foul fiend graven in copper. Such chairs are still occasionally to be found. In 1929 I saw a very fine specimen then in the possession of Mr. John Jennings. This was of mahogany, and inserted in the back showed the painting of a magician, holding his wand of power, and surrounded by demons. The picture was covered by an elegantly shaped shield of bevelled Vauxhall glass. On the arms and seat were various mystic devices inlaid and *piqués* in brass. Other instruments appertaining to Bolingbroke's craft and which had been found in his closet were displayed, stars, pentacles, cups, censers, images of silver and other metals, together with waxen mommets not a few. Thomas Southwell used to say Mass at an altar in the Lodge of Hornsey Park over " certain instruments fit for the craft of necromancy ". He had celebrated a requiem for the living king, and had also baptized a wax figurine of Henry, piercing it with a sharp bodkin. The case not being proved against Sir John Hume and Woodham, they were acquitted.

Even Jacquette de Luxembourg, Duchess of Bedford, and mother-in-law of Edward IV was attacked by evil tongues who declared that she had fashioned two puppets to compel the king to love her daughter. There were also rumours of a mysterious figure, the image of a soldier, about a finger's length, but broken in the midst and mended with wire which the lady used for purposes of magic. The Duchess made her plaint to the Privy Council, and the whole thing broke down utterly, which did not, however, hinder Richard of Gloster some years later when he was aiming at the throne reviving the scandals, and declaring that his brother's marriage with Elizabeth was invalid as having been contrived " by sorcery and witchcraft, committed by the said Elizabeth and her mother ". He also charged them together with that other witch of their counsel, Shore's wife, with wasting his body by their spells, and did not hesitate to pull up his sleeve and show his shrunken withered arm to the Privy Council, swearing that thus " yonder sorceress, my brother's wife " and her company had plagued him, whereas all present knew well that he had been deformed from birth. And so Jane Shore must do public penance therefor, and walk the London streets clad only in a shift, barefoot, and carrying a lighted taper.

Throughout the fifteenth century there were prosecutions of the smaller fry, and an almost continuous list of cases, year after year, might be recorded. Thus Richard Walker, a chaplain, is accused by the Prior of Winchester of sorcery, and is found to have in his closet a beryl stone for divining, two grimoires, and two dolls of wax. In 1444 there was publicly punished in London a man " the which wrought by a wicked spirit the which was called Oberycom, and the manner of his process and working was written and hanged about his neck when he was in the pillory ". In 1500 Thomas Wright, a Premonstratensian Canon of Sulby Abbey, near Market Harborough, came under grave suspicion for " using books of experiments ", and for having bribed a mysterious " vagabond " to teach him the way of occult science.

At the trial of the Duke of Buckingham, twenty-one years later, an accusation of sorcery supported the capital charge of high treason. He had consulted with Dom Nicholas Hopkins, a monk of the Hinton Charterhouse, of whom he inquired concerning the King's death—a fatal question, if true. It was also alleged that the Duke had been heard to say that Cardinal Wolsey was an idolater and sorcerer, nourishing a familiar, who advised him how to keep the royal favour.

When Henry VIII was beginning to grow a little weary of the gospel light that gleamed from Boleyn's eyes he whispered to some convenient friend that unquestionably he had " made the marriage seduced by witchcraft ", a self-evident fact since God denied him a son. Before the birth of Elizabeth indeed a whole horde of occultists had been consulted to determine the sex of the child. All plumped for a boy, and when the royal mistress was delivered of a girl it was felt to be to " the great reproach of the astrologers, sorcerers, and sorceresses ".

The very comprehensive " Bill against conjurations and witchcrafts ", 1542, by which all using occult arts, were it even to discover stolen goods, are adjudged guilty of felony with pain of death, was short-lived enough, being repealed in the first year of Edward VI, 1547.

It was at the beginning of the reign of Elizabeth that drastic measures were taken against the black art. Although drafted soon after her accession it was not until 1563 that the measure passed on to the statute-book and became English law. In 1604 this act was repealed under James I, and a new act passed. It may be convenient very briefly to sum up the provisions of the two acts. Both prescribe the death penalty for Employing or Exercising Witchcraft with the intent to kill or destroy. To hurt persons in body or to waste and destroy goods under Elizabeth for the first offence was punished with a year's imprisonment and the pillory " by the space of six hours " each quarter ; for a second offence imprisonment for life. Under James the first offence in this kind was punishable with death. To employ witchcraft to find treasure or stolen goods both Acts punished with a year's imprisonment and the pillory. A second offence of this nature meant perpetual imprisonment under Elizabeth ; under James, death. The same penalties were attached to the felony of provoking persons to unlawful love by witchcraft, or indeed to employing witchcraft for any ends whatsoever. By the Act of James the consulting, covenanting with, entertaining, employing, feeding or rewarding any evil spirit was punishable with death.

The same penalty was prescribed for invocation or conjurations of demons, as also for taking up any dead body from the grave, or securing any skin, bone, or part of a corpse to employ in any manner of witchcraft or enchantment. Such is the main tenor of these Acts. There are ancillary penalties ; forfeiture of property, loss of clergy. The Act of Elizabeth was automatically repealed by the Act of James I. The Act of James I remained law until the reign of George II, 1736.

It should be remarked that the death sentence for a witch was " to be hanged by the neck until he or she be dead ". It is generally, but most erroneously supposed, that in England the stake was the doom of a witch and that she was burned alive. Some few witches such as Margery Jourdemain under Henry VI and Mother Lakeland of Ipswich in 1645 were burned at the stake, but this was because they were guilty of treason. The former was convicted of high treason against the King ; the latter of petty treason, she had killed her husband by sorcery. In Scotland the witch was burned, sometimes alive, and sometimes after being strangled at the stake. This too was the general custom on the Continent. Sometimes also (but infrequently) witchcraft was combined with heresy, for which the penalty was fire. By an Act of Henry VIII poisoning was punishable by " death by boiling ", and the witches were adepts in the art of poisoning, but no case has been quoted (so far as I am aware) in English records where a witch was thus executed.

Statistics which have been very carefully investigated and compared show that there were more trials for witchcraft during the two and forty years of Elizabeth than throughout the entire seventeenth century. It may be remarked that during the whole reign of James I, twenty-two years, not more than forty executions for witchcraft have been traced. The popular tradition which so confidently affirms that the most responsible and prominent figure in the history of English witchcraft is King James I, whose accession from Scotland to the English throne fanned expiring embers into a blazing flame and fearfully energized a furious and long unbated flood of persecution sending literally thousands of crazy gaffers and doting beldames to torture and to death is, be it said once and for all, the merest figment of ignorance.

Under James there was only one material change in the existing law which could be termed more rigid, and it is significant that in 1622 when Edward Fairfax, the translator of Tasso, accused six women who were duly brought before the York Assizes of bewitching his two daughters, although the evidence seems conclusive and the jury found a true bill, the Judge after hearing several witnesses pronounced that the matter " reached not to the point of the statute ", stopped the trial and discharged the prisoners.

One of the most notorious of Elizabethan cases was that of the Witches of St. Osyth. This little village stands on a creek of the River Colne, fitly described as " the lonely waters of St. Osyth Creek with its derelict quay of rotting timber ". It is situated some four miles from Clacton-on-Sea, and a dozen miles from Colchester. St. Osyth, which derives its name from the daughter of an English prince, a pious maid who preserved her virginity even in the marriage state and who founded a nunnery in this place erstwhile called Chick, where

she was martyred by Danish pirates in 653—her feast
is kept on the 7th October—is one of the oldest inhabited
spots in the country, having been a Royal demesne of
King Cnut. To-day there is a population of between
fourteen and fifteen hundred.

Here at the end of the sixteenth century dwelt in a
wretched cottage with her eight-year-old bastard son,
Thomas Rabbet, a woman of ill repute, Ursula Kemp
alias Grey, who eked out a scanty maintenance by
acting as midwife, nursing children, harlotry, and
various kinds of magic, both black and white, which
included " unwitching " the sick. Davy, the son of
a neighbour, Grace Thurlow, a poor and needy woman,
fell sick, and amongst other gossips Ursula Kemp came
to see the child. Taking him by the hand she muttered
some mysterious words, and the lad was almost immediately restored to health. Her suspicions confirmed,
Grace Thurlow refused to allow Ursula Kemp to nurse
a newly born baby girl. Soon afterwards the infant
fell out of the cradle and broke its neck, an accident
the mother pretty plainly attributed to the vengeance
of the witch. Hereupon Ursula Kemp threatened her
with lameness, to which she made sharp reply : " Take
heed, Ursley, thou hast a naughty name." But soon
enough Grace Thurlow was crippled with pain, so that
she could scarcely drag herself about the room on her
hands and knees. Complaint was made to Mr. Brian
Darcy, high sheriff of the county, who promptly
examined young Thomas Rabbet, and there was soon
unripped a whole coven of Satanists. At length
Ursula confessed the crimes of witchcraft and murder.
The death of Grace Thurlow's baby would have been
easy enough to accomplish, and it seems quite plain

that Ursula Kemp, who was the chief of the St. Osyth's witches, had been initiated into all the secrets of poisoning, which horrid art was so universally practised by the wise-women and conjurers of the day, both at home and abroad.

Ursula Kemp herself entertained four puckrels or familiars ; two other members of the gang, Alice Hunt and Margery Salmon, the daughters of old Mother Barnes, a notorious witch, had two spirits, bequeathed them by their mother ; Elizabeth Bennett also had two familiars ; whilst Annis Herd nourished no less than six small imps. Terrible was the mischief the coven had wrought before they were discovered. Five murders lay to the count of Ursula Kemp ; Elizabeth Bennett killed two farmers and their wives and much cattle ; Elizabeth Eustace had slain seven cows and a number of pigs, wellnigh ruining their owner ; Joan Robinson overlooked geese and a litter of pigs, drowned cows, struck horses with spavins, and men with a wasting sickness ; Cecilia Celles, a labourer's wife of Clacton, and Alice Mansfield had burned ricks, standing corn, and a barn stored with grain. And so the trial proceeded with guilty confessions, accusations, bitter recriminations, and counter-accusations until sixteen persons were involved. Thirteen witches were convicted, ten at least of whom were guilty of murder by sorcery and were executed. The accounts are a little confused, and it may be that the whole thirteen suffered.

In a chapel of the south aisle belonging to the parish church of St. Peter and St. Paul, St. Osyth, is a mural tablet to Brian Darcy, High Sheriff of Essex, who died on 25th December, 1587. Outside one of the old cottages is affixed a notice " Step Right In Here to

See the Genuine Skeleton of a Witch. Admission
Three Pence ". In a deep pit at the end of the garden,
protected by timber rails and a wooden cover lies the
skeleton of a woman, a horrid sight ! Great iron nails
have been driven through the knees and ankles. They
were fixed years ago lest the unhappy soul should
reanimate those bleaching bones and send the terror
walking abroad in the night.

It must not be forgotten that in the days of Elizabeth,
and the two kings her successors there lived wise men
and seers whose practices very nearly trenched upon
witchcraft, if indeed they were not entirely necroman-
tical, but who were consulted and protected by the
great ones at court, aristocratic ladies and men of the
first quality. Such were the famous Dr. John Dee,
who was employed by Leicester as a conjurer and
figure-caster, and who was " continually busied about
one thing and another at the fancy " of Elizabeth
herself. It was he who named the 14th January, 1559,
as a happy day for her coronation. There were also
his scryers, Barnabas Saul, and the enigmatical Edward
Kelley, in whose story sober fact and wild romance are
so inextricably blended that it is hard to know what
to believe. There was Dr. Simon Forman who set up
in London as an astrologer in 1583, and obtained a
large practice amongst the amatory court gallants and
light wanton ladies, who was frequently imprisoned
at the instance of medical and other authorities, but
who was granted a licence as a physician by Cambridge
University in 1603. He was a magician professed,
and one who knew the guilty secrets of Somerset and
the Countess of Essex. The all-powerful favourite,
Buckingham, protected Dr. John Lambe, who was even

more notorious as a sorcerer than Forman. The
" Duke's devil " they dubbed him. William Lilly
and John Booker were in some sort of the same line
as these occultists, and one remembers the trick of
the scapegrace Earl of Rochester who masqueraded
as Alexander Bendo professing *inter alia* " Astrological
Predictions, Divination by Dreams ", and whose
lodging " in *Tower-Street*, next door to the sign of the
Black Swan, at a Goldsmith's House " was crowded
by the wits and lovely cyprians of the Whitehall of
Charles II. Even the celebrated Oxford mathe-
matician, Thomas Allen, of Gloucester Hall (Worcester
College) who died in 1632 was commonly reputed
to command familiars, and to have learned his science
from the astral spirits he could evoke at will.

I am inclined to believe that the case of the Lancashire witches—perhaps the most celebrated case in the
history of English witchcraft—may have gone far to
bolster the false idea that King James' reign was a
period of fanatical malevolence when " the judges and
magistrates, the constables and the mob began to
hunt up as their lawful prey " old women from every
nook and chimney corner.

The first trial of the Lancashire witches took place
in 1612. Some five and twenty years before that date
Elizabeth Sowtherns, better known as old Mother
Demdike, encountered in Pendle Forest an evil spirit
(whom she had probably invoked) to whom she sold
her soul. At once she became an active missionary for
the Satanists, and although at first the way was slow
about five years later she persuaded Anne Whittle
or Chattox " to condescend and agree to become
subject unto that devilish abominable profession of

witchcraft ". Henceforward these two wretches and
all their families practised witchcraft. Mother Demdike
brought in her married daughter Elizabeth Device,
and her grandchildren, Alison and James Device ;
Mother Chattox proselytized to evil her daughter,
Anne Redfearn. The infection spread, and even a
woman of some degree, Mrs. Elizabeth Nutter, joined
the coven. Later a violent quarrel took place between
the Devices and the Chattox family, each party
endeavouring to harm the friends and relations of the
other. Terrible mischief ensued, and the coven became
bolder and bolder, almost openly holding their Sabbats
at the lonely Malking Tower on the further slope of
the high hill which shuts in Rough Lee glen, not far
from the old road to Gisburn.

> Malkin's Tower . . . where
> Report makes caitiff witches meet to swear
> Their homage to the devil, and contrive
> The deaths of men and beasts.

A veritable reign of terror oppressed the whole countryside and everyone went in mortal fear of the witches.
At length towards the end of March, 1612, Mr. Roger
Nowell, a Justice of the Peace, caused old Demdike
and Alison Device, Mother Chattox and her daughter
to be brought before him. Their confessions were such
that he committed them to Lancaster Castle. Even
during their imprisonment the rest of the coven
proved so audacious as to hold a Sabbat at Malking
Tower on the following Good Friday. This led to
further arrests. At the Assizes no less than nineteen
prisoners were put on their trial, of which number
ten were executed, murder by witchcraft having been
clearly proved against them. Old Demdike had died

in gaol. They were shown to be guilty of every circumstance of sorcery, and were as dangerous a gang of Satanists as very well could be. As Dr. G. B. Harrison says : " the Lancaster trial reveals the practice of the witch-cult in its full horror . . . There seems, in short, to have been little injustice in the sentences passed at Lancaster in August, 1612."

The case of the Second Lancashire Witches occurred in 1633–34, and was to a large extent a recrudescence of the former Pendle scandals. The affair, which presents several interesting features, came to an end when, as many as seventeen suspected persons having been tried and condemned, all upon further investigation were pardoned by Charles I.

Towards the end of the reign of this monarch, almost immediately upon the outbreak of the Rebellion, a veritable epidemic of witchcraft swept through the Eastern Counties, and there emerges the extraordinary figure of Matthew Hopkins " commonly call'd Witch Finder Generall ". The Holy Scripture tells us that Rebellion and Witchcraft go hand in hand, and it is not surprising to find that during those troublous years the land was corrupt to the core with sorcery. Hopkins, the son of James Hopkins, minister of Wenham, Suffolk, had practised the law at Ipswich first, and then at Manningtree, Essex. It was in his own town that his attention was drawn to witchcraft for a whole coven, " seven or eight of that horrible sect of Witches living in the Town where he lived . . . with divers other adjacent Witches of other Towns " on Friday nights held their Sabbat close by his house, and " had their several solemn sacrifices offered to the Devil ". He at once proceeded

A YORKSHIRE WITCH AND HER IMPS
From a contemporary drawing, 1622

[face p. 224

to inquire into these mysterious doings with the result
that numerous arrests were made. This was in March,
1645. His campaign once begun, Hopkins who had
got great glory from the business, zealously extended his
operations and was eager to smell out witches in
every direction. Accordingly he commenced a kind of
visitation in which he was accompanied by his
lieutenant—so to speak—John Stearne, who
strenuously aided and abetted him, and also by an
assistant Goody Phillips whose special province lay in
discovering the witch-mark on the bodies of the
accused. It was a very profitable concern, and it has
been calculated that between them the trio must have
netted far more than a thousand pounds, a very
considerable sum in those days. The usual methods
employed by Hopkins were searching for the devil's
mark ; watching the witch, which meant that the
suspected person tied with cords in an uneasy posture
was kept without food or drink for twenty-four hours
and not allowed to sleep, since it was believed that
then her imps, in the shape of spiders or a fly or a
wasp were bound to appear ; walking the witch, that
is to say compelling a person to hurry up and down
a room at a great rate until of very weariness and pain
a confession was extorted ; and swimming the witch.
This last ordeal was greatly favoured by Hopkins
and his satellites, but so notoriously illegal was such a
test that he was at last compelled to relinquish it.
The old story that Hopkins himself was seized by
the irate people, accused of being a wizard, and
swum in a pond where he was drowned has no sort
of foundation in fact. He died peaceably at
Manningtree " after a long sickness of a Consumption

. . . without any trouble of conscience for what he had done, as was falsely reported of him ". The Church Registers record his burial, 12th August, 1647. From 1645 to 1647 he had brought at least a couple of hundred to the gallows. This is shown by Stearne, who in his *Confirmation and Discovery of Witch-craft*, published the year after Hopkins' death, writes how he was himself in part an agent in searching out witches, " being about two hundred in number, in Essex, Suffolk, Northamptonshire, Huntingdonshire, Bedfordshire, Norfolk, Cambridgeshire, and the Isle of Ely in the County of Cambridge, besides other places, justly and deservedly executed upon their legal trials."

It is not at all to be wondered at that during the Rebellion and under the Commonwealth the evil weed of witchcraft spread so rapidly throughout England and that sorcerers fouled the whole land since, as is now proved beyond any shadow of doubt, Oliver Cromwell was a Satanist, intimately leagued with the powers of darkness to whom he had sold his soul for temporal success. After 1642, indeed, as the historian Eachard has well remarked : " Blasphemies, Heresies, Enthusiasms, and Witchcrafts were in a full tide." In my *Geography of Witchcraft*, published ten years ago, I drew attention to the pact which Cromwell had made with the devil, and related his interview with the fiend before the battle of Worcester. In *The Occult Review*, April, 1936, Mr. S. Everard has an article " Oliver Cromwell and Black Magic " in which he presents irrefutable evidence that Cromwell derived his power from the exercise of black magic. Mr. Everard whose investigations are very

thorough treats the whole subject with great fairness.
He comments upon the quite unequivocal expression
of Denzil Holles, after first Baron Holles of Ifield,
who when addressing Cromwell and Oliver St. John
speaks of the " Sabbaths " when " you imparted to
your fellow witches the bottom of your designs,
. . . all your falsehoods, villainies and cruelties with
your full intention to ruin three kingdoms ". Even
more damning is a letter in which Cromwell unbosoms
himself to that impious wretch Hugh Peter and writes
how the day after he received his commission
" walking in the evening in Hyde Park the Devil
appear'd to me in human shape and upon promises
of assuring the always success over my enemies, the
honour thereof tempted me to sell my soul and body
to him ". The infernal pact was for thirty-nine years.
And when Cromwell died at three of the clock on
the 3rd September, 1658, there had raged for many
hours a fearful storm round Whitehall ; the Devil
had come for his own, folk said.

Mr. Everard makes a good point when he
emphasizes the horrible sacrileges and blasphemies
which were so common under the rule of Cromwell,
and as is well known actively encouraged and incited
by him. Churches were polluted and profaned in the
most revolting manner, since " the essence of Satanism
is desecration ".

The admirers of Cromwell have been absolutely
unable to answer these charges. At best they have been
forced to content themselves with sharp but not very
relevant reflections upon scholars who " burrow among
the lampoons of the Restoration ". I think I may
venture to claim some acquaintance with Restoration

literature and I can safely assert that the occult practices of Cromwell are not a theme with Restoration satirists, high or low. His witchcrafts are proved not by the censure and detraction of any opponent, but by historical documents whose genuineness cannot be called in doubt. It is commonly reported that either (as I hope) in bitter jest, or in earnest, all members of the House of Commons were advised to make a daily bow to the statue of Cromwell. This would be plain idolatry, and something worse. It is sad and shameful enough that a statue of Cromwell should ever have been erected, sadder still that it should be allowed to remain. Cromwell was a Satanist, and to my mind it is extremely significant that the Reds should carry a banner of Cromwell in procession.

The case of the Drummer of Tedworth which caused so great a stir shortly after the Restoration of King Charles II, the knockings and the sound of a drum which disturbed the household of Mr. Mompesson may more properly be said to belong to poltergeist hauntings than to witchcraft, although it is not disputed that sorcery played its part in the phenomena.

In Somerset during the year 1664 a coven of Satanists was discovered by Robert Hunt, a magistrate of the Wincanton district. Julian Cox, a fearful crone, who had signed a written pact with the devil, who had attended countless Sabbats in Brewham Forest, and who had wrought terrible mischiefs during her threescore years and ten was hanged. We are fortunate in having very full details of the Somerset coven since Robert Hunt entrusted Glanvil with his Book of Examinations of Witches. " It contains," says that learned divine, " the discovery of such an hellish Knot of them, and that discovery so clear and plain, that perhaps there hath not yet any thing appeared to me with stronger Evidence to confirm the belief of Witches."

The charges of witchcraft being proven up to the hilt two sorceresses, Amy Duny and Rose Cullender of Lowestoft, were hanged at Bury St. Edmunds in March, 1664. The trial is famous, largely owing to the fact that Sir Matthew Hale was the presiding judge who pronounced sentence, and Sir Thomas Browne, then Dr. Browne, testified to the undeniable truth of witchcraft, and gave it as his opinion that the victims of these evil crones were clearly bewitched.

In August, 1682, Temperance Lloyd, Mary Trembles, and Susanna Edwards were hanged at Exeter. All three had wasted and killed their neighbours by their malefic charms. All three had entertained familiars in filthy commerce.

The last execution for witchcraft which has been traced in England is that of Alice Molland, sentenced at the Exeter Lent Assizes of 1685.

The two cases which are still sometimes quoted, that of " two notorious witches " Elinor Shaw and Mary Phillips, said to have been burned at Northampton in March, 1705, and that of Mary Hicks and her little daughter, aged nine, supposed to have been hanged at Huntingdon in 1716, are purely fictitious. The pamphlets which profess to give details of these executions are mere catchpenny invention, the Northampton incident being nothing else than a hash-up of a Chelmsford witch-trial of 1645.

The last execution of a witch in Scotland took place at Dornock in 1722. The last witch-trial in Ireland, the Island-Magee Witch Trial, when five sorceresses were sentenced to a year's imprisonment and the pillory was in 1711. It is true that Mary Butters, the Carnmoney witch, was put forward for trial in 1808, but no bill was found. It should be emphasized that to quote the Clonmel case of 1895 as a "witch-burning" is altogether inaccurate. The woman was put on the fire in the belief that she was a fairy changeling, and that she would instantly vanish in the flames, whilst the real wife, kidnapped by the little people, would then return. The last execution in France appears to have been that of a warlock condemned by the Parliament of Bordeaux in 1718. At Kempten in Bavaria Anna Maria Schwägelin, who was perhaps lunatic, was beheaded for sorcery in 1775. The last time the law burned a witch in Spain was at Seville in 1781. In the Swiss Protestant canton of Glarus, Anna Göldi was hanged as a witch in 1782. Two carrion hags, notorious and rampant Satanists, were sent to the stake in Poland in 1793.

It is perhaps worth recording that the burning alive of five witches by the Alcade Ignacio Castello of San Jacopo in Mexico on 20th August, 1877, "with consent of the whole population" is a myth having no sort of foundation in fact.

Even to-day there are instances when the populace maddened by the malice of some witch take the law into their own hands, and sometimes with very deplorable results. Thus in November, 1929, six natives were sentenced to death by a special court in Swaziland. Their crime was the murder, with his three wives and three children, of an elderly *induna* (tribal leader), who had been " smelt out " by the

witch doctors as a wizard. The accused avowed their
guilt, but pleaded that the deceased was a black
magician, and that he had cast a spell on many of
their friends, who languished and died. They had
set fire to the *induna's* hut, and when the seven
occupants endeavoured to escape they were assegaied
and flung back into the flames.

In November, 1932, ten people were arrested at
Bogota, Columbia. The cottage of an old witch living
in the village of Sativa Norte had been set on fire
whilst she was asleep and she and her daughter burned
to death. In May, 1935, a beldame of seventy-five,
commonly believed to be a sorceress, was rescued
by the Mexican police from being burned at the stake.
Neighbours had seized her, and the faggots were
beginning to crackle and blaze when the authorities
arrived on the scene.

Towards the end of the seventeenth century and
during the first decade of the eighteenth cases of witchcraft still came before the English courts, but the judges
for the most part refused to convict. Sir John Holt,
Chief Justice of the King's Bench (1689–1710), showed
himself a notorious sceptic in these matters and secured
acquittal after acquittal. When Richard Hathaway,
the 'prentice to a Southwark blacksmith, accused
Sarah Morduck of having bewitched him much
trouble ensued. In the end, however, Hathaway
found himself charged with rank imposture and
Sir John Holt sentenced him to a year's imprisonment
and the pillory thrice.

The case of Jane Wenham, the " Wise Woman of
Walkerne " caused an immense sensation in 1711–12,
and became " the discourse of London town ". At

the trial in March the Hertford Assizes were thronged ; opinions were almost equally divided, and rivers of ink flowed. In spite of Mr. Justice Powell's direction and efforts to secure an acquittal the jury brought in a verdict of guilty of witchcraft. Jane Wenham was formally condemned, only to be reprieved and very shortly set at liberty. She lived until 1730 upon a small pension allowed by certain charitable people of quality.

The last witch-trial proper in England—or rather commitment for trial—was that of an old woman and her son at Leicester Assizes in September, 1717, before Lord Parker. The trial did not come on since the bill was not found.

The Act of James I was repealed in the ninth year of George II, 1736, and witchcraft ceased to be a statutory or (under English law) an ecclesiastical offence. This new Act also repealed the Act " Anentis Witchcrafts " of the Ninth Parliament of Queen Mary of Scotland, 1563. It was provided " That from and after the said Twentyfourth Day of June, [1736], no Prosecution, Suit, or Proceeding, shall be commenced or carried on against any Person or Persons for Witchcraft, Sorcery, Inchantment, or Conjuration, or for charging another with any such Offence, in any Court whatsoever in Great Britain ". To prevent and punish " any Pretences to such Arts or Powers " whereby ignorant persons are frequently deluded and defrauded, any Person who shall " pretend to exercise or use any kind of Witchcraft, Sorcery, Inchantment, or Conjuration, or undertake to tell Fortunes, or pretend, from his or her Skill or Knowledge in any occult or crafty Sciences, to discover where or in what

Manner any Goods or Chattels, supposed to have been stolen or lost, may be found ", is liable to a year's imprisonment and to be publicly pilloried once a quarter for the space of one hour.

I quote from the *Daily Mail*, Friday, 31st May, 1935. " Sorcery Charge Fails. For only the second time in the last 100 years a charge of sorcery was brought under the Witchcraft Act of 1736 at Carlisle Assizes yesterday.

" The accused woman, Mrs. Katie McGee, aged 35, who was alleged to have undertaken to tell the fortune of Mrs. Alice Rothesay, of Beckermet, was acquitted.

" Mr. Glynn Blackledge, for the prosecution, said that the last charge under the Act was brought in 1904, and Mr. Justice Singleton interposed : ' So this jury may be making history.' "

It may be observed that proceedings against professional fortune-tellers, palmists, and consulting mediums of any kind, are now generally taken under the Vagrancy Act of 1824, which includes : " Every person pretending or professing to tell fortunes, or using any subtle craft, means, or device, by palmistry or otherwise, to deceive and impose on any of His Majesty's subjects." From the wording of the Act it cannot apply to anyone having no intention to deceive, none the less it has been held by the divisional court that a person " telling fortunes ", however honestly, commits an offence within the Statute. Such an interpretation, it might well be argued, opens up the widest issues, yet although there is obviously need for a drastic reform of these vague and indeterminate Statutes one cannot but hope that, lest a worse thing happen, they will be left untouched until better conditions prevail and a saner outlook is reached.

Well might the Associate Presbytery in their annual Confession of National and Personal Sins lament " the Penal Statutes against Witches having been repealed by Parliament, contrary to the express Law of God ".

To estimate the number of executions for witchcraft in England from the accession of Queen Elizabeth in 1558 until the Repeal of 1736 is almost an impossible task. What can with perfect confidence be said is that nearly all writers have grossly exaggerated the figures, and multiplied by tens, even by hundreds. In his annotations on *Hudibras* (1744), the Cambridge antiquary Dr. Zachary Grey remarks : " I have somewhere seen an account of betwixt three and four thousand [witches] that suffered in the King's dominions, from the year 1640 to the King's restoration." Daines Barrington computes that a couple of centuries saw 30,000 executions ; Robert Steele in *Social England* says that 70,000 witches were hanged under the Act of James I. All these figures are grotesquely inflated and utterly unreasonable. Mr. L'Estrange Ewen, who speaks with greater authority, writes : " actually the number of executions for witchcraft in England from 1542–1736 may be guessed at less than 1,000."

CHAPTER VI

Part II of English Witchcraft from the Passing of the Statute of 1736 until the Present Day

I would yet have it plainly known that I am a sworn enemy to witches, and that I shall never spare them, for their execrable abominations, and for the countless numbers of them which are seen to increase every day so it seems that we are now in the times of Antichrist, since, among the many signs that are given of his advent, this is one of the chief, namely, that witchcraft shall then be rife throughout the world.

HENRI BOGUET.

Not many years ago a well-known writer inquired of me in the public press if I could inform him when and where the last Sabbat was celebrated. I did not reply, because my answer must have been " yesterday night " or " the night before yesterday " since, of course, Sabbats are continually being celebrated by Satanists at the present time. As to the place, it might be London or any other of the cities or small towns or even villages in England which are the centres of devil-worshippers.

On Wednesday, 10th September, 1930, there appeared in *The Times* an article entitled " The Last Witch. A Question for the Antiquary ", a question, moreover, which wisely enough the writer did not attempt to answer. We are informed that " there were many parts of the British Isles where belief in and reprisals for witchcraft still existed when " Sir Walter Scott's *Letters on Demonology and Witchcraft* " was published in 1830 for Murray's respectable Family

Library ". Evidently *The Times* correspondent knew nothing of witchcraft in England at a later date, and from one point of view the article, however interesting, was extremely futile and a full hundred years out-of-date. Accidentally it proved valuable, none the less, since it provoked a number of letters very conclusively showing that witchcraft is no mere historical fact of the past, but that it is active and malignant to-day. To talk of " The Last Witch " is absurd. Satanism, in some cases scarcely veiled, is rampant in our midst. Satanist and witch are identical terms.

To suppose, again, as with some almost seems to be the case that the crass materialism of the Act of George II (1736) killed witchcraft is folly. Rather it protected the warlock and the sorceress. The only result of this fatuous legislation was that those who had been injured in body or in property by a witch took the law into their own hands, and during the eighteenth century there are recorded from every part of England. a large number of examples of witches being swum by the populace. In June, 1736, the very year that the statute was passed certain witches were swum at Twyford in Leicestershire, an affair which gave the cue to the Rev. Joseph Juxon to preach " A Sermon upon Witchcraft. Occasion'd by the Late Illegal Attempt to Discover Witches by Swimming ". The scepticism, one might say the rationalism of the eighteenth century clergy is, of course, notorious. In July, 1737, a witch was swum in a Bedfordshire village. She floated like a cork three times, but subsequently when weighed against the Church Bible outbalanced it. At Monk's Sleigh, Norfolk, a witch was swum on the 19th December, 1748.

On 22nd April, 1751, occurred the notorious Hertfordshire swimming ordeal. John Osborne and Ruth his wife, witches of long continuance, who had destroyed a neighbouring farmer's stock and afflicted him with a strange sickness, were seized by an incensed mob and swum in Marston mere. Souse they flung the pair into the water, and Mother Osborne did not sink. The wretched couple, however, expired through exposure and ill-treatment, and Thomas Colley, the prime mover of this business, was arrested, tried for murder at Hertford Assizes, on Tuesday, 20th July, 1751, found guilty and hanged in chains on the following 24th August. A very shocking and deplorable outbreak, no doubt, but the statute is wholly responsible. The villagers could not be expected for their own safety sake to tolerate witches among them to rot and blast the whole community, and the infidels who framed the law are to blame in the first place for these riots and disorders which seem an almost inevitable consequence of their imprudence and presumption.

Witches were swum in Suffolk in 1752 ; in Leicestershire in 1760 ; in Cambridgeshire in 1769. Two witches who had forspoken and maimed cattle were swum by a number of irate farmers in the Hundreds of Essex in 1774. Two years later there was a case of swimming in Leicestershire.

In 1785 a poor woman, Sarah Bradshaw of Mears Ashby, who was suspected of being a witch in order to prove her innocence, voluntarily submitted to be dipped. She immediately plumped to the bottom of the pond, and this her neighbours took to be an incontestable proof she was clear of the accusation.

Ten years later a case of swimming is reported from
Suffolk.

In February, 1808, a girl named Alice Brown, who
lived at Great Paxton, Hunts, whilst endeavouring to
cross the Ouse on thin ice fell through into the water
and with great difficulty scrambled back to the bank
where a friend, Fanny Amey, awaited her. As might
be expected Alice Brown became exceedingly ill, and
owing to the fright Fanny Amey was in little better
state. A neighbour at once proclaimed that the pair
had been overlooked. He told a story of a town in
Bedfordshire where he had recently been staying.
There a doting crone was more than suspected of
causing a man to languish away by her evil spells.
Accordingly the victim filled a vessel with his urine
and heated it in a corked bottle. The result was that
the old woman was seen to enter the room ; she
hurried wildly to and fro grimacing and convulsed
as if racked with pain ; and then vanished with a
horrid yell. After a few days the witch died, when
the sick man was completely cured.

This story was repeated with immense effect.
Shortly it was bruited in Great Paxton that Alice
Brown, Fanny Amey, and Mary Fox were bewitched
and rumour pointed to Mrs. Anne Izzard, a farmer's
wife some sixty years of age as the sorceress. In vain
the Rev. Isaac Nicholson sternly rebuked his congregation from the pulpit. Two or three accidents
seeming to confirm their accusations, one Sunday
evening of May a crowd broke into the Izzards' house.
They scratched the unfortunate woman, pricked her
with pins, pelted her, and threatened her with ducking.
With difficulty she escaped their hands, only to be

assaulted the following day. The result was that a number of her neighbours were brought up before Mr. Justice Grose on a charge of assault. Several were sent to prison, and others were bound over to find security for their good behaviour, failing which they were remanded in custody. Even this did not entirely end the matter, for in the autumn of the same year a local magistrate committed two women, a mother and daughter, to Huntingdon jail for assaulting Anne Izzard and calling her witch.

A rousing "Sermon against Witchcraft" was preached in the Parish Church of Great Paxton on the 17th July, 1808, by Mr. Nicholson, who did not spare his language in his denunciation of the "Two atrocious attacks on the Person of Ann Izzard as a reputed witch".

In 1825 a poor old man, Isaac Stebbings, aged 67, was "swum for a wizard" at Wickham Skeith, Suffolk, and all but killed by an angry mob—*The Suffolk Chronicle* quoted in *The Times,* 19th July, 1825.

Two years later, at the Monmouth Assizes, four persons were found guilty of assaulting an old trot of ninety, Mary Nicolas, commonly accused of being a witch. She was alleged to have overlooked cattle so that the beasts died. They had scratched her with a briar to draw blood ; searched for the devil's teat, which they swore they had found ; and threatened to swim her in a pool.

Writing in 1861, Mrs. Lynn Linton spoke of an " old gentleman who died at Polstead not so long ago, and who, when a boy, had seen a witch swum in Polstead Ponds, ' and she went over the water like a cork ' ; who had also watched another witch feeding her three imps like blackbirds ; and who only wanted five pounds to have seen all the witches in the parish dance on a knoll together ".

A magistrate who wrote anonymously to *The Times* on 3rd April, 1857, related how in the previous November application was made to him by a farmer whose wife had been overlooked by old Mrs. C., demanding that the police might be instructed to swim her or at least search her for the devil's mark. When the magistrate remonstrated the man explained that urine had been warmed in a hermetically sealed bottle, and sure enough as it grew hot Mrs. C., tormented in her bladder, has come to their kitchen window and stood there grinning and mowing at them through the casement. He added that only a few years before a witch, Mother Pointer, had been swum in the village pond, and it was found she could not sink. One woman told the magistrate of a witch whom she had known when she was a girl. It was never denied that Betsy Norris had bewitched cows, pigs, geese, and people. The hag was swum more than once but could never sink. Place-names are not given in the letter.

In 1864 Emma Smith, the wife of a beer-shop keeper at Ridgwell, Essex, and Samuel Stammers, a carpenter, were convicted at the Chelmsford Assizes of common assault for swimming in the previous year an old Frenchman, called " Dummy ", who was generally reputed to be a wizard, and who had over-looked the female defendant. " Dummy," a deaf and dumb gaffer of nearly ninety, at least pretended to sorcery, and eked out a miserable living by fortune-telling and the sale of charms. On the night of

3rd August Mrs. Smith, who had been anæmic and ill for many months, encountered " Dummy " in the taproom of the Swan at Sible Hedingham when she loudly accused him of being the cause of her failing health. The crowd, led by Stammers, egged her on until she seized a stick and began to belabour the warlock, shouting : " You old Devil, you served me out, and I'll serve you out." Eventually the unfortunate wretch was dragged to a brook which ran down the side of Watermill Lane, and Stammers flung him into the water at a spot where it was particularly deep. The next day he died from shock and exposure. At their trial Stammers pleaded not guilty, whilst for her defence Emma Smith kept reiterating that she was bewitched. The bench of magistrates who committed them to the Assizes remarked that " the whole disgraceful transaction arose out of a deep belief in witchcraft which possesses to a lamentable extent the tradespeople and lower orders of the district ".

At Dunmow on the 23rd June, 1880, two men were convicted of assault for attempting to throw an old witch into a pond.

In 1931 there was living at Good Easter, Essex, a villager who in his youth had been before the magistrates charged together with several of his friends with an attempt to do grievous bodily harm. They had attempted to duck an old woman who was a notorious witch.

A parish doctor, who elected to remain anonymous, gives an account in *All the Year Round*, 5th January, 1867, of a witch living in his district, a village " two miles from a populous borough town ", within an hour's railway journey from London. Old Mother

Redburn, a hag of seventy-two, "was accredited with all the recognized powers of curse and spell and evil eye. She has bewitched pigs, and they have refused to fatten ; she has bewitched cows, and they have become dry or died ; children under her baneful influence have wasted away to mere skeletons ; young women have gone into decline ; young men have been lamed ; old men and women have become blind, deaf, bedridden, palsied, a prey to every human woe, all owing—in the popular belief—to the ill-will of Old Mother Redburn.   Cabbages, corn, turnips, and potatoes have all in their turn withered and rotted before her curse." Shortly after he commenced practice in the place the doctor was called in to see Mrs. Smith, who was blind with cataract in both eyes, deaf, and bedridden. He could discover no reason why she should not be able to stand and walk, but a neighbour shrewdly hinted : "Ah ! *we* all think that Mother Redburn has most to say to it." At last Mr. Smith decided to leave the neighbourhood, "to give the missus a chance by movin' of her" to another place. "I suppose," queried the doctor, "you think Mother Redburn prevents her getting well?" "No one else, sir, darn her !" was the reply. "Many years ago Mrs. Redburn, sir, came to our back-door to borrow some taters which my wife refused. Words ensued, and a day or two after the wife's eyesight began to fail. There was another dispute over some cabbages, and then my old woman became blind, deaf and bedridden, all through offending Mrs. Redburn." Certain it is that from the very night of settling in their new home, Mrs. Smith improved in an astonishing manner. She was at once able to sit up, and shortly began to walk about briskly enough, whilst her hearing returned. The cataract, however, remained.

The Daily Chronicle, 15th February, 1879, records a case of witchcraft at Caergwrle. Mrs. Braithwaite supplied a Mrs. Williams with milk, but suddenly refused to serve her. The reason was that Mrs. Braithwaite had always been very successful with her butter until she offended Mrs. Williams, when her butter would not come try as she might. She declared Mrs. Williams had overlooked the churn, and called after her, " Out, witch ! witch ! If you don't leave the place, I'll shoot you." Mrs. Williams applied to the bench for protection as everyone in the district believed her to be a witch. The magistrates directed an officer to caution Mrs. Braithwaite against repeating the threats.

Writing in *The Times*, 20th September 1930, Mr. Andrew Innes, of High Tenter Fell, Kendal, relates several recent exploits of a Caithness witch. On one occasion when a farmer refused to sell her a young cow, saying he needed the milk himself, the witch charmed the animal so that she could yield no more milk, but remained dry.

The Leigh Chronicle, 19th April, 1879, reports the case of William Bulwer, of Etling Green, who was charged at the East Dereham Petty Sessions with assaulting Christiana Martins, a girl of eighteen. Recriminations of the filthiest description passed between the two and from words they came to blows. The defendant stated : " Mrs. Martins is an old witch, gentlemen, that is what she is and she charmed me, and I got no sleep for her for three nights, and one night at half-past eleven o'clock, I got up because I could not sleep, and went out and found a ' walking toad ' under a clod which had been dug up with a three-pronged fork. That is why I could not rest ; she is a bad old woman ; she put this toad under there to charm me, and her daughter is just as bad, gentlemen. She would bewitch anyone ; she charmed me, and I got no rest day or night for her, till I found this ' walking toad ' under the turf. She dug a hole and put it there to charm me, gentlemen, that is the truth. I got the toad out and put it in a cloth, and took it upstairs and showed it to my mother, and ' throwed ' it into the pit in the garden. She went round this here ' walking toad ' after she had buried it, and I could not rest by day or sleep by night till I found it."

Mrs. Martins also bewitched by a curious look or side-glance, a form of spell noticed in the *Malleus Maleficarum*. I have no doubt that Bulwer's story, clumsily told, was entirely accurate, and that the toad was one of the woman's imps.

In 1886 there happened to be found hidden away in the belfry of an English country church a long cord tied in elaborate strands and interwoven with the feathers of a black hen. Obviously it had been made for some definite purpose and presently an old woman in the village identified it as a " witch's ladder ", proof positive that some persons in the neighbourhood knew something of the traditional occult lore and were endeavouring to cast a spell.

In 1911 a poor woman was tried in Ireland for killing an old witch, who by means of a familiar, a rat, had tormented her to madness. *The Irish Times*, 14th June, 1911.

At the Glamorgan Assizes on the 27th July, 1920,

before Mr. Justice Avory, William Davies, a hawker, and his wife Mary Jane Davies, were sentenced to terms of imprisonment with hard labour for obtaining sums of money and articles of value from various persons " by pretending to exercise witchcraft ". David James, an old farmer living at Twynygarreg Farm, near Treharris, said that he and his family had been suffering from a skin disease. Mary Jane Davies told him that they were bewitched and the cattle also were overlooked. She undertook to cure the household, but first demanded a number of articles she scented as having been " cursed ". They also paid her considerable sums in cash. A neighbouring farmer, James Williams, who likewise had illness in his family was warned by the female Davies that his house was under malign influences. He gave her money to avert the working of the charm. The two families fully believed that some witch had cast an evil spell upon them, and it was contended for the defence that the accused had been called in to remove the ban and that no false pretences were used. It is, of course, quite possible that the Davies, witches, had in the first instance brought disaster upon the two households and then cunningly contrived that they should be summoned actually to undo their own mischief.

In July, 1929, Eugene Burgess, a taxicab driver, was arrested at Kalamazoo, Michigan, for the murder of Mrs. Etta Fairchild, aged seventy-five. This woman, who was undoubtedly a witch, bragged of the numbers of people (including her own husband) whom she had killed by her foul enchantments. Burgess invited the woman who was the inmate of a charity home to his house and then brained her with a piece of lead piping and a hammer. Mrs. Burgess, who had been overlooked by the witch, said : " I stagger lots of times and have pains and aches and trouble in breathing. It was either her life or ours." Mrs. Fairchild had also bewitched the seventeen year old daughter of Burgess, and intended to waste her to death.

Thus in the *Daily Express*, 22nd January, 1934, there is an account of a man in a remote Dorset hamlet who has been bewitched and is dying slowly although physically there is nothing the matter with him. " Doctors have examined him from head to toe. They pronounced him perfectly healthy in wind and limb. Yet they are powerless to save him." The local physician said : " The man is doomed. We can do nothing for him, as he is determined to die." The victim is described as a tall, gaunt man of middle age. His cheeks were sunken and pasty ; he was so weak he could scarcely stand. For about two and a half years he had been ailing. A gipsy came to the door, and when he asked her if she could suggest a remedy, she told him that someone, a woman, had " looked over " him. Yet since the repeal of the law of James I the witch must go scathless and scot-free.

In July, 1935, a man who lived near Taunton committed suicide because he had been " overlooked " by a witch.

Witches are as numerous, as malign and mischievous in England to-day, as ever they were in the sixteenth and seventeenth centuries, and legislation is as much needed now as then.

In one part of the Empire, at least, in Jamaica the laws against witchcraft (obeah) are happily in full force.

By the *Encyclopedia Americana* (1829–1833 ; vol. iv, 1832), the word Obeah is thus defined : " a species of witchcraft practised among the Negroes, the apprehension of which, operating upon the superstitious fears, is frequently attended with disease and death." We remark then that the result of Jamaican and English witchcraft is the same. Fr. Joseph J. Williams, S.J., the eminent authority upon voodoo and obeah, observes that " real obeah must be regarded as a form of Devil-worship " since the agent (the witch) is the servant of the Sasabonsan or the Devil invoked and relied upon to produce the desired effect. Obeah " is professedly a projection of spiritual power with the harm of an individual as an objective. Practically, its end is attained through fear, supplemented if needs be by secret poisoning ". This might well stand for a definition of European witchcraft, for the two things are one and the same.

The obeah-man fears the priest as one who can exercise a more powerful influence. In their own fashion the coloured folk think that the Catholic Church controls the strongest obeah. The devotees of the obeah cult, says Fr. Williams, believe that a priest can give evidence of his dominance by " lighting a candle on them ". " Fadder take pin and Fadder take candle, and him stick der pin in der candle ; and him light der candle on you. Der candle him burn and him burn and him burn. And you waste and you waste and you waste. And when der flame touch dat pin—you die." The threat made in jest by a priest " I think I'll have to light a candle on you " will bring the stoutest black to his knees.

Fr. Williams quotes a number of reports from *The*

Daily Gleaner of Kingston to show that witchcraft (obeah) is widely prevalent and most obstinately practised throughout the island. Moreover the majority of cases that come before the Court are mixed up with a deal of imposture, low money-grubbing, and gain. In his real professional practice the obeah-man is as secret and close as the witch of three centuries ago. A little gamble with luck he will chance. He will help in love affairs or effect a cure or clear a haunted house, and if he is caught at any of these games he pays the penalty, and then returns to his trade exercising a trifle more caution, asking his clients for a rather higher fee. But when it is a question of real obeah he will take good care to assure himself of inviolable secrecy, for he will never run the risk of having a capital offence proved against him.

Thus on 24th November, 1933, Vitelleus Brown was charged with practising obeah. He said he could cure a swollen knee, which he attributed to obeah in the first instance. Someone " had set hand " on the sufferer, who was to be healed for three pounds. On the following day Alexander Brown was charged with the same offence. A man and woman consulted him, declaring they were very sick. He informed the woman that a policeman had put a ghost upon her, and asked a fee of three pounds to " take off the duppy ". On 14th December of the same year at Spanish Town there was " Six Months for Obeahman ". David Simon was convicted of contracting to remove the duppies from Ada Bogle's house, which she swore was beset with spirits who scratched and rapped and pelted the place with stones. Simon's job was to drive away the unruly ghosts.

On the 9th January, 1934, George Washington Pitt was fined £12 10s. for practising obeah. He had been heard to boast that : " He could cure ; he could kill ; he could get his clients good positions." This vaunt betrays a knowledge of the darkest secrets of obeah, the art of dealing out death and decay.

In *Chambers's Journal*, 11th January, 1902, an article entitled " Obeah To-day in The West Indies " points out that " In many countries superstitious rites are practised to bring good luck ; but that is not the case as a rule with *obeah*. Its root idea is the worship and propitiation of the Evil One : it is essentially malevolent. A Negro usually goes to the obeah-man to harm his neighbour, not to do any good to himself ; and that is why the law regards the matter so seriously ". The Jamaican legislation of 1760 provides against " the Wicked Art of Negroes going under the Apellation of obeah-men and obeah-women pretending to have Communication with the Devil and other Evil Spirits " and enacts that " any Negro or other Slave who shall pretend to any Supernatural Power and be detected in making use of any . . . materials related to the practice of Obeah or Witchcraft in order to delude or impose upon the Minds of others shall upon Conviction thereof before two Magistrates and three Freeholders suffer Death or Transportation ". *The Times* of London, 5th December, 1818, quotes " a recent Act of the house of Assembly (Barbados) " which punishes negroes or slaves wilfully, maliciously and unlawfully pretending to any magical or supernatural charm or power, or who use and carry on the wicked and unlawful practice of obeah, with death, transportation, or such other penalty as the

Court may decide. Obeah, European witchcraft in the past, Satanism in England to-day, are all one and the same thing, essential evil, malignant, destructive, accursed by God, hateful to man, the cult of the Devil.

The Daily Express, 20th January, 1937, says that " Voodooism, with its strange, awful rites, is still flourishing in Michigan ", and reports how a negro woman and her child sought the protection of the police, since her husband, Verlen McQueen, was going to sacrifice them to Satan in a huge jar of boiling water. The man, when arrested, was found stirring a great cauldron of water set over a fierce fire. In 1932, a voodoo magician, Robert Harris, beheaded another negro upon an altar. Harris was confined in an asylum. Negro children are actually being sent to secret voodoo schools.

The Church Times, 21st December, 1928, quoting the latest number of the diocesan magazine of the Bishop of Mauritius, says : " I wonder how many people in Mauritius realize what a strong hold sorcery in some form or another has on quite a large number of persons in Mauritius, by no means all of whom are of the uneducated classes, and all of whom profess some form of Christianity. Although prosecutions for witchcraft *qua* witchcraft have ceased, indirectly it is still dealt with under other names by the penal codes of every civilized country. In Mauritius those involved are prosecuted for swindling. I am assured by those qualified to give accurate information that witch-craft or Petit Albert is practised by many thousands of persons in Mauritius. No one professing the Christian Faith can, without mortal sin, have anything to do with any form of witchcraft. Petit Albert is nothing less than the cult of the Devil." Here the Bishop gives three examples of invocations.

" The petitions are for personal gain or injury to enemies, and are often of an erotic or obscene character. Sacred names and phrases are used in a blasphemous way. These intercessions are accompanied by various ceremonies, in which a skull, a dagger, camphor, and flowers figure. Engravings of saints have pins stuck in various parts of the figure ; I have seen a picture of the Sacred Heart covered with such pins. A crucifix is also frequently used in these blasphemous rites. It has been known in Mauritius for a newly-interred female corpse to be dug up and used for horrible purposes. To take part in such practices, and at the same time to pose as a Christian, is, in my opinion, perilously near committing unforgivable sin."

Not without reason has Rumania definitely banned magic in every form. *The Daily Mail*, Wednesday, 1st April, 1936.

In *The Times* of Thursday, 21st January, 1932, was published an extraordinary—and to my mind a disturbing—article entitled " A Satanist Picture ". There was at Burlington House an Exhibition of French Art, including a picture of " The Annunciation " loaned from Aix-en-Provence. The writer stated that this was locally acknowledged to be the work of a Satanist painter. It hangs in a " dark chapel " in the Church of the Madeleine. " It has always been there. Who painted it ? " A Satanist who concealed his name through fear of the Inquisition ? " Did the picture enter the church under the auspices of that Robert Mauvoisin, Archbishop of Aix, who, accused of sorcery and convicted of having celebrated Black Masses with the blood of little children was condemned at Avignon by Pope John XXII ? Or was it offered to the parish by Rodrigue de Lune, nephew of the Antipope Benedict XIII, who vowed himself to the devil ? " " This is quite conceivable ! "

Better still ; " Is it not possible that it was surreptitiously hung in its niche by the Abbé Gaufridi, who, during the minority of Louis XIII, was burnt alive in the Place des Prêcheurs for having convoked a whole convent of Ursulines to Witches' Sabbaths ? "

All this is very alarming. The picture is examined in detail. " Here the announcing angel has owl's wings ; the ray of light emanating from God the Father, before reaching Mary, falls on a monkey crouching on the edge of a lectern. In the groining, instead of doves and larks, flutter bats and vampires. From the trefoils of the arches horned devils peep. In the vase beside the lily stand three evil herbs, basil, foxglove, and belladonna, and, indubitable sign of Satanic consecration, both God the Father and the angel, instead of raising fingers in the orthodox attitude of benediction, advance the thumb between the third and middle fingers according to the obscene and malefic gesture which Spanish wizards termed *hacer figa*, and with which, according to mediæval demonologists, the devil often opened Sabbaths.

" In the shutters of the triptych two pious figures are standing beneath shelves laden with books. These will keep their secret, and we shall never know their titles. Let us wager, however, that they spell Cabal, and that the priest and deacon keeping vigil in this singular sanctuary were reading, not the Breviary, but the ' Malleus Maleficarum ', the ' Daemonomania', or the 'Livre des Charmes, Sorcelages et Enchantements'" [*sic*].

This is a regular thrill. Unfortunately some details in the very picturesque description are a trifle inaccurate. The announcing Angel, St. Gabriel, has not owl's wings. The rays of light do not more than pass over the lectern of which the finial is a monkey. The bats and vampires instead of fluttering in the groining, flutter only in the writer's imagination. A fluttering vampire is a novelty, to be sure. There are no evil herbs beside the lily, no foxglove, no belladonna. What may be clearly seen has been identified as the blue columbine, which obtains its name from a pretty fancy as resembling a nest of doves, and a red flower which is either the rose or the poppy. The thumb of the Father is not " advanced between His third and middle fingers ", in fact it is scarcely visible, nor indeed is that of the Angel who is not blessing at all. One would be glad to know which mediæval demonologists state that the Devil opened the Sabbath with the gesture, *hacer figa*. Reference, please. The " two pious figures " will not and do not desire to keep their secret. The name of one, *Jeremias propheta*, is quite legibly inscribed beneath him. The name *Isaias propheta* is by chance out of sight. We are told of two possible donors of the fourteenth century. In this case it is hardly likely that the " pious figures " would be reading works written respectively at the end of the fifteenth and sixteenth centuries. Nor is it probable that the picture " entered the church under the auspices " of an Archbishop condemned by a Pope who was dead more than a hundred years before it was painted. True, an alternative is suggested.

But is there the slightest reason for supposing that the
sorcerer Louis Gaufridi, executed in 1611, has any
connexion whatsoever with the picture ?

I may remark that it is impious—although doubtless
no offence was intended—to speak of a Saint, St.
Sara, as the " patroness of fairies, witches ".

The whole article " A Satanist Picture " is—to use
the mildest terms—founded upon a complete mis-
apprehension, but such a mistake may leave a very
ugly impression. There are " Satanist Pictures ", but
not such as this, and my late friend, the Provost of
Eton, Dr. M. R. James, both in a private letter to
myself and in a letter published in *The Times*,
25th January, 1932, expressed himself as aggrieved
that the Mystery of the Annunciation should have
been made the subject of such an imputation.

Satanism is alive to-day. It is a power in the land.
Mysterious, unseen, wholly evil.

I myself have been shown two ancient candlesticks
of great value upon which in a secret place was inscribed in Hebrew characters the Most Holy Name
of God,—but inverted. They had been used at the
hideous celebration of a diabolic Eucharist.

In 1899 Mons. Serge Basset, a well-known French
journalist, who unhappily fell in the Great War, was
present at a Black Mass, and his account of the ceremony appeared in *Le Matin* of 27th May of that year.
The circumstances were peculiar. Mons. Basset had
contributed an article to *L'Éclair* expressing himself
entirely sceptical concerning the practice of Satanic
Masses to-day, whereupon he received a letter requesting him in very plain terms to meet the writer at
9 o'clock on the following Thursday in the Place Saint-

Sulpice, whence he would be conducted to a Black Mass and see for himself. Suspecting a practical joke he did not reply, and even ignored a second and more pressing communication. A few evenings later there called at his flat a lady, heavily veiled, who told him that it was she who had been his correspondent, and who invited him, if really in earnest, to accompany her—unless indeed he were afraid. "You do not believe in us," she said. "Very well, I will convince you." A car was waiting, and full of curiosity he agreed to go. Such precautions were taken that he was unable to gather their route, nor could he guess the name of the lonely street where they stopped, as he was immediately hurried into a large house, which seemed in complete darkness. Here he was ushered into a lofty room of some size, fitted up as a chapel. About twenty or a couple of dozen persons were present, of whom seven or eight were women. Amongst the men several appeared quite young, almost boys. At the far end of the room, dimly lighted by one faint lamp, he could half-discern an altar, and when six black candles were presently lit he saw that they were equally ranged on either side of a monstrous figure, a hideous goat, squatting on its haunches, bearded and lewd, with great red staring eyes. It butted with its huge protudent horns the tips of which glowed with a dull crimson flame. The walls of the room were painted with esoteric designs, curious triangles of gold within silver circles, pentacles, many-rayed stars, Hebrew and Greek characters, all intermingled with vividly designed scenes of the most shameless obscenity. A sombre chant was heard in low, mournful tones *Gloria in profundis Satano ! In profundis Satano Gloria !*

More candles were lit, and there approached the altar
a tall man vested in a richly laced alb and a cope of
flaming scarlet embroidered with gilt cones and
pomegranates. The server was a woman, a horrible
hag, raddled and scarred with villainy. From unseen
braziers the fume of heady incense mixed with pungent
herbs began to load the heated air. The voices of
celebrant and server alternated in low muttered tones :
*Introibo ad altare dei nostri Satanis. Ad Deum qui nunc
oppressus resurget et triumphabit.* Suddenly a girl, hardly
beyond her teens, darted forward, and stripping off
her clothes knelt stark naked before the altar. *Quid
velis ?* (What would you ?) asked the celebrant. *Ad
sacrificium corpus meum offero* (I present my body as the
place of sacrifice), she cried. He bowed his head
silently, and at his gesture she mounted on the altar
where she lay at full length covered with a black veil.
In hideous parody of the Offertory a jewelled ciborium
was presented whence the celebrant drew a large black
host and elevated it with the ritual prayer. *Accipe
etiam sanguinem nostrum* (Receive also our blood),
clamoured the frenzied worshippers. The ceremony
continued. From time to time the woman stretched
on the altar uttered hysterical screams and moans.
Suddenly the celebrant turned and scattered a number
of black hosts to the devotees who rushed towards him
with mænad fury. By this time all, or nearly all, were
in a state of nudity. It seemed as if worse horrors were
to follow, and Mons. Basset clapped his hands before
his eyes with a cry of disgust. At that moment two
men who had been standing in the shadow intently
watching his every movement sprang forward and
caught him by either arm. " Get out of here," they

shouted, hustling him towards the door. "Get out. You've seen too much already."

He was hurried down a long dark passage, up some stairs across a garden, and through a door which was slammed and bolted behind him. He found himself in a narrow back street, whence it was with difficulty that he made his way to a district he recognized and knew. At the time his story was questioned in some quarters, but although he steadily refused to give further particulars—he was undoubtedly bound by an oath of secrecy—Mons. Basset pledged his word that the details he related were in every respect exactly true. Nor would it be at all hard closely to parallel this scene in London and in many another English city to-day.

The following experience which,—with the suppression of actual names, an obvious precaution—I am allowed to relate, happened less than ten years ago to the sister of a personal friend of mine. This lady who is a Catholic and a medical doctor was persuaded by two acquaintances to accompany them to a "fortune-teller" in Merthyr Tydfil. They made their way to a little house in a poor street and were admitted by a woman who seemed obviously demented, so wild-eyed was she and so eccentric in her gestures and behaviour. An old grey-headed man appeared from within, ready to interview them. He promptly denied that he was a "fortune-teller". "I am not a Christian," he said, "nor a Jew. I belong to the oldest religion in the world." He then fastened his attention upon my friend's sister and accused her of being his enemy. "You are carrying a rosary with you," he cried, and such was in fact the case. He next invited all three of his visitors downstairs to a basement. My friend's sister at first refused to go, but when she found herself left alone with the woman who had admitted them and who began to laugh and mutter in a menacing fashion she preferred to descend, and joined the rest who were in a chapel, the altar of which blazed with candles. Above in the centre was suspended a pair of horns, and queer objects were ranged on the altar-table. This lady had no knowledge and little suspicion of the truth. The old man spoke to her for a few minutes and asked her to lay her hand on the altar and say : " In the Name of the Father." This she refused to do, and she forthwith insisted upon her companions leaving the place with her. The warlock had already told her several things concerning herself and her family. He cried : " I cannot prevent you going for you are protected by the constant prayers of an old man whom I see reclining in a chair and telling his beads." This, no doubt, referred to the lady's father, an invalid who spent his day in a chair, and was extremely devout, passing the hours in prayer and intercession.

Up and down England there is hardly a village without a witch. In our great cities, our larger towns, our seats of learning, Satanists abound and are organized (as of old) into covens of wickedness. Black Masses are celebrated in Mayfair and Chelsea ; in Wapping and Shoreditch ; in Brighton ; in Birmingham ; in Liverpool ; in Edinburgh. Under conditions of peculiar horror a Black Mass was celebrated in the ruins of Godstow Nunnery near Oxford. A band of Satanists have their rendezvous not far from the city of Cambridge.

During the Helsingfors scandals of 1931, a veritable

outburst of Satanism and necromancy, it was commonly bruited (and stated in the newspapers) that the Finnish police had called in the help of Scotland Yard since London was believed to be the headquarters of the infernal society, the Black International.

Who shall say that the statute of James I was severe? Rather did it not incline to clemency.

The Divine Law has spoken : " Thou shalt not suffer a Witch to live."

" Certain London cults practise the Black Mass, where black bread, black wine, and black candles are used, worshippers confess every good deed as a sin, and do penance."—*The Daily Mail*, 14th April, 1934.

Lady Peirse has well written : " They may call it psychism or occultism ; they may learn to cast curses or spells ; they may invoke the help of the powers of evil, but it is practically the same thing, and its lure to mankind is as old and mysterious as the wind that blows over the earth, urging them with strange elusive thrills to recapture and use the old powers of the Serpent."

" I am perfectly certain that there are witches to-day —both men and women who do a great deal of harm by their foul practices and bring ill-luck to people. I do not consider this is superstition at all but just common sense." I spoke those words at a public meeting in February, 1933. The next day the newspapers blazoned their headlines : " Modern Faith in Witches. Clergyman thinks they Exist." " Priest believes in Witches. Common Sense ! "

Now and again some gang of devil-worshippers may be—almost by accident—broken up and dispersed, but there are (I fear) few persons who realize how far-spread and how cunningly organized are these Societies of Evil. To the ordinary man Satanism often seems incredible, or at any rate a myth of the remote Dark Ages. He does not realize, and he is happy in his ignorance, the devil's fires that burn just a very little way beneath the thin and crumbled crust of our boasted modern civilization.

INDEX

INDEX 263

British Goblins, 26
Brocken, the (Blocksburg), 125
Brown, Alexander, 248
Brown, Alice, 238
Brown, Vitelleus, 248
Browne, Sir Thomas, 229
Bruges, 179
Buckingham, Edward Stafford, Duke of, 215
Buckingham, George Villiers, First Duke of, 62, 221
Bubb-Dodington, George, (Lord Melcombe), 185
Bulmer, Desirée, 202
Bulmer, Johann, 202
Bulwer, William, 243-4
bunn (familiar), 25
Burchard, of Worms, 142
Burgess, Eugene, 245-6
burning at stake, 217
Burroughs, Rev. George, 99, 111, 183
Burton-on-the-Wolds, 128
Burtree House, Stocksfield-on-Tyne, 108, 131
Bury St. Edmunds, 229
Bush of Barton, Mother, 197
Butcher, Elizabeth, 133
butter bewitched, 53
Butters, Mary, 230
Buxen, the, 187-8
Bwiti, 134

Caergwrle, witchcraft at, 243
Cæsarius of Arles, St., 116
Caithness, witchcraft in, 54, 243
Caister Castle, near Yarmouth, 133
Caligula, 7
Callcott, Lady, 73
Cambridgeshire, witchcraft in, 37-8, 50, 128, 226, 237
Canary Isles, familiars appear in, 32
cannibalism of witches, 156-7
Canon Episcopi, 103-4, 142-3
Carbonell, Mrs., 66

Cardiganshire, witchcraft in, 52
Cardrona, 75
Carmelite scapular, 17-18
Carnmoney witch, the, 230
Carrier, Martha, 183
Carvajal, Cardinal Bernadino (Lopez de), 33
Cassiel, 87, 88
Castello, Ignacio, 230
Catherine of Siena, St., 136
cattle bewitched, 53-4, 65
Caverne des Trois Frères, Ariège, 116
Celles, Cecilia, 220
Cervantes Saavedra, Miguel de, 32
chair, a magic, 213
Châlons, 179
Chambers's Journal, (cited), 249
Chantelouve, Madame, 179, 194
Charles Albert of Bavaria, 83
Charles I of England, 133
Charles IX of France, 17, 164
Charmillon, Marianne, 175
Chattox, Mother (Anne Whittle), 109, 222-4
Chelmsford, 39
China, witchcraft in, 139
Christian Council of the Gold Coast, the, 206
Chrysal, 187, 190
Church Times, The, (cited), 51
Churchill, Charles, 185
Clavicula Salomonis, 81 ff.
Clement of Alexandria, 199
Clerc, Gentien le, 161, 189
Clonmel case, the, 230
Clovesho, Second Council of, 205
Cnut, King, 121, 206, 219
coaches, phantom, 132-3
cock crowing ends Sabbat, dissolves enchantments, 201-2
Coirières, 124
Coke, Sir Edward, 3, 62
Colas, Antide, 122
Colchester, 66-7
Colley, Thomas, 237